# New Wings for Daedalus

# Some Other Titles from Falcon Press

Christopher S. Hyatt, Ph.D.
*Undoing Yourself with Energized Meditation and Other Devices*
*Techniques for Undoing Yourself (audios)*
*Radical Undoing: Complete Course for Undoing Yourself*
*Energized Hypnosis (book, videos & audios)*
*To Lie Is Human: Not Getting Caught Is Divine*
*Secrets of Western Tantra: The Sexuality of the Middle Path*

Christopher S. Hyatt, Ph.D. with contributions by
Wm. S. Burroughs, Timothy Leary, Robert Anton Wilson et al.
*Rebels & Devils: The Psychology of Liberation*

Christopher S. Hyatt, Ph.D. & Antero Alli
*A Modern Shaman's Guide to a Pregnant Universe*

S. Jason Black and Christopher S. Hyatt, Ph.D.
*Pacts With the Devil: A Chronicle of Sex, Blasphemy & Liberation*
*Urban Voodoo: A Beginner's Guide to Afro-Caribbean Magic*

Antero Alli
*Angel Tech: A Modern Shaman's Guide to Reality Selection*
*Angel Tech Talk (audio)*

Peter J. Carroll
*The Chaos Magick Audios*
*PsyberMagick*

Phil Hine
*Condensed Chaos: An Introduction to Chaos Magic*
*Prime Chaos: Adventures in Chaos Magic*
*The Pseudonomicon*

Joseph Lisiewski, Ph.D.
*Ceremonial Magic and the Power of Evocation*
*Kabbalistic Cycles and the Mastery of Life*
*Kabbalistic Handbook for the Practicing Magician*

Israel Regardie
*The Complete Golden Dawn System of Magic*
*The Golden Dawn Audios*
*The World of Enochian Magic (audio)*

Daniel Allen Kelley
*Behind the Veil: The Complete Guide to Conscious Sleep*

Steven Heller
*Monsters & Magical Sticks: There's No Such Thing As Hypnosis?*

**For up-to-the-minute information on prices and availability, please visit our website at http://originalfalcon.com**

# New Wings for Daedalus

## Wilhelm Reich, His Theory and Techniques

by
Francis Israel Regardie

with contributions by
Nicholas Tharcher
MobiusFrame
Calvin Iwema
Fernando P.

THE *Original* FALCON PRESS
TEMPE, ARIZONA, U.S.A.

Copyright © 2018 C.E. by Israel Regardie

All rights reserved. No part of this book, in part or in whole, may be reproduced, transmitted, or utilized, in any form or by any means, electronic or mechanical, including photocopying, recording, or by any information storage and retrieval system, without permission in writing from the publisher, except for brief quotations in critical articles, books and reviews.

International Standard Book Number: 978-1-935150-70-1
ISBN: 978-1-61869-700-4 (mobi)
ISBN: 978-1-61869-701-1 (epub)
Library of Congress Catalog Card Number: 2018949747

First Edition 2018
First eBook Edition 2018

Cover by Krys Koseda

The paper used in this publication meets the minimum requirements of the American National Standard for Permanence of Paper for Printed Library Materials Z39.48-1984

Address all inquiries to:
THE ORIGINAL FALCON PRESS
1753 East Broadway Road #101-277
Tempe, AZ 85282 U.S.A.
(or)
PO Box 3540
Silver Springs NV 89429 U.S.A.
**website: http://www.originalfalcon.com
email: info@originalfalcon.com**

"Love, work and knowledge are the well-springs of our life. They should also govern it."
— Wilhelm Reich


"In the heart of every neurotic there is a hope…beneath neurosis lies the prior background of health where this hope always remains latent. Somewhere there is the place, the person, the work, the secret that can restore health."
— L.L. Whyte

# Dedicated

with profound respect and admiration to
WILHELM REICH

# TABLE OF CONTENTS

**PREFACE**
    BY NICHOLAS THARCHER .................................. 11

**PSYCHIATRY, THEN AND NOW**
    BY MOBIUSFRAME, M.D. .................................. 15

**TOWARD A BLANK SLATE**
    BY CALVIN IWEMA, M.A. .................................. 27

**INTRODUCTION**
    BY ISRAEL REGARDIE .................................. 35

**CHAPTER I**
    REBEL .................................. 44

**CHAPTER II**
    ARMOR .................................. 72

**CHAPTER III**
    METHOD I .................................. 99

**CHAPTER IV**
    METHOD II .................................. 122

**CHAPTER V**
    THEORY .................................. 147

**CHAPTER VI**
    TETANY .................................. 166

**CHAPTER VII**
    ABREACTION .................................. 185

**CHAPTER VIII**
    TRANSFERENCE .................................. 213

**CHAPTER IX**
    AFFECTS .................................. 236

**CHAPTER X**
    GOAL .................................. 262

**CHAPTER XI**
    SELF-REGULATION .................................. 281

**AFTERWORD**
    BY FERNANDO P. .................................. 309

# Preface

## by Nicholas Tharcher

**Background**

Though Francis Israel Regardie (1907–1985) is best known for his writings on the Western magical/mystical system known as the Golden Dawn (see *The Complete Golden Dawn System of Magic*), that is not how he made his living. He was a Doctor of Chiropractic (D.C.) under which license he practiced the psychotherapeutic methods of Wilhelm Reich, M.D. (1897–1957).

Reichian Therapy, also known as *vegeto-therapy*[1], was a revolutionary approach to dealing with psychological issues. Reich, who had once been an associate of Sigmund Freud, had developed important extensions to the talk-therapy methods of the day (e.g., *Character Analysis*), and theory (e.g., *The Function of the Orgasm*). But in a clinical setting he and others were continually faced with the intractability of many patients against the therapeutic methods—such as Freudian analysis—then in use. He came to believe that this "armoring" was not simply a "head issue," but was also elaborated in actual physical armoring of the musculature. In time he developed a novel, and highly successful, approach to psychotherapy: rather than just *talk* with his patients, *he manipulated and attacked the muscular armor directly*. But today we see almost nothing of his methods. Why is that? For a partial answer, see the prefatory article of this book, "Psychiatry, Then and Now".

Reich's downfall can be seen as analogous to that of Timothy Leary, Ph.D. He had already gone well outside the box with his vegeto-therapy, but went totally off the psychiatric reservation with

---

[1] Sometimes called *Orgonomy*. However, this term more appropriately refers to Reich's theory of "Orgone Energy". [Ed.]

his theory of a universal life energy he called "Orgone"[2], extraterrestrials, weather manipulation, and other *outré* notions. Eventually, his promotion of "Orgone accumulators" (which he claimed could collect and harness Orgone Energy) attracted the attention of the U.S. Government which, in 1957 prosecuted and imprisoned him and burned *all* of his books (which they claimed were nothing more than advertising for Orgone accumulators—which they held to be quackery). Reich died in prison in 1957, and it is against this backdrop that Regardie was finishing the first draft of this book.

Regardie was unusual at the time as he did not come to practice Reichian therapy in the "approved" fashion. Reich insisted that all practitioners be medical doctors who, in turn, had to be trained by his organization. Regardie was neither. To be sure, he was well qualified as his chiropractic training gave him great understanding of physiology—particularly the muscular-skeletal systems—and he had been trained by someone who had come through Reich's school.

One of Regardie's patients was Alan Miller (1943–2008) who later took the name Christopher S. Hyatt. Alan, like Francis, was practicing as a psychotherapist, and was intensely interested in mystical systems as well as human psychology. It was a perfect match, and they became close friends and colleagues. Regardie taught Alan vegeto-therapy which became a significant part of his successful practice in West Hollywood, California.

I was introduced to Alan by a mutual friend in 1971 when I was seeking a therapist. I immediately entered a course of Reichian Therapy with him which continued for some time. Alan also held a weekly group of a few of his patients in which we learned about other aspects of psychological testing and practice. Several of us became close friends with Alan and both socialized and worked with him—something which today would be legally dangerous, if not impossible for a therapist. Even then, the licensing boards were cracking down on such "dual relationships" and, seeing the writing on the wall, Alan retired from the formal practice of psychotherapy in the late 1970s when he was in his mid-30s.

---

[2] The concept of a universal life energy is, of course, quite common throughout the world, but seems to have been unacceptable in psychiatry, at least in the United States.

Around that time Regardie was in a legal dispute with his book publisher. Eventually he regained the rights to some of the titles they had published, but what to do with them? He approached Alan with the idea of publishing them, even though Alan had no experience in the field. Thus was born Falcon Press.

In addition to the titles that Regardie had gotten back from his former publisher, one of Falcon's earliest publications was Hyatt's *Undoing Yourself with Energized Meditation and Other Devices*. Hidden within this seminal work was the beginning of what eventually became *Radical Undoing* (often called *RUDY* today), Regardie and Hyatt's system of therapy based largely on Reich's methods.

**Other Resources**

- A Glossary of Terms
  http://www.wilhelmreichtrust.org/glossary.html

- The Wilhelm Reich Infant Trust was established in Reich's Last Will and Testament, signed on March 8, 1957. The Trust operates the Wilhelm Reich Museum in Rangeley, Maine; manages Reich's Archives at the Countway Library of Medicine at Harvard University; and makes the writings of Wilhelm Reich available through this website and at the Wilhelm Reich Museum Bookstore.
  http://www.wilhelmreichtrust.org

- The Wilhelm Reich Foundation is a fund-raising organization aiming to support projects, which further the qualitative development and promote the establishment of body psychotherapy (BP).
  http://www.wilhelmreichfoundation.eu/index.html

- The United States Association for Body Psychotherapy was founded in 1996 as an umbrella organization for the emerging profession of body psychotherapy.
  http://usabp.org

- The European Association for Body Psychotherapy [EABP] is the accrediting organization for Body Psychotherapists and the established authority in its field.
  http://www.eabp.org

- Bioenergetic Analysis is a specific form of body-psychotherapy—based upon the continuity between body and mind—rooted in the work of Wilhelm Reich and founded by Alexander Lowen (1910–2008).
  http://www.bioenergetic-therapy.com/index.php/en/

## BIBLIOGRAPHY

Relevant titles by Christopher Hyatt (all available from The Original Falcon Press)

### Books
- *Dogma Daze*
- *Energized Hypnosis*
- *Secrets of Western Tantra*
- *Sex Magic, Tantra & Tarot*
- *Taboo*
- *Tantra Without Tears*
- *To Lie is Human*
- *Undoing Yourself with Energized Meditation & Other Devices*
- *Undoing Yourself Too*

### Audios
- *The Energized Hypnosis Audios*
- *The Extreme Individual*
- *An Interview With Christopher Hyatt*
- *Shotgun Tantra*
- *Techniques for Undoing Yourself Volumes 1–2*

### Videos
- *The Energized Hypnosis Videos Volumes 1–4*
- *Radical Undoing Volumes 1–6*
- *The "You" Meditation*

# Psychiatry, Then and Now

## by MobiusFrame, M.D.

### Modern Psychiatry

I am a board certified psychiatrist in the U.S. Until the time of his death Alan Miller (aka Dr. Christopher Hyatt) was my primary mentor and a great support to me throughout my training. He often spoke of Francis Israel Regardie, Wilhelm Reich, and the bodywork he learned from Regardie which he ultimately reformulated and called "Radical Undoing". It is from this perspective that I was asked to write an Introduction to this book by Regardie, about Reich's body-work methods.

Since this book was written, psychiatry has undergone enormous changes. In modern times, most psychiatrists make diagnoses and give medications, while psychotherapists do the "talk therapy." Classical Freudian psychoanalysis is not in common practice. Some psychiatrists are trained in a variety of psychotherapies, but it seems most are not. The most common form of psychotherapy taught to psychiatrists is probably "supportive psychotherapy" and crisis management, but perhaps I'm too optimistic. There are different kinds of psychiatry residency training programs: some have psychotherapy training and some do not. I specifically chose a psychiatry residency program that has training in supportive psychotherapy, Cognitive Behavioral Therapy (CBT), and psychodynamic psychotherapy. We were evaluated by a panel of Ph.D. psychotherapists, Licensed Clinical Social Workers (LCSW), Licensed Clinical Professional Counselors (LCPC) and Registered Nurses (RN). Most of the psychiatry residents I knew found the psychotherapy training onerous and unnecessary as they will rarely do actual psychotherapy in the real world. The most common basic triad of psychotherapy in modern times is supportive psychotherapy, CBT, and psychodynamic psychotherapy. I was taught that psychoanalysis has a low efficacy rate for remission of most of the common major mental illnesses, and could be harmful to those with psychosis. We were taught instead, Psychodynamic Psychotherapy which incorporates the basics of Freudian thought, but is generally considered less useful and more abstract than A. Beck's CBT.

The average psychiatrist today knows nothing of Reichian body therapy as modern psychiatry has almost entirely outsourced "psychotherapy" to a range of non-medical providers: Ph.D., LCSW, LCPC and others. Psychiatrists in America today largely prescribe medications and treatments (such as Electro-Convulsive Therapy [ECT] and Transcranial Magnetic Stimulation [TMS]), and deal with a variety of medical crises (things that are somewhat covered by insurance and pay the bills), while psychotherapy is ordered as a treatment to be carried out by others.

While the average psychiatrist probably read and was tested on psychoanalytic theory in a basic form, at least once, they would analyze the scenarios and vignettes in this book differently than did Reich or Regardie. For example, a the modern psychiatrist is trained in the "bio-psycho-social model"—i.e., what is the behavioral or developmental issue and what kinds of medications, psychotherapies, and social services, etc., would best help the patient to be healthy? These treatments would then be ordered and the orders carried out by nurses, therapists, social workers and the like.

Child and adolescent psychiatrists and psychotherapists are probably more likely to be aware of psychoanalytic theory. However, I think "all this Freud stuff" is considered archaic and minimally useful to the average M.D. psychiatrist. This book is steeped in Freudian theory and Regardie makes many references to Freudian thinking in reference to Reich, e.g., "There may also be some accusation, in true Freudian clichés, of my having castrated Reich." Obscure psychoanalytic concept, this "castration." Hyatt often made such comments and when I asked him to explain he'd tell me to go read this or that book. Usually something from Edmund Bergler.

I was mildly familiar with Reich when I entered psychiatry residency and hopeful that I would get some training in "body-work." *It became quickly apparent that physical contact other than a handshake, or a touch on the shoulder or forearm for comforting the severely distressed, is forbidden and a punishable offense.* Reich's work should have been, and still should be, scientifically investigated, but it is largely considered harmful fantasy. We see these days some physical work from physical therapists, osteopaths, chiropractors, and the like. Rebirthing and primal scream therapies are more psychotherapeutic variants of physical work, but are largely considered ineffectual by the Evidenced Based model of medicine. If it doesn't exist in a peer-reviewed journal article, it is not a medical treatment. During my training I asked numerous psychiatrists and psychotherapists if they had ever heard of Wilhelm Reich, and only one, an 80-year-old retired psychoanalyst from the east coast, who taught classes at the university just for fun, had. I think most modern "biological" psychiatrists would consider this book so much psychoanalytic garble, already deemed useless and potentially harmful.

**Historic Psychiatry**

The techniques of the asylum era (roughly 1800's–1970's) included cold/hot baths; wrapping people tightly in wet sheets; forcing people to work or exercise; and chemical, and then Electro-Convulsive Therapies. Hypnosis came of age around the 1800's when the first person to use hypnosis for clinical purposes was a surgeon, Dr. James Braid.

When this book was written there were few psychiatric medications. Chlorpromazine (Thorazine) came of use in severely psychotic patients in the early 1950's. It was discovered accidentally after being used for anesthesia with surgeons noting improvement of psychotic symptoms in large numbers of patients.

With few medicines available prior to 1950, talking and manipulating the body were the primary treatments—along with simple detainment. Other common major psychiatric treatments available at the time of the writing of this book are listed by Regardie, including:

**ECT (Electro-Convulsive Therapy):** Still widely practiced today, Electro-Convulsive Therapy is considered the method of last resort in many of the most severe mental illnesses. Initially doctors noticed improvement in patients who had a seizure related to diabetes. Later the doctors induced seizures using insulin or other chemicals, but the death rate was high. Electro-Convulsive Therapy is much less likely to cause death. In fact it is considered safe during pregnancy.

**Lobotomy/Leucotomy:** Scrambling up the frontal lobes with an ice-pick was all the rage for a short while (1940's–1950's). There are modern incarnations of this used to treat severe seizures that don't respond to medications, but they are full surgical procedures and not some dude with a pointy object and a hammer.

**Hormonal/Endocrine Therapy:** Still in use to some degree. For example, refractory depression can be treated with, or at least other medications augmented with, thyroid hormones.

**Chemotherapy:** This is a reference to using medications. At the time this book was written, as mentioned above, there were literally no well-known psychiatric medications. LSD was new. Recent research (which has largely been impeded by legal rather than medical constraints) has shown that psilocybin, MDMA, Ketamine and LSD appear to have at least some therapeutic value. This is in addition to all the usual suspects: Prozac, Zoloft, Paxil, Amitriptyline, Lithium, etc.

**Hydrotherapy:** In the old days severe mental illnesses were often treated by forcing someone to sit in hot water or steam rooms for hours, often wrapping them tightly in wet sheets.

**Carbon dioxide:** This is an outdated treatment modality. As people were desperate for a psychiatric fix for the masses of anxious, depressed, hallucinating people they tried anything and everything, often with the goal of inducing a seizure.

Since the abolishment of the asylum mental health model around the 1970's, the new paradigm is that of "community mental health centers." Initially, the asylums of the 1800's were staffed with the most educated doctors, nurses, practitioners who were using the most modern treatments. However, the asylum system became so decayed and abused by the 1950's–1960's that most asylums were shuttered in favor of the "State Psychiatric Hospital," and its surrounding county-based "Community Mental Health Centers." Legislation was geared towards "reintegrating" mental health patients into their communities, and treating them in their communities with goals of increasing socio-occupational functioning: employment, marriage-family, independent living, paying taxes rather than relying on welfare. However, during the 1980's–2000's, federal funding for these institutions steadily decreased. When I started psychiatric residency in 2010 there were community mental health clinics in every town with a courthouse, and there were, in my state, approximately six state psychiatric hospitals, and something like 10 large facilities for housing the severely intellectually disabled. By the time my residency completed in 2014, there were only two state psychiatric hospitals, roughly 80% of all community mental health clinics were shuttered, and roughly 90% of all large facilities for the housing of severely intellectually disabled people were closed. The patients were then largely without any treatment which led to their going to an emergency room and being seen in general hospitals and their associated clinics—all with ever-decreasing federal funding or insurance parity. Nowadays if I talk with a surgeon they will say "I pay your salary." This is because something like 95% of my patients have no job, no home, no insurance, no way to pay for treatment, but by federal law, they must not be denied emergency treatment. The whole system has the feeling of polishing the brass on the Titanic. I model the situation as: the system is collapsing, it is my job to extract function from what is left of it.

**Psychiatry vs. Psychotherapy**

At one time all mental illnesses were categorized as either "neuroses" (software problems) or "psychoses" (hardware problems). The distinction was made between the severely mentally ill—essentially, institutionalized "psychotic"—patients, and everything else, which was called a "neurosis." (Neurosis is now considered an archaic term.)

A little anxiety here and there, or a mild seasonal depression (without suicidal ideations, obsessions-compulsions, dissociation, etc.), would be considered milder neuroses. For Regardie, Reichian therapy appears to be very effective at removing armors and the protections one has built inside—thereby freeing up emotional expression—and is much gentler than the other treatment modalities available at the time. Moreover Regardie considers Reich's methods effective for the more severe neuroses which even modern medications find a hard nut to crack.

Many people hold on to their traumas and wear them as a badge of honor. They're not sure what they would do without their bag of wounds to show to everyone they meet. The basic presumption of psychotherapy is that people need to express and feel certain emotions to properly process life events. There is the theory that if feelings are not fully experienced or integrated they cause chronic changes to the physical structure of the human. This is the curious crux of the human issue: that we are not at all in control of either logical or emotional faculties within our own bodies. Insight is important for psychotherapeutic healing, but it is not the only important factor.

The theory of this book is that chronic posturing of the personality and defense mechanisms, based on temperament and traumas, themselves based largely on chance, will lead to tensions, strains and blockages in a human body. Much like chronic cigarette smoking leads to reasonably reproducible and predictable changes in a human, so do chronic beliefs, worldviews, fears, tensions and feelings.

**Reich's Sexy Magic Forces**

Reich's Orgone Energy work and theorizations are largely considered to be psychotic delusions of magical powers. Since we do not have much objective evidence that orgone exists, it likely more efficacious to focus on the aspects of Reich's work that had measurable value, mainly his body-work psychotherapeutic methods. A balanced view might see character armor as serving a purpose, but in general removing armor, tension and restriction will lend to the health of the human, but not necessarily to satisfaction with one's culture, religion, family, etc.

It's important here to note that both reductionism and holism have value and need to be balanced as do empiricism and objectivism, rule of law and anarchy. Overall the human species cannot contemplate most things without involving dualistic evaluations of "good" or "bad." However, duality is the illusion that must be overcome and moved beyond. (But it is only one of the most primitive illusions generated by the human mind; there are so many others.) On the other hand, the "physical nameless wordless world" was your first world. You knew many things before you learned to speak. Some of them you learned, some were "reflexes," but what's the difference?

Again and again in this book we see Regardie's sagaciousness, as well as an adroit display of the basic machinations of psychoanalysis. Humans seem to carry their traumas (even the minor petty ones) from childhood throughout their life unlike the other animals on the planet, and psychoanalysis is all about digging down to the hidden motivations generated by the traumas and their unfolding.

**Working with the Vegetative Body**

All body-work involves touching and other physical manipulation of the body. In psychiatry residency I was specifically instructed that there are only two places that it is ever appropriate to touch a patient: the shoulder or the forearm. Furthermore, that touch was only to be used for comforting extreme distress, but is otherwise inappropriate. The thought of working with an unclothed patient is completely verboten in modern psychiatric and psychotherapeutic venues. This highlights one of the primary changes over time in psychiatry and psychotherapy: a majority of modern treatments involve noticing the body and acknowledging responses and sensations, but the kind of undressed session of Reichian therapy would lead to endless lawsuits for sexual harassment, and is considered completely inappropriate in most modern professional circles. Especially today. A vast majority of modern mental health providers will look at you like you are crazy if you mention "Reich." Then they will read up on him online and then they will be *certain* you are crazy.

I often ponder that as an adult in contemporary American society, it is easy and often likely that a human will go decades without any form of compassionate, caring touch. They might shake a few hands, give a few hugs and have sex with a few people, but consistent healthy touch is nearly absent. Ours is a sterilized society of simulacra and proxies. Also in trying to reclaim his genital function, man has substituted ideas for intuition, feeling and curiosity such that pornography, one night stands, and generally having sex with anything and everything one can has become an equally disruptive but blind reaction. Alas, I get the sense that we are all far more rigid than we know—I think if you ask a fish how it enjoys living in water, the fish will say, "what water?"

It would be interesting to ask what would have come of Reich's therapies and theories had he not been impeded. I get the sense that Reich had sort of two contributions to the world: his body focused therapy techniques vs. his "magic sexual energy fantasies." My best guess is that his body work has significant value. I don't know about orgone accumulators and the like. I think most scientists find it so preposterous that no one even thinks to test the orgone stuff out in a lab.

What little I know of orgone theory sounds similar to many religio-cultural constructs such as Hindu Prana and the abundant other energies they address. I think it is important to remember that no one knows what is happening here. Some of Reich's theories are empirically absurd, but nonetheless remain without any form of objective refutation. Maybe he could change the weather, but this is not the focus of this book.

**Rebellion**

Reich's imprisonment and the burning of his works is reminiscent of Timothy Leary's ostracism from organized psychiatry and psychology. In general, if you think outside the norm, be prepared to keep it quiet. Reich was so far ahead of his time that he was ahead of *our* time. He has a much more balanced view about the need to have good work and good play. Even now religious common folk believe sex is largely for reproduction, likely should not be enjoyed much, and should only occur between husband and wife. This conservative viewpoint was even more rampant and culturally ubiquitous in the 1950's. But Reich was a rebel. This is the distinguishing characteristic of Reich, and the thing that killed him and scattered the shards of his work. He seemed to think that the simple adjustment to cultural law was not healthy, and that the base instincts, even the human body itself had been relegated to the living recycle bin, while concepts such as "your soul, your country, your family, your career, your god" became the primary concern. This absurdity is the largest progenitor and nurturer of this emotional plague. For more on this topic see the writings of Max Stirner.

Examples of Reich's brazen rebelliousness include his views on marriage. Marriage is one of the primary mechanisms used by the state and religion to control the breeding and taxation of humans. To attack this culturally sanctioned institution outright was foolish in my view, especially in the 1950's, and especially if one enjoys having a job and not being in prison. Nonetheless, rebellion is necessary for the long term health of the human species. Repeatedly we see that Reich was not the type of person to simply accept what the authorities call "Truth".

We must remember that the sexual liberation and women's liberation movements of the 1960's–1970's, and subsequent explosion of the pornography industry have markedly impacted, for example, what I consider sexually normal, but this is less of a liberation than a desensitization. I don't spend much time contemplating sexual inhibition or liberation as that is but one fruit of a much larger poisonous tree. Genuinely open, compassionate sex, and the ability to be intimate and without armor—to love someone else truly—are fantastic goals, but most people absolutely do not love or respect themselves and prior to growing into a sexual or emotional adult, one I think should start with how to treat, love, and care for oneself.

Rebellion is one of the most important attributes of an unfettered mind. In most cultures rebellion is nearly completely unsanctioned, if not outright forbidden, and to the degree it is accepted at all, it is in some watered down version that resembles a field of bleating sheep. "Modern man functions like a machine" is the primary model of human consciousness in much of the world today. It is the rare human who tries to break out of the robotic strictures of society, culture, religion and establishment dogma (scientific or otherwise). Rebellion, chaos, conflict and non-conformity have brought most of the positive changes to humans throughout time, but also are constantly dissuaded by culture, indicating that culture itself—in any form—is a temporary solution to a long term human problem. Furthermore, culture itself is a form of, or set of, strictures. Therefore, one can see how easily the "removal of strictures" can equate with rebellion against culture, religion, etc.

These are also the primary channels through which a new rebellion must flow. Each new wave of information or understanding is first required to overcome the cow mind that goes into a defensive position, condemning new art, science, religion and literature, until the new is also old and bored and insufficient.

There are many "traps", the most basic of which is that as soon as you became a living thing, you were bound to die. Of course, Leary and so many others discussed that we may one day overcome the need for death, but this is the plague: *most people do not want to overcome death.* So, we get what we ask for, on average, en masse.

I agree that a human cannot be extricated from its traps if it is too armored. Some mystics would say the ultimate liberation from the need to be born and die requires the complete divestment of one's armor. As an extremely armored monkey, myself, I almost cannot fathom the total removal of my armors. This raises the question then: who am I, my armor or the thing that requires the armor? Regardless, I think the issue of Einstein's early hypotheses being rejected by the older established scientists is illustrative. In some ways, Einstein simply had to wait for enough of the old scientists to die off before his radical new ideas could be truly evaluated for veracity. Perhaps Reich simply didn't wait for long enough to introduce his orgone concepts as I suspect they would have been perceived as less "toxic" by a post 1960's human. But, in the 1950's he was perceived as truly harmful and insane to the degree that his trace has been essentially entirely removed from modern psychiatry and psychotherapy.

While it is beneficial to be able to temporarily adjust to the ambient culture and social structures, Christopher Hyatt's goals of "free time and free space" to cultivate one's own morality and society of self are far more important. But the constant pressure to conform to arbitrary social norms, over time, leads to physical changes in the human. Chronic high stress and feelings of dysphoria lead to hormonal changes that ultimately shorten life span. I tell some patients that I suspect I am giving them a pill that will allow them to tolerate the life they already despise, rather than encouraging them to rebel against their oppressors in any guise.

I'm not sure how often I've assessed my "plasmatic mobility," as referenced in the text, but it is known that chronic adrenaline release lends to chronic spasm/contraction of vascular smooth muscle and is thought to contribute to things like heart disease and hypertension, and that prolonged stress hormone release (e.g., adrenocorticosteroids) can diminish neuronal turnover in places such as the hippocampus. My best guess is that chronically swimming in stress hormones causes genetic, epigenetic, and physical changes in a human. Again, the physical cannot be separated from the characterological as decreased physical turnover of neurons, for example, is likely to have a direct impact on memory, cognition, executive function and overall personality. We humans are simply simpletons who have just stepped out of the jungle. We are children in adult bodies, full of dreams and simplifications, hysterics, prone to fancies.

The damage to brain function associated with chronic stress and trauma is reasonably well documented in the scientific literature. Psychosis is in simplest terms defined as "Impaired Reality Testing." Most commonly when one says "psychosis," one is referring to auditory hallucinations, visual hallucinations, delusions, and formal thought disorder. However, huge masses of humans routinely hallucinate a variety of gods, demons, devils and superstitions and are nonetheless considered "normal." I think in fact psychosis may be the default operating state of the human mind and the goal is to use technologies to augment our rudimentary perceptual apparatus, the brain, as it is prone to continuous psychosis.

Thousands of years of mass serfdom and slavery has had quite an impact on the inherently sheepish human. What other animal on the planet has such a protracted childhood? At least 15–25 years of being a child is common for human cultures. Snakes are born ready to inject venom, know how to swim, and are completely self-sufficient. Alas, they do not have such a large limbic system to deal with, with its constant suffusion of emotion and memory into each situation. This again points to the need for balance of the robotic reductionist human brain with the holistic, symbolic, visceral human totality.

I would argue that this chronic human need to believe in some system is a major part of the sickness of our species. The primary purpose of religion and culture is to control your production of orgasms and offspring, as well as your time, space and resources. The other primary purpose of culture, religion and society is to keep you pre-occupied, exhausted, and in a constant state of fear. This way you will cling to religion, patriotism, political movements and entertainment, and never will you stop to listen to your thoughts or feel your body. Fear is used to control the human. With enough fear, a person can be made to perpetrate war, rape, lynchings, stonings, and ultimately a mass of fearful monkeys can be motivated to genocide based on threats that are inflated to appear emergent.

I think this "plague" is the primary human attribute that will lead to our species ending itself. The human is so constantly in a state of—at least—mild emotional alarm and fear that it cannot conceive of a new idea. The human clings tightly to simple premises, outdated laws, explanations, dogmas, social norms and mores in a frantic and futile attempt to "make sense of" its life—which is almost by definition, nonsensical. The crux of the issue is that most humans are sheep who crave a shepherd, and very much enjoy being sheared and avidly await their slaughter for the lord's supper. A few humans do not like to have parents, authorities, or the chronic sacrifice (to god, family, country, etc.) to the degree that one's life is a living death. Choose whatever dogma you like, the fact remains that we as a species have little if any understanding of anything within or without.

\*\*\*

It had been difficult to find manuals of Reich's methods and other body-work techniques until the publication of Christopher Hyatt's *Radical Undoing* books, audios and videos (Falcon Press), and now, this book. I've also found that most therapists who employ body-therapies, don't like to talk about the techniques or their purposes or meanings. Dr. Hyatt did not like discussing the "why" of most of the techniques he promulgated, saying that it allows people to *theorize* about the work instead of *doing it.* I find curious Freud's optimistic speculation of a time when a biological route to the treatment of the neuroses could be developed. This gave rise to the current dogma that you have a "chemical imbalance," and the priests of psychiatry have a pill that will fix it. Which is every bit as bizarre and simplistic as Freud rehashing the principles of newly discovered electricity, applying it to human behavior, and calling it psychoanalysis. Reich, Regardie and Hyatt stand in a long line of humans intent on freeing the human from itself.

# Toward a Blank Slate

## by Calvin Iwema, M.A.

I came to know the UnDoing work (also known as **RUDY**, the **R**adical **U**n**D**oing of **Y**ourself, or as Regardie refers to it in this book, *vegeto-therapy*) from the time I spent as a student and co-author with Dr. Christopher Hyatt. The idea of getting back to a true blank slate, the *tabula rasa,* although somewhat idealistic, is something that we shared in common. We looked with optimism at the permutations the world might take if given free rein to explore and evolve. Imagine serious and unrestricted research on genetics for life-extension and physical regeneration and adaptation. What about the philosophical maturation and evolution of the human to learn to cohabitate and negotiate resources with more skill than a wounded, scared and angry ape? We also shared and enjoyed the rebel's perspective, which puts loving and honoring the self as a *much* higher priority than average instead of worshipping dogma and following rules of a game which serves a select few, disguised as "the common good." The rebel is willing to do whatever it takes to meet his objectives, and in the case of UnDoing, Reich, along with Regardie and Hyatt have certainly done that. You will find that the material in this book goes quite a few steps farther than what was commonly accepted back when it was written, let alone today. It disturbs me that we still live in such a fearful, naïve, prudish and restrictive society which makes continuing this work, for the simple and noble cause of elevating the human back to something generative and creative, so difficult.

So many claim and exclaim that they are *free*, operating under their own free will as rebels, sinners, iconoclasts and pioneers when in fact they neither behave that way physically nor accomplish as much as their superior self-evaluation would lead you to believe. Having the personal and therapeutic goal of reaching past normalcy and delving into my potential is what brought me to Hyatt and to this work in the first place.

What I have learned through experience (I have practiced as a psychotherapist) and have come to appreciate more over time is that there is only so much that talk therapy and analysis can accomplish on its own. While there is great value in understanding how I got this way and why I am thus at this current state, it is not the end-in-itself I thought it was when I first started my journey. Understanding the big "whys" and "hows" is often when the work really starts. One you have had the "aha moment" you still need to get on with life, pursue directions, and achieve goals. The UnDoing work helps you to get more done at a faster pace with less suffering. It allows you to have an organic and unedited expression of yourself and to undo the emotional double-binds—the go/don't go messages that constantly remind you to limit your reach.

The muscular tensions and correlated emotions that serve as a steering and limiting mechanism operate at a level outside of the story we put together that contains the whys, hows, causes, excuses and beliefs. As Regardie shows that sound itself (think along the lines of a cooing mother, growling father or different types of music) becomes linked with emotion and muscular tensions linked to memory, we realize just how much of this programming and learning takes place outside our conscious mind's own commentary and awareness. An oversimplification is to say that the thinking isn't necessarily a part of the wiring, or that the software doesn't have sufficient impact on the hardware. This is where UnDoing shines as a unique and very special type of therapy. It is one of the few psychotherapies that operate and interface directly with the body. By operating on this level directly, it helps the *body* process, integrate and reset itself to be in support of the organism in its current context instead of being stuck with past programming. Talk therapy aims at helping the *mind* process and re-learn, which does not translate nearly as directly to the body as we would wish. This reminds me of experiments where you attempt to write down the instructions for tying your shoes, rather than showing someone physically how to do it, which is much more expedient and direct.

The emergence of UnDoing sheds light and can help lessen a self-diminishing social belief around what is "bad" and impolite about our bodies. UnDoing's focus on the body allows the body to be elevated to its rightful place in the hierarchy of personal and social importance. The Victorian era, and what came before, has done enough damage with shame and guilt surrounding the body. The philosophy underlying the UnDoing work surpasses this antiquated thinking and encourages healing in both mind and body by closing the artificial gap between the elevated mind and the lowly body. Reich, Regardie and Hyatt all stressed that the body and its functions take precedence and should not be edited or shamed. If you have to burp, fart, yawn, sneeze or tingle…this should be not only permitted but welcomed. Society has long said otherwise and has blamed the individual for their natural bodily functions as if they are shameful indiscretions. As these functions are resisted and blocked they become tensions and corresponding emotions. At some point this leads to belief systems and legislation, either in the individual to himself or society to itself, with the guilty party being nothing other than what is natural and healthy for the body. It doesn't take much to connect the dots and come to the conclusion that society at large still supports the notion of the original sin of being born a dirty and naughty human.

There are a few things that come to mind when considering the perspective of the therapist. First, the goals of therapy for Reich, Regardie and Hyatt are somewhat different than that of the normal population. This is elevated further when you look through the perspective of their involvement in the occult. Most cringe at the use of the word occult and equate it to witches, wizards, magic, psychic phenomena and evilness (and, unfortunately, orgone as well). I urge you to think in terms of *hidden.* The true occult has long stood for free thinking and rebellion against the status quo and power elite— along with their superstitions and social games intended to increase their power, wealth and influence. What the pioneers of evolution in the field of philosophy, medicine and, later on, psychology were looking into and discussing *had to be hidden* for their own safety. Consider the fates of Socrates, Galileo, Leary and Reich along with countless others who were ostracized and disposed of quietly. The difference I am pointing at is that Reich, along with Regardie and Hyatt, didn't seek to be included in the sample of "normal population," but strove forcefully and deliberately to supersede it. Their standards of human health and performance are greater than that of the average Joe. Their openness to free thought, free will and exposing human games put them at risk with authorities. Their drive, along with the occult backchannel is why this work has survived, been improved upon and is currently being published. It all could have just as easily been lost in the odd footnotes of research.

The goal of Reichian therapy is the maximization of the human to fully capitalize on freedom, creativity and overall personal evolution. You can see from Regardie's writing that he interfaced with the general public much more in alignment with these goals than most (dare I say, almost all) therapists do today. It is the state of psychology today that the risks of litigation, censure, loss of license or worse... often overriding any benefit to the patient...has become a major focus of the therapist. Their own career risk management takes a much greater priority than doing work that creates *real change.* This is in part due to the fickle nature of common man—that even with the advances in psychology and medicine, the possibilities of this type of therapy take a back seat to political correctness. The possibility of causing some level of temporary upset in a client, even though there is tremendous upside and long term return on investment, is to be avoided. To suggest to the average client that they remove most of their clothes, lie down on a true working couch (bed) and then breathe and move in certain ways that will stir up a great deal of emotion seems more than a little preposterous these days. On top of that, we have the practitioner helping the client position their body with their own hands, and at times press, poke, prod and slap them. Regardie even talks of holding clients. For what diabolical ends the concerned public and licensing boards might ask? To help clients become aware, re-process and re-align with their own bodies (thus, their hardware and software) at a deep level. In other words, to assist their clients so they can *heal.* These days, touching a therapeutic client even when they are crying and falling apart, is highly limited and all but forbidden. As you read through the book with the explanations of technique and case studies, you will quickly see how this would put a current practitioner into a predicament when viewed through the pampered, histrionic lens of John Q Public.

Second, the level of psychological analysis you find in these case studies and the level of psychological and anatomical acuity and dexterity is not at all common in your average therapist, let alone the educational programs that create them. While much of Freud's psychoanalytic analysis and the psychodynamic field that followed is not as prevalent as it once was, it is important that the baby not be thrown out with the bathwater. The human mind functions in a highly symbolic way, and the psychological difficulties people have—limitations, fears, guilt, anxieties—are often responses to their conceptual inner world whether they or their therapist is conscious of it or not. The neurological mechanisms and connections between the human response to metaphor and analogy are not easily, if at all, pinpointed…yet continues to exist. We can see that most people respond to the semantic difference between "up" and "down", "forward and behind" as well as create a personal identity with all combinations of metaphors. I think that psychological analysis still has room to help a patient understand their own inner workings through understanding and re-deciding what and how they label themselves and how those concepts serve as the foundation for their neurotic dysfunction. There is no current reason that one's psyche need be a black box with its functioning completely unknown to them, even if that functioning is explained and known as a metaphor. This is somewhat at odds with current medicine, which needs a different level of proof to generate prescriptions. To be clear I am not against medication, but in favor of a balance of personal power and hard work *along with* prudent medical assistance. What I find difficult in this is that the current state of psychological and/or medical practitioners cannot balance the side of the equation presented in this book *because they are completely unaware of it, and generally do not value it anyway.*

To experience or practice UnDoing therapy, one must dig deep to find and understand this material as well as finding an avenue to experience it live and be taught how to do it. With that said I am thoroughly thankful that I've had the opportunity to experience this work firsthand…both on the couch and looking over it.

One of the maxims that both Regardie and Hyatt stressed are for the client to "make haste slowly." The overall goal of the work is that it should be self-enhancing to the client and support their progress in life, not completely disrupt it. The techniques are powerful, and one should approach UnDoing with the respect and caution it deserves. While Regardie was rigorous on the level of training that should accompany the practitioner, Hyatt saw the trends and wanted to preserve the work and get it into the hands of the solo practitioner. While he liked to say "Become Who You Are, There Are No Guarantees," one can also posit that you can put the odds of success in your favor by not pushing too hard too fast. Your nervous system can only process and adapt so fast, so lots of extra work does nothing but slow the entire process down.

UnDoing is a therapy that works well in conjunction with other therapeutic techniques. Often the results of various techniques inform each other, which helps one make more progress at a quicker pace and enhanced accuracy. Progress in therapy should be measured not just in terms of how good you feel, or how bad you don't feel, but in terms of how much work you can accomplish. This includes both therapeutic work—which requires resiliency—as well as the external work required to build the life that you desire to have. (Alas, I may be among the minority who thinks that building a great life is the end result of good therapy.)

Psychotherapy—talk therapy—is the most obvious overlap of UnDoing, and as evidenced by Regardie's writing, they are intertwined and often performed in close succession to each other. As body armor and tension are lessoned, memories and past decisions are more easily accessed and processed. The patient doesn't need to push against their own tensions and fears as much as they do with talk-based therapy alone.

Hypnosis is another therapeutic technique that is synergistic with UnDoing. The body and mind are more easily relaxed through UnDoing, especially following an UnDoing session. This also seems to help the mind to be more receptive to suggestions, which in this case are pro-health, continued learning and unlearning.

Meditation is also enhanced through UnDoing work. The "sensing and feeling" component of UnDoing, along with the insistence that the patient stay present and in-the-moment during the session, has a direct and intentional correlation to meditative practice which shares this direction in common. It is often said that tension is thought and thought creates tension. Since deep meditative states and the transformations that occur in them are free of thought, and thus free of personal stories and metaphors, it is easy to see why a therapy that reduces tension and "thoughting" is extremely valuable to the practitioner.

Yoga, physical disciplines and sports that require flexibility and the overcoming of fears and limitations are also enhanced through UnDoing. Considering that yoga, as well as some martial arts, have a spiritual underpinning to them as well is another overlap of the results and goals of the UnDoing work.

If you were to combine all of the disciplines I just mentioned, and performed them regularly over time, what do you think you might accomplish? I will leave it to you to connect the dots and to see the depth and breadth of the work that Regardie and Hyatt were involved with. As you read on, you will see the component that Reich pioneered.

**Calvin Iwema** is an author and consultant in the world of personal and professional development. He is an executive coach and leadership development consultant, and has worked as a licensed psychological counselor. His entry into the world of psychology was with hypnosis and NLP before pursuing formal education in it. Calvin was a long-time student of and coauthor with Dr. Christopher Hyatt and continues to further their work. On occasion he works with individuals in the same manner that Dr. Hyatt did. You can contact him through his website:
        http://www.bestmindforward.com

# Introduction

## by Israel Regardie

In the summer of 1956 I wrote a letter to Dr. Wilhelm Reich asking permission to quote at some length from various of his writings. There was no answer. Under the pressure of everyday clinical practice and the task of revising this manuscript, I momentarily forgot all about the enquiry. By the time it became necessary to obtain permission from other authors and publishers for the many quotations to be included in this book I once more wrote, in the spring of 1957, to Dr. Reich.

Several weeks later the following letter came in the mail:

June 15, 1957

Dear Dr. Regardie:

Dr. Wilhelm Reich is imprisoned since March 11, 1957, on a contempt of court charge, obtained by a corrupt government agency, on the basis of an unlawful, unconstitutional court order (1954) which enjoins *all* literature concerning the discovery of the Cosmic Life Energy.

The injunction specifically forbids communication regarding the subject of Orgone Energy with anyone else. You may find yourself acting as the tool of a conspiracy to destroy the Discoverer and the Discovery of the Life Energy in publishing about it at this time. We are not in a position to advise you further than to recommend you study the records in this case for the true background of the situation:

U.S. District Court, Portland, Maine Southern Division, Civil Case 1056
U.S. District Court, Portland, Maine Southern Division, Criminal Case 5003.
U.S. Court of Appeals for the First Circuit, Appeal 5160.
Supreme Court of the United States, October 1956, No. 588.

See Injunction, in Volume IV. Record Appendix to Briefs for Appellants, Case 5160, page 67a-72a, especially points 5) page 70a, and i page 72a... "That the defendants refrain from, either directly or *indirectly,* in violation of said act, disseminating information pertaining to the assembly, construction, or composition of orgone energy accumulator devices to be employed for therapeutic or prophylactic uses by man or for other animals..." The works you wish to quote from are considered labeling of a misbranded device!

A copy of this letter will be forwarded to the FBI, together with some others of similar nature.

Sincerely yours,

/s/ Eva Reich, M.D.<br>
(Daughter of Dr. Wilhelm Reich<br>
Power of Attorney)

Hancock, Maine

I do not consider myself a tool of any conspiracy, real or imaginary, to destroy any cause—least of all Reich and his discovery. He commands too much of my most sincere respect, as this book should indicate. I would not lend myself willingly to any such smear. This book does not relate in any way to the accumulator nor to the cosmic life energy. There is no attempt to disseminate information pertaining to the assembly, construction or composition of the orgone accumulator. Therefore, it does not violate the terms of the federal injunction.

I do not and have not practiced orgonomy. Nor do I know anything about the accumulator above and beyond what has been overtly published by Reich. As his critics allege, it may be quite worthless in the treatment of cancer. I personally do not know. However, his writings should have been studied and given due consideration before some of the more grotesque criticisms about him were penned.

It must be emphasized here that I am not a partisan of any cause. I do not favor by any means the cruel and malicious opposition that dismisses Reich's contributions as delusions and he himself as paranoid. Nor, on the other hand, do I adhere unequivocally to the current Reich viewpoints.

After receipt of Eva Reich's letter, I proceeded with the task at hand—to complete the revision of this manuscript preparatory to publication, and to incorporate the quotations I had assembled for due acknowledgment in this introduction.

Then came the news in the fall of 1957. Wilhelm Reich had died in jail. This was indeed a great shock. I think we are the losers here. Reich was a great innovator as well as a creative and experimental clinician. It is a blot against the intellectual climate of our society that he has been denied the freedom of expressing and disseminating his ideas, whatever they were. It is an even greater crime against freedom of scientific thought that he was imprisoned—regardless of the fact that he had violated a legal injunction and then refused to adequately defend himself. He felt no court of law was fit to adjudge scientific discovery and progress.

I am deeply concerned about this infringement of the basic freedom of expression of scientific thought and creativity. We run the risk, if it is continued as it was in his case, of becoming imprisoned in a police state where not only our ordinary activities and secular movements are controlled and regulated, but our thinking as well. This is a condition which violates the basic mental climate and attitudes of the fathers of the American revolution. Perhaps Thomas Paine and Thomas Jefferson today might have been considered subversive individuals and subject to investigation by a government agency.

The lifework of Wilhelm Reich can be divided for the sake of convenience into at least five well-defined epochs. The first stage of this lifework found him operating as a psychoanalyst, apparently very efficiently. This has been written about at great length by others so there is no need on my part to discuss it. In the second stage, he elaborated his technique of "character analysis"[1]. Many psychoanalysts now admit that these contributions have become incorporated, wholly or in part, into the mainstream of psychoanalytic thinking.

Vegeto-therapy[2] was the third phase. Altogether apart from Reich's own writing on this subject, there has been little attempt to organize, consolidate, or reinterpret this material. I am unable to determine what the motives for this silence are, though a fair guess might be fear of abuse if the technique should fall into the hands of

---

[1] See Reich's *Character Analysis,* first published in 1933. It has been republished in several editions since then. [Ed.]
[2] Reich's term for his body-oriented therapeutic methods which are intended to directly attack the "body armor". [Ed.]

one untrained in the method. Here, as in psychoanalysis, it is categorically asserted that the proper employment of the therapy is impossible unless one has gone through a protracted course of therapy oneself. Otherwise the therapist's own unresolved character problems will unduly modify the clinical responsiveness of the patient.

I rather fancy that there is also a fear of ridicule and misinterpretation because most of the work done is with the patient in a relatively unclothed state. It is not difficult to imagine how many abuses could follow by an irresponsible therapist taking advantage of a patient under such circumstances. There would also be some apprehension that the technique, frankly aggressive at times, could readily be distorted and perverted into the grossest brutality and sadism.

*Physical Dynamics and Character Structure* by Alexander Lowen, M.D.[3], (Grune & Stratton, New York, 1958) is a work about the pre-orgone therapy of Reich. It is a splendid piece of work. It attempts to fit many of the Reich concepts and methods into the general framework of psychoanalysis. It, however, suffers from the major defect already mentioned—there is no adequate description of the technique involved. There are hints and many clues, but these become intelligible only in the light of having known what the methodology really amounts to.

I strongly maintain that some of the creative approached made to the vexing problem of neurosis by Reich are so significant and so valuable that they must be given broader circulation in the professional field. He has made some timeless contributions, altogether apart from orgonomy, which can solve several of the therapeutic problems that we encounter daily in clinical practice. Many people on either side of the fence may strongly criticize both my exposition of the vegeto-therapeutic technique and my tentative neurophysiological hypothesis which puts the burden of explanation upon hyperventilation. But I rather fancy that there will be a far greater number who will welcome with open arms and with equally open minds this manual of a specific therapeutic approach.

There may also be some accusation, in true Freudian clichés, of my having castrated Reich. I can only comment that one abstracts

---

[3] Lowen was a student of Reich's and developed his own variation of the therapeutic methodology called "Bioenergetics." [Ed.]

from one's environment what one needs, or what can be fitted into one's own frame of reference. Or else one uncritically swallows a mass of dogma wholesale without digesting it and making it one's own personal property, thereby losing one's human identity in the phenomenon of becoming a fanatical follower.

This book has taken some years in preparation. It has been frequently revised, edited and criticized. Some areas have been expanded and others deleted—constantly being modified by my own clinical observations and experience. I am especially indebted to several friends who have gone to the trouble of reading it and extending their literary criticisms and technical suggestions. I am happy to acknowledge therefore the gracious assistance of Dr. Henry Platov, Dr. Ursula Greville, Dr. George Steeples and the late Dr. Robert Lindner for the vast help and understanding they have given in what was for me a mammoth task of writing. Without their encouragement and aid it would have been far less readable and organized than it may appear to be now. I am very grateful to them.

To all the authors and publishers who have courteously given me permission to quote from their books I must acknowledge my indebtedness. In some instances permission has been given by the author, in others by the publishers, and in a few by both author and publisher. I list them all—author, publisher and title—in tabulation below.

## BIBLIOGRAPHY

1. *American Journal of Psychotherapy* (for news item about Reich) VIII, 3. New York.
2. Gerhard Adler. *Studies in Analytical Psychology.* New York, Norton & Co. 1948.
3. Mark D. Altschule. *Bodily Physiology in Mental and Emotional Disorders.* New York, Grune & Stratton, 1953.
4. Edouard Ascher. "Motor Attitudes and Psychotherapy," in *Psychosomatic Medicine,* July-August, 1949.
5. C.E. Best and N.B. Taylor. *The Physiological Basis of Medical Practice.* Baltimore, Williams & Wilkins, 1950.

6. Trygve Braatøy. *Fundamentals of Psychoanalytic Technique.* John Wiley, 1954.
7. Charlotte Buhler. "The Process-Organization of Psychotherapy," in *The Psychiatric Quarterly.* Utica, N.Y. April, 1954.
8. Stanley Cobb. *Emotions and Clinical Medicine.* New York, Norton & Co., 1950.
9. D. Cameron Ewen. *General Psychotherapy.* New York, Grune & Stratton, 1950.
10. Otto Fenichel. *The Psychoanalytic Theory of Neurosis.* New York, Norton & Co., 1945.
11. W.E. Fenn, H. Hahn, A.B. Otis, and L.E. Chadwick. "Physiological Observations on Hyperventilation" in *Journal of Applied Physiology,* 1:11, May 1949.
12. Robert Fliess. *The Psychoanalytic Reader,* Vol. I, New York. International Universities Press. 1948.
13. Sigmund Freud. "Analysis Terminable and Interminable," *Vol. V. Collected Papers.* London, Hogarth Press, 1950.
14. Bertrand Frohman. *Brief Psychotherapy.* Philadelphia, Lea & Febiger, 1949.
15. Martin Gardner. *Fads and Fallacies in the Name of Science.* New York, Dover Publications, 1957.
16. Donald F. Geddes. *An Analysis of the Kinsey Reports.* New York, Mentor Books, 1954.
17. Ernest Gellhorn. *Autonomic Regulations.* New York, Interscience Publishers, 1943.
18. E.L. Gibbs, Gibbs, Lennox and Nims. "Regulation of Cerebral Carbon Dioxide." *Arch. Neurol. & Psych,* 47. June, 1942. Chicago, Illinois.
19. Frederick A. Gibbs. "Value of Electroencephalography" in *Modern Medicine,* July 15, 1954.
20. L.A. Gillilan. *Clinical Aspects of the Autonomic Nervous System.* Boston, Little Brown & Co., 1954.

21. Roy Grinker. "Hypothalamus Function in Psychosomatic Interrelations." *Studies in Psychosomatic Medicine,* edited by Franz Alexander and Thomas N. French. New York, Ronald Press, 1948.
22. Henry Guze. "Compensatory Behavior as Completion of the Sensori-Motor Cycle." *Journal of General Psychology,* 1953, 83.
23. Carl G. Jung. *Two Essays On Analytical Psychology.* Bollingen Series, XX. 7. Translated by R.F.C. Hull. New York, Pantheon Books, 1953.
24. S.H. Kraines. *Therapy of the Neuroses and Psychoses.* Philadelphia, Lea & Febiger, 1943.
25. Bernard I. Lewis. "The Hyperventilation Syndrome." *Annals of Internal Medicine,* 38, 1953.
26. Robert Lindner. *Prescription for Rebellion.* New York, Rinehart, 1953.
27. Margaret Mead. "What is Human Nature." *Look,* April 19, 1955, New York.
28. Bela Mittelman. "Psychosomatics." *Encyclopedia of Psychology.* New York, Citadel Press, 1946.
29. Henry J. Montoye. "Breath-holding as a Measure of Physical Fitness." *The Research Quarterly of the American Association for Health, Physical Education and Recreation,* 22:3.
30. M.F. Ashley Montagu. *Anthropology and Human Nature.* Boston, Porter Sargent, 1957.
31. Clifford J. Morgan. *Physiological Psychology.* New York, McGraw Hill, 1943.
32. Ruth Monroe. *Schools of Psychoanalytic Thought.* New York, Henry Holt & Co., 1955.
33. Norman Munn. *Psychology.* Boston, Houghton Mifflin Co., 1946.
34. P.P. Pavlov. *Conditioned Reflexes and Psychiatry.* New York, International Publishers, 1941.

35. Frederick Perls, et al. *Gestalt Therapy.* New York, Julian Press, 1951.
36. Francis M. Pottenger. *Symptoms of Visceral Disease.* St. Louis, Mosby Co., 1944.
37. *Psychiatric Quarterly* (for book review.) 22:4, 1948. Utica, New York.
38. Carl R. Rogers. *Counselling and Psychotherapy.* Boston, Houghton, Mifflin Co., 1942.
39. Leon J. Saul *Emotional Maturity.* New York, Lippincott, 1947.
40. Ernest Schachtel. "On Memory." *A Study of Interpersonal Relations.* New York, Hermitage Press, 1941.
41. John M. Schimmenti. "Hyperventilation Syndrome in Women." *Modern Medicine,* May 15, 1954.
42. Charles Shagass and Robert B. Malmo. "Psychodynamic Themes and Localized Muscular Tension during Psychotherapy" in *Psychosomatic Medicine,* XVI, 4. 1954.
43. Sir Charles Sherrington. *Man on His Nature.* London, Cambridge University Press, 1940.
44. Nathan W. Shock. "Physiological Factors in Behavior," *Personality and the Behavior Disorders,* Vol. I., edited by J. MCV. Hunt. New York, Ronald Press, 1944.
45. William V. Silverburg. *Childhood Experiences and Personal Destiny.* New York, Springer Publishing Co., 1952.
46. A.D. Speransky. *A Basis for a Theory of Medicine.* New York, International Publishers, 1934.
47. Wilhelm Stekel. *Conditions of Nervous Anxiety and Their Treatment.* New York, Liveright, 1933, and *Technique of Analytical Psychotherapy,* New York, 1950.
48. William Steig. *The Agony in the Kindergarten.* New York, Duell, Sloan & Pearce, Inc., 1950.
49. Clara Thompson. *Psychoanalysis: Evolution and Development.* Hermitage Press, 1950.

50. George N. Thompson and J. M. Nielson. *Engrammes of Psychiatry.* Springfield, Ill. Thomas, 1947.
51. Mabel Elsworth Todd. *The Thinking Body.* Boston, Branford Co. 1948.
52. W. Grey Walter. *The Living Brain.* New York, Norton & Co., 1953.
53. Robert Wartenberg. *The Examination of Reflexes.* Chicago, Year Book Publishers, 1945.
54. Carl A. Whitaker and Thomas P. Malone. *The Roots of Psychotherapy.* New York, Blakiston Co., 1953.
55. L.L. Whyte. *The Direction of Human Development.* New York, Mentor Books, 1950.
56. Benjamin Wolstein. *Transference.* New York, Grune & Stratton, 1954.

Finally, an acknowledgment must be made to Wilhelm Reich and his publishing organization. Though no direct permission has been obtained to use quotations from his various writings because of present legal complications, nonetheless I feel impelled to register my profound gratitude. I know of no other way of expressing my appreciation than by dedicating this manual to him with the hope that perhaps it may restimulate scientific interest in his creative contributions to psychotherapy. I do not know whether he would welcome this, were he alive today. But this is beside the point. It is my own sense of deep obligation and appreciation that requires some form of expression.

## Chapter I

### Rebel

"Rebellion is...the instinct that, by participating in all the
activities of the organism, is the vehicle of evolution."
— Robert Lindner

Every present-day form of psychotherapy has evolved from the parent stock of psychoanalysis. That is to say one of the earliest colloquialisms given to Freud's method was "the talking cure." So it has remained to this day. Psychoanalysis and its derivatives are conceptualistic approaches to emotional problems and neurotic conflicts. The few advances made in recent years remain fixated by-and-large on the same level. And this despite Freud's optimistic speculation of a time when a biological route to the treatment of the neuroses could be developed.

Though this hope for a biological approach has not yet been fulfilled, voices are being raised testifying to the frustrating impasse that has arisen in the field of psychotherapy. Many critics have expressed the belief that a verbal psychotherapy for the neuroses has fallen far short of what was expected of it. In the severe obsessional and compulsive neuroses, no matter how much intellectual insight the patient achieves, neither the anticipated improvement nor the emotional release occurs. The term "affect-lame" has been justly used with regard to such neurotically blocked patients. No verbalistic therapy appears to alter the clinical course of their malady.

Psychoanalysis has had a leavening effect on almost every phase of our cultural life. In one way or another, the world has become different because of Freud's dynamic contributions to our understanding of personality and motivation. Medicine, history, anthropology, philosophy and all the social sciences have been profoundly impressed. Despite this, current professional criticism is that psychoanalysis leaves much more to be desired in the treatment of some of the neuroses.

A tempest has been stirred up by these criticisms, but nearly everyone has overlooked a dynamic non-verbal therapy which is a step in the direction of Freud's anticipation of a biologically oriented therapy. It was developed in the 1930's by Wilhelm Reich. His contribution has almost been relegated to the dust heap of oblivion for a variety of dubious motives which need to be exposed as inadequate and unworthy of the scientific world. A small number of contemporaries gifted with sharp perception have recognized our indebtedness to Reich. Prejudice and fear have darkened their counsel however and hampered their efforts to enrich our thinking.

In this thesis, I propose to give a brief history of Reich in order to place his work in the proper perspective of psychiatric endeavor and to indicate the possible motives for his ostracism and repudiation by modern psychoanalysts. Fuller biographical data may be explored in *Wilhelm Reich* by David Boadella (Vision Press, England, 1973), a fine introduction to the man and his work. Also I suggest reading *The Quest for Wilhelm Reich* by Colin Wilson (Anchor Press/Doubleday, New York, 1981), a critical and revealing portrait of Reich and a challenging re-assessment of his ideas and his life work.

It will be necessary to review some of his theories concerning character, personality and neurotic development, and to describe at length the specific nature of the unique psychotherapy he evolved for the treatment of severe and chronic neuroses. I propose further to replace his debatable theory about "orgone energy", which has encountered opposition from medicine, with a neurophysiological interpretation. The latter should prove a more satisfactory frame of reference for the clinical phenomena encountered in the application of Reich's methods. This interpretation could lead in time to come to as many innovations in therapy and the social sciences as did the psychoanalytical contributions of the early part of this century.

One hundred years ago Braid separated hypnotism from the unacceptable terms of "animal magnetism" and so paved the way for the evolution of psychoanalysis. In 1950 Dollard and Miller of the Yale Institute of Human Relations attempted a reinterpretation of Freud's techniques in terms of the learning theories derived from experimental psychology (5). They contended that this step permitted establishment of psychotherapy on a more sound scientific footing, permitting new developments in precision technique and prediction of results. What was once attempted with hypnosis, and more recently with psychoanalysis I now wish to do with Reich's concept of the character-muscular armor and his technique of vegeto-therapy. Since the clinical facts are valid and experimentally verifiable, the proposed re-evaluation should disclose scientific possibilities that were inconceivable or improbable with the former theory.

Reich has presented a body of principles and reliable techniques which in many ways meet current scientific requirements. They are of special value in the severe obsessional and compulsive neuroses producing personality reorganization where everything else has previously failed. Psychoanalytically oriented, since it has evolved out of the work of a former Freudian, vegeto-therapy is essentially a biological rather than a conceptual approach to therapy. Its use yields data which may shed new light on hosts of social problems, history, anthropology, comparative religion and human behavior as a whole.

What are the reasons for development of a non-verbal psychotherapy? When employing conventional psychotherapy, one often encounters situations where a severe affect-lameness has impeded the successful course of therapy. To dismiss such problem situations as being due to "resistance" is merely dodging the basic issue. Consider the many incidents narrated by a patient relating to the early loss of a parent where grief and sorrow were experienced. Again and again, the therapist has contrived—on the theoretical basis that frequent and intense verbalization might elicit a reliving emotionally of the painful situation—to help the patient feel the situation he is discussing. All too often he finds himself up against a blank wall of emotional sterility and lameness.

For example, there was a girl whose father had died many years previously. Bereft and grief-stricken because he had been her only remaining love object, she was horrified upon his death by her desolation, emptiness and inability to cry. At the funeral, the spectacle of friends and relatives weeping freely left her feeling frozen. During therapy no matter how often this event and its pertinent psychodynamics were investigated, she was still blocked emotionally.

Another patient, a male passive-feminine character, sent off to a health camp at the age of 10 years because of a suspected tubercular condition, became attached to the matron who had shown him the first overt affection he had received in his life. About 18 months later, she left to take a job elsewhere. Pierced within by a feeling of being left behind, rejected by the one person he had begun to love, he felt he wanted to cry. Try as he would, however, there were no tears. He felt hard, cold and dead inside. It seems as if he knew the flow of tears would relieve his grief; the demonstration of sorrow would assuage his sense of isolation. It was not until after 30 years of frustration and bitterness that he was able to shed a few of those repressed tears with the aid of non-verbal psychotherapy. He had previously talked about it, discussed it with me. He could vividly recall his frustration, but up to the time non-verbal therapy was started nothing had brought any kind of affective response.

A 48-year-old chronic anxiety neurotic who had been plagued since the age of 10 by feelings which convinced him he was going crazy, narrated that he had a strict Catholic upbringing. In parochial school, there was the prolonged emphasis by the Sisters that anything to do with sex was vile. This conclusion they buttressed by teaching in history classes that many of the Roman emperors who indulged in sex debauches became insane. At this time he was masturbating often and he began to experience guilt about this habit. His family was undergoing some financial hardship so that sleeping accommodations at home were limited. In one bedroom were three beds. He slept in one, his sister in another nearby, his parents in the third. At first he had few recollections about home life. Yet shortly after beginning therapy, he recounted a dream in which he was in bed with his somewhat older sister, playing with her breasts and saying, "How about a little incest?"

During discussion, this dream was wholly without significance to him. Probing into historical details of his life, analysis of the dream, the transference relationship, all failed to elicit adequate feeling response. He was utterly rigid from his bald head and perpetually wrinkled forehead to his ankles and feet. Though he was a weekend athlete of sorts and played a fair game of golf, he was somatically stiff, unyielding and tense. This rigidity was his *armor,* behind which or in which he had congealed those damaging feelings of boyhood. Conceptualization of any kind and for any duration was unavailing.

These are problem situations that have plagued the best of therapists. These are people one can never quite reach. Emotionally inaccessible, they hold themselves aloof from the therapist's efforts to induce some emotional reaction. Even the crucial transference situation never quite succeeds in rendering the relationship more than an intellectual one. Defensiveness, the keynote of such patients, is used so skillfully and with such frantic necessity that in many instances the analyst's insight and effort are fruitless.

The opposite is also true. A charming, nervous little woman, quiet and reserved, a chain smoker, suffered from a variety of tics which fluttered across and distorted her face. She visited a psychiatrist for relief from the tics which had become aggravated by a current marital problem temporarily being "solved" by a legal separation. After a few sessions, the psychiatrist advised that she did not really need intensive psychotherapy. "You're an intelligent woman," he remarked. "You don't need therapy. If you couldn't think out your problems for yourself that would be something else again. But you're capable of doing it yourself."

Such psychiatrists consider a neurosis to be a problem relating to reason or intelligence, and believe that therapy must approximate the approach of Dubois on the level of logical persuasion. They almost act as if Freud had never lived, having never heard of or understood anything about unconscious motivations and displacement of drives and feelings. The equivalent of Stekel's phrase "disorders of instinct and emotion" seems never to have occurred to them.

Only recently a psychologist admitted to me his bitterness and disillusionment about his personal experiences in psychotherapy. His many neurotic symptoms—homosexual tendencies[1], oral eroticism, counting compulsions—were intact and in fact were getting progressively worse, despite his ever-increasing knowledge of psychodynamics, psychopathology and psychotherapy. As a teacher he was

---

[1] It was not until 1974 that the American Psychiatric Association declassified homosexuality as a mental disorder. The World Health Organization did not do so until 1990. It is also worth noting that masturbation was a diagnosable psychological condition in the U.S.A. until 1968. [Ed.]

superb. He was said to be efficient as a therapist. But his own adventures in therapy were attended by nothing more than frustration and disappointment.

This is not a rare experience. No attempt is being made here to criticize any special group of analysts, or the therapeutic method of any particular school. All of us, if we are honest, may murmur *mea culpa.* The problem is not to attack or to exclude any specific analytical method or approach. We need desperately to devise an adjuvant technique which all therapists may employ with confidence and assurance.

Reich was confronted by similar clinical situations in the 1930's. They are the therapeutic problems that still haunt us. Edouard Ascher in *Psychosomatic Medicine* (2) expressed a similar conclusion not long ago. "One sees the occasional patient who has an amazing understanding of the dynamics of his personality functioning but nevertheless is severely maladjusted. The same applies to those whose social conduct shows marked improvement at the expense of inner turmoil."

A writer who attempted a popular formulation of a therapy based upon reconditioning, also took several nasty quips at psychoanalysis. He cited the case of a masochist who after years of conventional psychoanalysis did achieve a keen understanding of his condition. But the symptoms of his masochism persisted unchanged. It was the value of this insight that the author questioned and ridiculed.

Jung was impressed many years ago by the detailed accuracy of a young man's report about his own history, symptoms and psychodynamics. Jung called attention to the fact that despite such clear intellectual grasp, the patient's symptoms continued without alteration by such perceptiveness (10). Finally, Sargent and Slater have stated categorically that often years of psychotherapy fail to produce anything worthwhile by way of improvement in such patients.

Despite these testimonies to the inadequacy of the conceptual approach, very few have accomplished anything that approaches a satisfactory non-verbal psychotherapy for the neuroses. There are several types of somatic therapy already in psychiatric use. We might list the following[2]:

**1. Shock therapy.** The electrical or chemical methods produce coma and/or convulsion and are employed largely in the treatment of psychoses. The general impression, outside of the few using electro-narcosis, is that it is useless for the treatment of neuroses.

**2. Lobotomies and leucotomies.** A court of last appeal when all other methods fail to achieve improvement. Rather than condemn a patient to lifelong confinement in an institution representing a life wasted both to the family and to society, psychosurgery can now be performed without impairing the patient's intellectual faculties, so it is said—though I have many doubts.

**3. Endocrine therapy.** Primarily of value as an adjunct to other forms of treatment. Some of the newer research with regard to ACTH and cortisone, in relation to the recent stress theory of Selye, offers considerable promise in time to come.

**4. Chemotherapy.** Sedation as with barbiturates and excitation as with Benzedrine, for example, are commonly employed. Experimental work with the newer tranquilizers[3]—lysergic acid diethylamide (LSD) showing more and more promise—is underway on an extensive scale[4]. It is safe to assume that even now chemotherapy

---

[2] In the years since this was written, most of these "therapies" have (thankfully) been abandoned (although "electro-convulsive therapy" is still in use). More commonly in use is what the author calls "chemotherapy" (i.e., the use of "chemicals", "drugs" or "medications"), which is used primarily for the long-term treatment of *symptoms* and which has become the predominant therapeutic methodology in the psychiatric field. In short, most practicing psychiatrists seem to have largely abandoned the aim of "curing" psychological problems; instead their focus has primarily become the goal of "symptom relief." [Ed.]

[3] Characterization of LSD as a "tranquilizer" is, of course, inaccurate. It is more correctly referred to as a "psychedelic" or "hallucinogen". [Ed.]

[4] When this book was written, the psychiatric use of LSD showed great promise as a methodology that could lead to actual, persistent behavioral and psychological change. That it was sometimes used recreationally led to its wholesale legal prohibition and that ended almost all research and clinical application. Since then other potentially valuable substances, such as

has hardly come into its own. A promising future might be in store for this particular phase of the healing arts.

**5. Occupational therapy.** This again is largely an institutional procedure. However, some individual psychotherapists do encourage their patients to weave, paint, build, model and seek out other avocations as forms of emotional outlet and as techniques for the mobilization of unused energies and creative abilities. It is almost entirely an adjunct to other therapies.

**6. Hydrotherapy.** This, too, is almost entirely confined to institutions, though apparently it is not as extensively used as it once was. It comprises the use of tubs, showers and hoses for mentally disturbed patients needing sedation or stimulation as the case may be. Physical medicine can be included under this category though full evaluation of its efficacy has still to be made.

**7. Carbon dioxide.** This is an inhalation therapy developed by Meduna. The gaseous mixture is administered with a face mask, and rapidly induces heavy accelerated breathing and, eventually, a brief narcosis. Meduna's claim is that for some of the neuroses it is a complete therapy, requiring anywhere from a dozen to 100 treatments. It is alleged that with this treatment no conventional psychotherapy is required. Professional opinion is still divided as to whether or not these claims are valid. There is little doubt, however, that it has already begun its decline, and I fancy will soon disappear from the therapeutic scene. Its claim to value was that it facilitated emotional discharge on a purely physiological level.

However useful these methods may be, none applies to the particular problem discussed here. Reich's vegeto-therapy is the only effectual solution to the affect-lame case. Why is it, then, that a man whose work contains such potentialities should have been ignored by so many members of the profession? Little insight is gained when enquiring of most psychiatrists and psychologists. Most appear to be unfamiliar with the facts in the case and seem to care less. A few were prone to ridicule him and his theories. When questioned closely, however, some frankly admitted they had never done Reich

---

MDMA, Ketamine and psilocybin have incurred similar legal wrath. At this writing, however, there is a glimmer of hope that this may change... [Ed.]

the scientific courtesy of experimenting with his techniques to obtain data similar to that from which he formulated his functional constructs. Others confessed to having been frightened away by his cumbersome theories of orgastic potency, cosmic energy, the orgone accumulator and the cancer cure. It is presumptuous to assert that these theories are false or otherwise. Not dogmatic statements, but systematic and unprejudiced research must prove the validity or error of Reich's contributions.

Here and there an acknowledgment of indebtedness by the psychological profession to Reich's earlier contributions has appeared. A few years ago Robert Fliess expressed the belief that

> "The significance of the three papers on psychoanalytic characterology to follow—all by Wilhelm Reich—can hardly be overrated. There are few contributions to be called as unhesitatingly as are these, a 'must' for the student; there are in spite of their looseness of style, perhaps occasionally even of theoretical thought, few to be as emphatically recommended for periodic rereading in the first decade of any analyst's clinical work; and few that will spare the beginner in analysis as much avoidable disappointment—a disappointment which frequently causes him to look to 'advanced' analytical schools of Adlerian, or neo-Adlerian description, for assistance." (6)

In a review of Reich's *The Function of the Orgasm,* Masserman (14) gave full credit in the admission that some of Reich's formulations concerning the neurotic character and the analysis of the negative transference were now part and parcel of modern psychoanalytical technique. But, like so many others, he peremptorily dismissed Reich's theories regarding orgastic potency and the biophysical concept of orgone energy.

The several writings of Frederick Perls also give evidence to his familiarity with and current usage of Reich's technical material. Though he is occasionally critical of the orgastic potency theory, nonetheless his deep respect for Reich is patent and often expressed (16). Many chapters in Gestalt Therapy could readily serve as commentary on the efficacy of phases of vegeto-therapy. His students who attempted some of the recommended exercises have there described personal psychosomatic responses.

Neither must that arch-Freudian Otto Fenichel be forgotten. In his encyclopedic book *The Psychoanalytic Theory of the Neurosis,* there are more than a score of references to the pre-orgone writings of Reich. These references can hardly be construed as being damned with faint praise.

Lewis Wolberg gives a relatively sympathetic view of Reich's work in his book *The Technique of Psychotherapy.* It provides a broad frame of reference to include most of the therapeutic ideas taught in seminars at the Post-Graduate Center for Psychotherapy in New York City. While Wolberg does state that the orgone concepts have not been accepted by most psychiatrists, his account of vegeto-therapy is not inaccurate nor altogether unfavorable.

*Man Above Humanity* by Walter Bromberg also deserves a place in this account of public acknowledgment of Reich's work. Bromberg's book (4) purports to be a semi-popular history of psychiatry, containing a relatively short description of what Reich has contributed to our understanding of man. He not only mentions the early psychoanalytical contributions of Reich, but also gives a sympathetic account of the later work with orgone energy.

Trygve Braatøy's *Fundamentals of Psychoanalytic Technique* (3), is the only major work I know that attempts to deal overtly with the current psychoanalytic "silent treatment" of Reich. Braatøy's penetrating insight must be recommended to every psychotherapist. He even makes some attempt to cope with the patient's sensations of bio-electric pulsation which Reich explained by means of orgone. Braatøy apparently does not believe that ignoring Reich wipes out the acrimonious and vicious dichotomy that has arisen within the psychoanalytic field. Whereas most modern analysts scrupulously avoid Reich's writings, Braatøy on the other hand strongly urges that every candidate-analyst read them carefully.

There is in that book a fascinating discussion in which Braatøy vindicates one of Reich's earliest and most provocative viewpoints. As part of his technique of character analysis, Reich would often crudely mimic a patient's attitude in order to facilitate the patient's recognition of unconscious mechanisms in relation to the analyst. Some contemporary psychoanalysts ridiculed Reich, believing the procedure not only useless therapeutically but comical and nonsensical in theory. Braatøy thinks otherwise. As a representative of the psychoanalytic profession, his writing proves that it has taken 20 years to vindicate this approach of Reich, though admittedly he is highly critical of Reich in connection with other matters. This particular vindication is well-taken because many of the current criticisms and vilifications of Reich are based upon events in the 1930's which eventuated in Reich's repudiation by the psychoanalytic profession. The slander has never been permitted to die and it required courage on the part of Braatøy to be honest in the final recognition of a really creative thinker.

The headmaster of Summerhill, a school in England where A.S. Neill attempted to prove some of Reich's contentions in the education of problem children, is an ardent and enthusiastic supporter of Reich. In one of his books (5) many of this theories about education are uncompromisingly flavored with the rich findings of Reich's long years of clinical and social experience.

The famous cartoonist William Steig, whose creative drawings have earned him acclaim far and wide, is yet another who has paid homage and tribute to Reich. Several books of his devastatingly biting cartoons mention Reich specifically by name, and in the foreword of one the following paragraph appears: "I want to express my gratitude to Wilhelm Reich, to whom I am indebted for much of my insight into the sickness described in the following pages, as well as for the phrase 'Mama, mama!' which I heard him use in characterizing infantile attitudes of 'love'."

There are also many of Steig's cartoons in a late book by Reich (22), a caustic diatribe against the society which so unthinkingly rejected and persecuted him. A review without a byline in the *Psychiatric Quarterly* had this to say about *Listen, Little Man!*:

> "Reich hopes and has faith, not only in the life work which has brought the lighting crashing around his head for decades, but in the future of man himself... This reader thinks that all social scientists, regardless of their views of Reich's theories, owe it to themselves to read this brilliant and blazing work." (17)

On the basis of these tributes, it is not possible to dismiss Reich merely as a crackpot or disturbed neurotic as some have misguidedly done. Nor can we give any credence to the vicious gossip-mongers who have disseminated rumors to the effect that he was a schizophrenic, a paranoid, or that he was once confined to an institution from which he was later released after having achieved a "cure." These are evidences of a disease in those who malign him, a disease which Reich later came to call *the emotional plague.* Such rumors may have harmed Reich's personal reputation it is true. In the long run, they cannot damage his basic scientific contributions.

\*\*\*

In exploring the motives for this anomalous situation, clarification can best be achieved by formulating the different periods of Reich's professional career. In each one of these periods he evolved a different set of ideas. Like Freud he was never averse to changing his mind nor to discarding a theory when he found it no longer coincided with facts. For the sake of convenience, his lifework can be classified under five major headings:

1. That period prior to 1925 when he was an orthodox psychoanalyst. No comment need be made about his ability. It is well known that at the very least he was a competent analyst.

2. In 1925, he indicated the possibility of the reductive analysis of neurotic character traits in much the same way as had previously been attempted with symptom analysis. This reached its logical conclusion with the publication of *Character Analysis* which has been widely hailed as an important contribution to the technique of psychotherapy.

3. The next period is characterized by development of his concept of the muscular armor being functionally identical with neurotic character attitudes. Once this notion had appeared, the first systematized attack on the neurosis by physical means was thereby made possible.

4. In 1940, he expounded the existence of orgone radiation in the atmosphere and the soil, and this led to his uncompromising stand on orgonomy. The attack on the muscular armor liberated specific energies which could be directly experienced by the patient as well-defined body sensations of a bio-electric nature. When Reich theorized later that these energies also existed outside of man, in the

external world, he formulated the view that there was a cosmic stream of orgone energy, the basis and source of life.

5. Later research became summarized under the initials "C.O.R.E."—Cosmic Orgone Engineering. This began with an investigation of the possible use of the "orgone accumulator"[5] as an antidote to destructive atomic radiation. His discoveries encouraged him to speculate about smog, weather in general, drought and desert conditions. From all of this, there emerged a tentative technique for the production of rain in arid areas of the country. Admittedly, this is a far cry from psychotherapy. But, as one friend has reminded me, Leonardo da Vinci's monoplane notes were also a far cry from the Mona Lisa!

Current criticism suggests that Reich became bogged down in a complex maze of new terminologies and bizarre concepts which have received no corroboration from other scientific disciplines. Reich's emphasis on orgastic potency, cosmic energy and the cancer cure have so frightened these over-cautious critics that they never examined what could have been a valuable addition to the proven body of psychological knowledge and methodology.

The exposition undertaken here of non-verbal psychotherapy is based on Reich's creativity in the third phase of his thinking.

\*\*\*

According to a hostile critic, Martin Gardner, "Wilhelm Reich, the discoverer of orgone energy (or 'life energy') was born in Austria in 1897. He received the M.D. degree in 1922 from the University of Vienna Medical School, became a protégé of Freud, and for the next eight years rose rapidly in psychoanalytic circles. He held several important teaching and administrative posts in Vienna

---

[5] "Orgone accumulators" are devices intended to collect and store orgone energy from the environment—for the improvement of general health or even for weather control. The U.S. Food and Drug Administration (FDA) obtained a federal injunction barring the interstate distribution of orgone-related materials on the grounds that Reich and his associates were making false and misleading claims. It was after Reich was held to have violated the injunction that he was jailed...and all of his writings burned. [Ed.]

psychoanalytical organizations, and contributed to their periodicals." (8)

To have become a protégé of Freud could only carry the meaning that his mental equipment and abilities were far from mediocre. How was it, then, that such a man could have become so completely ostracized by many of his fellow workers? It is not enough to say that he became involved in controversy about orgone and cancer cures. Too many men have weathered similar storms of scientific controversy and emerged to a position of recognized strength.

It is my contention that his enthusiastic conversion to communism first laid the ground for his final repudiation by society and by his fellow scholars and analysts. This is the crucial factor behind the social and professional ostracism. Robert Lindner suggested in 1952 that our present-day analysts and psychotherapists are inevitably part and parcel of the conformist social structure which has nurtured and trained them. Their character-structure, with its consequent social orientation towards maintaining the *status quo,* has its roots in the mores and conventions of the social organization from which they sprang. Inevitably they preach the gospel of adjustment to society as we find it here and now. Lindner complained that

> "this concept enjoins men to conform, to adopt an attitude of passivity and a philosophy of resignation. It requires that each of us make such efforts as he can to align his thinking, feeling and acting with situations as they are presented to him; that he recognize and submit to existing 'realities' ordinarily described as inevitable; that he make peace with things as they are; that he perform such actions and engage in such behavior as will result in the adaptation of his self to conditions; and finally, that he abjure all protest not only as vanity but also as harmful…" (12)

None of the great innovators of history held this acquiescent viewpoint. Almost all were rebels against the established order of things. Adjustment culminates in adoption of a rigid personality armoring, leading to the cessation of all creativity. Rejection of social adjustment leads either to neurosis, more often than not, or else to a high degree of creativeness. When Otto Rank was obliged to sever his connections with the psychoanalytical field, he too had arrived at a similar conviction. Freud was certainly no exception to the above rule. He rejected the conventional adjustment theory. And while it is true he did develop considerable neurotic anxiety as Ernest Jones' magnificent biography indicates, his genius is unquestioned. Much the same was true of Reich. He, too, was a rebel. But there was a difference. It was this disastrous difference which has plagued Reich from the late 1920's even until today.

Lindner has leveled a powerful indictment against those who ostracized Reich. It was not Lindner's intention to rally to the defense of Reich's rebelliousness, but the effect was the same. Lindner vehemently charges:

> "That a vast new body of knowledge is being misused and misapplied hour by hour by the bulk of the psychotherapeutic fraternity, and especially by the psychoanalysts;
>
> "That the tacit 'therapeutic' hypothesis of most practitioners of the arts of psychotherapy—although it may never be mentioned by name for what it is—is adjustment in one of its many forms and disguises;
>
> "That, by and large, the scientists of the mind, physicians of the 'soul' and doctors of the spirit have entered somehow into a collusive conspiracy with power seekers everywhere to stamp out and destroy with their various techniques the rebellious among us, and to aid in the promotion of a hive psychology;
>
> "That the most that is ever accomplished with the perplexed, anxious and problem-ridden who offer themselves to psychotherapy today...is the substitution of another neurosis for their original complaint...the neurosis of conformity, surrender, passivity, social apathy and compliance." (13)

*Prescription for Rebellion* could well serve as a preface to a special study of Wilhelm Reich and his contributions to psychotherapy.[6]

---

[6] There are at least two derogatory references to Wilhelm Reich in the above-named book, because of which I entered into a correspondence with Robert Lindner. His reply to my criticism is dated April 23, 1953, and has always impressed me as being an honest admission of error. "You are correct about my too-hasty dismissal of Reich. If I ever do another edition of R I intend to correct this. I, too, have great respect for the earlier formulations of Reich. As for his therapeutic techniques, I confess to a lack of personal experience with them."

Reich's *Function of the Orgasm* contains many chapters dealing with his personal struggle to extricate himself from the bonds of conformity and apathy, and to permit the expression of his own revolt against a diseased society. This led, as he himself narrates, to the adoption of the Communist philosophy. Regarding this step, Martin Gardner says:

> "Politically, Reich was active in the Austrian Socialist Party until he broke with them in 1930, and moved to Berlin where he joined the Communists... He was a Freudian Marxist... Reich failed, however, to convince the comrades of the revolutionary importance of his views. Moscow branded his writings 'un-Marxist rubbish,' and it was not long until he had severed his connections with the Communist movement... Having written in 1933 a book attacking German fascism as the sadistic expression of sex-repressed neurotics, Reich was not looked upon kindly by the Nazis when they came to power." (9)

But this phase of his life is far more clearly dealt with by Colin Wilson in his book about Reich.

Disregarding the known facts that he repudiated the Communists after he had recognized their utter bankruptcy, and despite the further fact that he indicated the Nazis as brutal sexual psychopaths, Reich was still subjected to the odium that attaches itself to all those who become smeared by the Marxist brush. Society will have none of them, and sustains the old truth—no matter how out of date that truth may have become. Conservatism, in this sense, is positively dangerous and vicious.

Because he was once a Communist and because he was vitriolic in his attack on Fascism, Reich showed that he was a rebel through and through. A conservative society could not accept this kind of rebel. Much of the inner social and political turmoil that he experienced is well described in a privately distributed book of his, *People in Trouble.* It is a simple, honest and sincere account of his gradual evolution from an ivory-towered psychoanalyst to a serious social scientist involved personally in some of the most severe problems of our day.

As so many others had previously done, Reich rebelled against formal psychoanalysis. Adler, Jung, Stekel and Rank, for example, had also withdrawn from the Freudian circle, but although they were subjected to severe criticism, they did not suffer the calumny which became attached to Reich. He was vilified not only because of all these several factors, but because he took seriously Freud's earlier theorems about sex. It is curious to reflect that despite all the groundbreaking that Freud and many others have done to destroy some of the taboos surrounding this subject, only a minor dent seems to have been made in the current social outlook. Kinsey, too, experienced the abuse and condemnation which our sex-negative culture heaps on anyone attempting to open the doors revealing truths about the sexual inclinations of men and women today. This is what Reich has called "the emotional plague."

By this apt phrase, Reich implies that kind of social behavior which grows out of the individual armoring process which, in turn, produces affect-lame people. The affect-lame person, or the character neurotic, can only employ the dynamics implicit in the neurosis itself. That is to say he will fantasize, repress, project, displace and create reaction-formations in which are invested much libido. All his psychic activities, therefore, are bound to be colored by distorted perceptions. And out of these distorted perceptions only distorted motor activities can proceed.

Much of what Reich implies in the term "emotional plaque" is somewhat covered by the general use of the term "paranoid." The individual is suspicious, hostile, spiteful, jealous, insecure and fearful. These affects may result in the development of delusional states, mild or severe as the case may be. Usually these states are relatively mild. Only the more severely afflicted seek treatment or are institutionalized. The others "function" within the confines of the environment in which they have developed, wreaking mischief and malice on those unlucky enough to be in contact with them.

These people are more numerous than one might be inclined to believe at first sight. Social, educational, economic and class distinctions apparently form no barrier to them; they are found on every level. All forms of society are affected and afflicted by them. These "bad apples" affect all the other "apples" in the crate, and in turn make them "bad." Their effect is ubiquitous. It is their widespread maliciousness, in terms of social and group psychological activity, which makes for the emotional plague. It is the direct consequence of individual and social armoring.

Reich believed that an organism which is constantly impeded in its natural way of locomotion from birth develops *artificial forms of locomotion,* limping or moving on crutches. Similarly an individual moves through life by means of the emotional plague if, from birth, his natural self-regulatory life expressions have been suppressed. An individual afflicted with the emotional plague *limps, characterologically speaking. The emotional plague is a chronic biopathy of the organism*; it is an epidemic disease, like schizophrenia or cancer, with an important difference: it manifests essentially in social living.

Reich would know—he was horribly victimized by it. He observed that *as soon as one touches upon the motives of the plague reaction, anxiety or anger inevitably appears*, but a plague reaction is accessible to genuine character-analytic therapy and can be eliminated. The real motive is always concealed and replaced by a seeming motive.

Though a few of the followers of Reich might be inclined at times to use the term rather uncritically, it is nonetheless a useful concept. Instead of accepting judicious responsibility for their own psychosomatic problems which may develop from time to time, or for the professional or social difficulties which may occur, the emotional plague is blamed. Sometimes this is too easy. I do not wish to imply that Reich or many of his disciples are in this category. But it is fairly evident that the very concept of the plague, useful in itself, can and does lend itself to a personal distortion of facts and to the evasion of individual responsibility. In fact, this is a major symptom of the plague itself as Reich has shown. The therapist requires to be especially careful of the concepts that he employs to describe the pathological behavior both of his patients and society as a whole. There is no doubt that the concept is of supreme value—but like all diagnostic and categorizing tools it requires the label "handle with care!"

Nevertheless, it must be understood as describing a diabolical phenomenon against which many great men—from Freud to Kinsey *et al.* in our own era—have collided and by means of which they have been sorely hurt. The world of armored people with the diseased characteristic of the emotional plague is, to Reich and his protagonists, a trap. Art, science, religion, literature and all the fine accoutrements of our culture are all so many devices to make life in the trap more tolerable or comfortable—and perhaps more beautiful. But a trap it remains, regardless of how we disguise it and dress it up. No way out of the trap is possible save by dealing directly with the pernicious armoring of the human animal. Steps have to be taken not merely to protect the few healthy individuals in a community but to segregate and treat those who are already diseased. The technique is similar to that employed in handling contagious diseases—individually by isolation and vegeto-therapy, and socially by wise, liberal legislation and social reform calculated to respect the growing child and adolescent in their basic experiments with reality. Only in this way can viciousness and the heartbreak of the trap be destroyed.

Meantime we are trapped in the deceptive and illusory world of armoring where, because of the emotional plague, love and sincerity and honest naturalness have become distorted into world-hate, hypocrisy and perversion.

Reich believed that sexual inhibition based upon our irrational social mores had more than a great deal to do with the growth of the emotional plague. He suggested that free and healthy sexual outlets would go far towards maintaining the integrity of the individual.

*He felt that in the course of thousands of years of mechanical development the mechanistic concept has anchored itself deeply in man's biological system and has actually altered human functioning to be machine-like. In the process of killing his genital function, man has become biologically rigid,* armoring himself against that which is natural and spontaneous. He has lost contact with the biological function of self-regulation and is filled with a strong fear of what is alive and free.

Reich noted that *biological rigidity* is expressed primarily in a general rigidity of the organism and a demonstrable reduction of plasmatic mobility. Intelligence is damaged, the natural social sense is lost and there is a general psychosis. So-called civilized man is in fact angular, machine-like, without spontaneity. He has become an automaton and "brain machine." Man not only *believes* that he functions like a machine, *he functions like a machine.* He lives, loves, hates and thinks like a machine. With his biological rigidity and the loss of the natural function of self-regulation, he has acquired all those character attitudes which reached their pinnacle in the pestilence of the dictatorships.

According to Reich this tragic machine-like aberration did not develop without its counterpart. Deep down, even the rigid human has remained a living animal. No matter how immobile his pelvis or how stiff his neck and shoulders, no matter how tense his abdominal muscles, deep down he feels that he is a part of living nature. But as he denies and suppresses this nature in every possible way, he cannot recognize it rationally and factually. Hence, his needs *must experience it as something mystical, supernatural, other-worldly,* be it in the form of religious ecstasy, a cosmic soul, or in the form of the sadistic surging of the blood.

Reich thought *the relationship between the sexual life and work achievement is significant,* and considered erroneous the belief that the more sexual energy is diverted from gratification the more work is achieved. He thought the opposite is true. The more satisfactory the sex life, the more full and more pleasurable is the work achievement. After sexual gratification the sexual energy turns to interest in work and urge for activity. Conversely, work is disturbed in various ways if sexual needs are not gratified and the sexual energy is dammed up. Therefore, a basic principle of work hygiene in a work-democratic society should establish the best external conditions and also the inner life conditions if the biological urge for activity is to fully develop. The safeguarding of a fully gratifying sexual life of the working masses is the most important prerequisite for joyful work. The degree to which work in any society serves to kill *joie de vivre,* the degree to which work is presented as duty (no matter whether towards "the father land," "the proletariat," "the nation" or whatever the illusions may be called) is a sure indication of the anti-democratic character of the leading strata of this society. Just as "duty," "state," "propriety," "sacrifice," etc. go inseparably together, so do *"joie de vivre,"* "work democracy," "self-regulation," "enjoyment in work" and "natural sexuality."

Some psychoanalysts, despite their apparent dedication to intellectual if not social reform, have continued to make their neurotic compromises with the sex-negative conventions of contemporary society. This has gradually resulted in the rejection of the instincts and the over-emphasis of personality adjustment in a society whose sexual standards are patently diseased. Reich would have none of this. He regarded a full sex life as indispensable to physical and mental health.

Marriage, as an institution as we know it today, became one of his targets for incisive attack. His book *The Sexual Revolution* was so telling an attack that the pillars of society could only regard him as a threat, as a dangerous firebrand whose creed spelled doom to their most cherished beliefs and customs. His condemnation of the legal form of marriage to be preserved when only hatred and spitefulness were the survivors of a former love, evoked retaliatory measures from the armored animals he so mercilessly exposed. His writings on this topic must have served as a major factor leading to his rejection by the therapeutic profession, and this naturally freed him still further to progress in as yet uncharted territory.

Another issue which brought things to a head and culminated in the final break with Freud and the inner circle of psychoanalysts revolved about Freud's enunciation of the death instinct in the early 1920's. It was Reich's contention that careful clinical investigation did not warrant meta-psychological speculations of this type. He would not and did not accept them. Making a special study of the problem of masochism, he evolved what appeared to him, and many others since then, a theory more in accordance with clinically verifiable facts than was the *Thanatos* theory. Reich's opposition to Freud and his followers on this particular topic led to much personal antagonism from his hitherto admiring colleagues. A chasm came to separate him from the main body of European analysts and was responsible for his final repudiation by the psychological field.

There is an ironic sequel to this. Many years later, Reich, in his scrutiny of the cancer problem, enunciated concepts which were just as dichotomous as Freud's postulation of *Eros* and *Thanatos*. Reich, of course, did not use these psychoanalytic labels. Instead he employed dualistic concepts such as the *Todt* bacillus and the *Bion*. The former was defined as the ultramicroscopic vesicle found in the erythrocyte and the carcinomatous cells, and which was responsible for the living putrefaction which was cancer. The *Bion* was the blue-glowing life vesicle, the presence of which, in adequate quantities, was the antidote to the cancerous process and which *per se* spelled the presence of good biological health.

By using the analytical method it might be possible to account for this theory. A great many significant questions could be raised. Did Reich develop father-hostility to the aged patriarch Freud? Did he reject the *Thanatos* theory entirely on intellectual and clinical grounds? Or was there in the background the substratum of unresolved infantile hatreds and death-wishes against his own father that, transferred to Freud, created the split that subsequently developed? Following the schism, after years of persecution and professional ostracism, did the repressed elements of earlier years return in only slightly modified form when Reich emerged as an adult in his own right? Given a new terminology, is it possible to perceive them to be essentially the same conceptualizations of Freud's own bipolar theory of *Eros* and *Thanatos*?

It is necessary to call attention to this particular controversy because, altogether apart from Reich's reformulation of Freud's *Thanatos* as the *Todt* bacillus and *Eros* as the life-sustaining *Bion,* the bitter squabble is certainly a significant one in Reich's personal history. It must play an important role in his rejection of psychoanalysis. By the same token it must have meaning for his later "functional thinking" which culminated in his exclusion from the contemporary scientific world.

Besides his contribution of character analysis to the mainstream of psychoanalytic development, he departed still further from orthodoxy by evolving a physical approach to psychotherapy. It was Reich who developed the thesis that is the mainstay of this book: *that muscular tensions are requisite to emotional inhibition, that the muscular armor is essentially identical with the character armor.* That, in a word, defense is defense, whether it be somatic or psychic. As part of his analytical work in freeing the emotional life of the patient, he gradually came to pay attention to the muscular attitudes of the patient. The sequelae of these observations led to an ever greater distance separating him from the orthodox stand of the main body of psychoanalysts.

Since he was a pioneer, there was no social or intellectual group with whom he could identify himself. He found himself completely excluded from all because he rebelled against psychoanalytic doctrine, procedure and current sexual mores.

As he pursued this investigations into vegeto-therapy, he encountered problems and phenomena for which he was unprepared. Among them was the problem of apparent energy-flows which resulted from the breakdown of muscular tensions. Patients invariably described weird sensory phenomena of tingling, pulsing, electricity and streaming in such a way as to force him to develop a theory about a new kind of energy. Conservatively at first, he thought he was dealing with an actualization of the Freudian libido. Yet libido was merely a theory enunciated by Freud to clarify certain theoretical considerations called for by his developing psychoanalytical knowledge and experience. It was realized at all times to be purely a hypothetical necessity, not in any way related to that kind of reality coped with by physics and chemistry. Reich came to believe that these bio-energetic phenomena revolved not merely around the libido but with an energy which he had finally been able to prove real in the above scientific sense of the term.

Once again the psychoanalysts repudiated him, ridiculing the whole concept. Most of these rejections unfortunately were voiced without investigation into the experimental data which he had accumulated. The judgment was *á priori.* If ever there were a violation of the scientific spirit, this was it.

How badly this ridiculous and vicious treatment must have made him feel can barely be guessed. It must have been humiliating almost beyond endurance.

He later said he would likely have desisted from any controversy with this ocean of psychic filth, but would not withdraw to the comfortable academic viewpoint of splendid isolation. The stakes were too high and, although not vengeful, he did not wish to deny himself the triumph of emerging from this hell, this Dantian inferno of human existence, with a whole skin, unbroken and unsullied, although severely hurt with many scars from painful and dangerous insults to his honor, to the pride of his scientific accomplishment, and shocking defamation on the part of biopathic individuals.

When Freud was subjected to similar slander, abuse and vilification he became bitter, morose and pessimistic. In his later days, he withdrew from society, partly because of his serious illness, but also out of disillusionment and hurt, even though he had by then achieved a high degree of world fame and acceptance. I do not believe this emotional reaction occurred to Reich. He was still able to fight the emotional plague.[7]

It has been assumed that compensatory trends unconsciously pushed him into obscure realms of endeavor out of which came the hypothesis that this body-energy or libido had its counterpart also in an all-pervasive life-force extending throughout the cosmos. By this means he argued that man was not isolated from the rest of nature. All structures, organic and inorganic, were bound together by this life energy which he called "orgone". A viewpoint such as this was bound to have momentous repercussions as to goals of therapy.

The orgonomic goals, therefore, were shifted from merely helping man free and express his emotions and hitherto repressed instinctual drives toward the realization of man's kinship with all of nature. The intent was to aid him in feeling his unique place in the world, as a part of the throbbing, living cosmos around him. Reich conceived it to be a living, vital world of universal energy that beat with man's own heartbeat, pulsed with the warmth of his own blood, and breathed with his own breath. It was an attempt to end the vicious dichotomy of man and nature, and so to bring man back into his own.

It all sounds curiously familiar. In its own way, it is reminiscent of D.H. Lawrence, as, for example, when he rhapsodically cried:

> "We are perishing for lack of fulfilment of our greater needs, we are cut off from the great sources of our inward nourishment and renewal, sources which flow eternally in the universe. Vitally, the human race is dying. It is like a great uprooted tree, with its roots in the air. We must plant ourselves against the universe...
>
> "The world of reason and science, the moon, a dead lump of earth, the sun, so much gas with spots; this is the dry and sterile little world the abstracted mind inhabits..." (11)

---

[7] He died in prison, brokenhearted, in 1957. See Jerome Greenfield's book *Wilhelm Reich vs. USA* (Norton & Co., NY, 1974).

It is very much like Reich. The principal difference is that while Lawrence cried out in bitterness and frustration but was unable to contribute anything by way of method or technique, Reich demonstrated a way. Some may be critical of theory or goals. But the technique, in its own frame of reference, is altogether beyond reproach.

Still later, new developments led him to construct a special box which he believed would accumulate or concentrate this atmospheric orgone energy to be used in the treatment of cancer and other biopathies. He wrote a book describing in considerable detail the various experiments and events which occurred—events which cautiously instigated the belief that cancer was "curable" by means of the "accumulator." Few critics have troubled to duplicate his experiments. Most sneered and condemned.

Here was a man who not only had wholly unconventional views about life, psychotherapy and society, but who now came forward with an unorthodox cure for cancer. This idea encroached upon the special preserves of orthodox medicine with all its hidebound, traditional and conservative approaches to disease, research and therapy. His final experiments caused him not only to be ridiculed and persecuted by his colleagues, but a federal injunction was issued to prevent dissemination of material relating to the cancer cure by the orgone accumulator. Many believe this violates the very principle of free speech. "According to a permanent injunction order issued on March 10, 1954, by the Federal District Court at Portland, Maine, (Judge John D. Clifford) 'Orgone Energy' devices misbranded with curative claims were barred from interstate commerce…" Commissioner of Foods and Drugs Charles W. Crawford said, "Dr. Reich has long contended that only the hopelessly ignorant could disagree with his theories or doubt his miraculous cures with Orgone Energy Accumulators. Repeated challenges were issued in literature… The Food and Drug Commission accepted the challenge and has concluded that there is no such energy as orgone energy and that Orgone Energy Accumulator devices are worthless in the treatment of any disease or disease condition of man." (1)

This commission's conclusions are in remarkable conflict with the findings of the Atomic Energy Commission, a correspondence with whom was published by Reich in *The Oranur Experiment.* In all honesty we have to admit that there is still much that we do not know, and prejudicial judgments will not help very much to clarify basic issues. Reich felt compelled to develop the orgone hypothesis to answer certain difficulties which he felt other theories failed to do. There can be no satisfactory theory ultimately which does not take into account the experiments which Reich performed and reported in *The Cancer Biopathy.* Anyone wishing to discount the orgone theory must first repeat these experiments. When done, it will then be possible to determine whether he was justified in his theory. My neurophysiological theory of vegeto-therapy is offered solely as a stepping-stone. If, by its means, others can be persuaded to use and experiment with the method and thereby prove its value, then perhaps they may be encouraged to go still further to prove or disprove other of Reich's contentions.[8]

Meanwhile, his technique of vegeto-therapy is most certainly effective as a non-verbal psychotherapy comprising a new dimension of a highly dynamic nature. It is so important and valuable that in order to preserve it for posterity it might be advisable temporarily to dissociate the technique from the sad social stigma attached to the cruelly rejected man himself. By this means perhaps a new *modus vivendi* can be found for it. It should survive and be utilized afresh without the encumbrance of special theories.

---

[8] An honest investigator would have to become aware of the research work conducted by Burr and Northrop and the Yale School of Medicine, Section of Neuro-Anatomy, which has shown unequivocally that an electromagnetic field could be demonstrated in all living systems. Experimental studies show that feeling and behavioral deviations in human beings are related to measurable aspects of this field. Ravitz has written: "Rather than 'psyche' acting on 'soma', 'mind' on 'body,' and other such naive conceptions, both manifestations are postulated to result from changing intensities and directions of energy, natural energy which can be precisely defined in relative terms and objectively recorded without spurious distinction between 'organic' and 'functional'."

Except for language, ever a stumbling block, Reich's orgone energy is defined not too dissimilarly to the concepts involved in the Electrodynamic Field Theory of Burr and Northrop. But see the symposium in *Main Currents in Modern Thought,* September-October, 1962, Vol. 19, Number 1.

One last word: some critics may misconstrue my motives here. I did not know Reich personally. I never met him. There are aspects of his orgonomic work which will receive little attention here. Of some others I am frankly critical. But in this book I deal with one facet of his creativity. And this I do deliberately without reference to any later contributions. I do not consider that he needs defending. There may be some scientific and imaginative errors in his work. He is only human. But these errors can best be discovered by honest experiment—not by *á priori* judgment.

He has been smeared as psychopathic and his work labelled as bizarre. This ridicule is too frequently encountered to be lightly dismissed. Therefore, it is better to provide a rational and objective presentation of one branch of his work so that the facts may be evaluated. His vegeto-therapy has proven of inestimable value, effective and important, both to me as a person and to my patients. I come neither to bury Caesar nor to praise him. I wish only to appraise that part of his work which I have proven and which should be protected from the threat of extinction.

## Bibliography

1. *Am Jnl. Psychotherapy.* VIII:, p. 506–7. New York.

2. Ascher, Edouard. "Motor Attitudes and Psychotherapy," *Psychosomatic Medicine,* July–Aug, 1949.

3. Braatøy, Trygve. *Fundamentals of Psychoanalytical Technique,* New York, John Wiley, 1954.

4. Bromberg, Walter. *Man Above Humanity.* New York, Lippincott, 1954.

5. Dollard, John and Miller, Neal E. *Personality and Psychotherapy.* New York, McGraw Hill, 1950. p. 7.

6. Fliess, Robert. *The Psychoanalytic Reader,* Vol. I., New York, Int. Univ. Press, 1948, p. 127.

7. Fulton, John F. *Frontal Lobotomy and Affective Behavior.* New York, Norton & Co., 1951.

8. Gardner, Martin. *Fads and Fallacies,* New York, Dover Publications, 1957, p. 250–1.
9. Gardner, Martin. *ibid,* p. 250 *et seq.*
10. Jung, Carl G. "Postulates of Analytical Psychology," *Modern Man in Search of a Soul,* New York, Harcourt Brace, 1939, p. 223.
11. Lawrence, D.H. *Apropos of Lady Chatterley's Lover,* London, Mandrake Press, 1930. p. 51.
12. Lindner, Robert. *Prescription for Rebellion.* New York, Rinehart, 1952, p. 11.
13. Lindner, Robert. *ibid,* p. 112.
14. Masserman, Jules. *Psychosomatic Medicine,* Jan–Feb, 1946. p. 75.
15. Neill, A.S. *The Problem Family.* New York, Hermitage Press, 1949.
16. Perls, Frederick, *et al. Gestalt Therapy.* New York, Julian Press, 1951.
17. *Psychiatric Quarterly,* 22:4, p. 761, 1949. Utica, New York.
18. Salter, Andrew. *Conditioned Reflex Therapy,* New York, Creative Age Press, 1949.
19. Sargent, W. and Slater, E. *Physical Methods of Treatment in Psychiatry.* Edinburgh, Livingston, 1944.
20. Steig, William. *Agony in the Kindergarten.* New York, Duell, Sloan & Pierce, 1950.

# Chapter II

## Armor

> "...the Persona...is the mediator between the naked ego and the outer world. If all the inner life has been sacrificed to the building up of a Persona image, there comes a time when one seems almost to have been encased in a magnet or shell which draws everything from the center to the periphery."
> — Frances G. Wickes

Some years ago, Leon Saul defined psychotherapy in these terms:

> "The aim of therapy...is to help the patient recognize and appreciate as fully as possible, his true impulses and desires, to free them from the automatic operation of the inhibiting forces and bring them under the purview of conscious realization and judgment, so that rigidity and automaticity of reaction can yield to greater flexibility, conscious choice and the reopening of this hitherto blocked part of the personality to further development." (8)

As description of a process it is particularly applicable to non-verbal psychotherapy. With the basic premise that a rigid musculature serves as the physical ground on which all automatic inhibition subsequently operates, it offers assurance of the feasibility and possibility of a direct attack on the inhibiting mechanism. This armor is more accessible and immediate than are the classical mental mechanisms. Ordinarily much time has to be consumed in verbalizing historic events and inner attitudes in order to determine how this rigidity of response has developed in the past and operates now. *In this approach there is a frontal assault on the inhibiting structures themselves.* By dealing with the muscular armor first, rather than with the mental mechanisms, the pent-up affects of years ago may be abreacted in a relatively simple and direct manner and the repressed memories which by more conventional methods take so much time to unleash, arise spontaneously.

It is orthodox belief now that defective training of one kind or another in childhood is responsible for the inability of the patient to tolerate his feelings and impulses. Parental attitudes have been such that fundamentally normal needs and desires are rejected. The child learns that certain feeling responses are not acceptable to his parents. They are thus forced into inhibition and then utterly repudiated. If he expresses them at all, he will be punished one way or another. Either he will be directly punished corporeally or he will be ignored, or sent away, or not loved. Rejection is intolerable to all of us. It contravenes basic survival feelings. As the years elapse, rather than risk rejection, these feelings and their related body sensations must be blocked off. Since inhibition does not imply annihilation, they clamor for expression, fighting against the trained cortical and muscular control that has had to be established. Given no normal outlet, they force a surreptitious exit by devious substitutive routes, gradually creating what we conveniently call the neurotic character—the fertile soil from which neurotic symptoms emerge.

These psychoneurotic symptoms are the products of a group of emotional relationships or attitudes to life-situations which have developed through much earlier family settings, the soil wherein grows and develops the personality of the child. According to Ewen Cameron,

> "The influence exerted upon the personality structure by the long period of dependency has great significance for psychotherapy, since the way in which the child relates himself to parental figures greatly affects not only the way in which he will relate himself to others, but also the way in which he will relate himself to the therapist during treatment. From these primary parental relationships may be derived, for instance, a fear of excessively close relationships, or a pattern of relationship in terms of hostility, or a tendency towards excessive dependency." (1)

Whatever attitudes child had to develop within the family circle early in life, he will continue rigidly to react with later. At first he learns a pattern of response to the most significant people in his immediate environment, a pattern which later extends to others. These early events unmistakably influence the development of character, which is the product of diverse environmental pressures and the reaction of the personality to them. The various psychic defense mechanisms—mechanisms to defend the child not only against threats in the environment but against inner responses to them as well—become integral parts of his character structure. Flexibility in adjustment is gradually lost in those early years because of repression, displacement, identification and reaction formation. The personality becomes rigid and unyielding; a stereotyped pattern of response is employed thereafter in many life-situations where it is unwarranted. *Rigidity is congealed emotion.* Thus comes into being what Reich so eloquently called the character armor. According to his description in *Character Analysis*,

> "The ego, the exposed part of the personality, under the continued influence of the conflict between libidinal need and threatening outer world, acquires a certain rigidity, a chronic, automatically functioning mode of reaction, called 'character.' It is as if the affective personality put on an armor, a rigid shell on which the knocks from outer world as well as the inner demands rebound. This armor makes the individual less sensitive to unpleasure but also reduces libidinal and aggressive motility, and his capacity for pleasure and achievement. The ego becomes more rigid, less mobile and the extent of the armoring determines the extent of the ability to regulate the energy economy. The character armor consumes energy, for it is maintained by the continued consumption of vegetative energies which otherwise would create anxiety."

Much of the theoretical framework of psychoanalysis is based on the antagonism of the pleasure principle to reality. Sandwiched in between, the Ego has to "master" the Id by postponing or forgetting its demands for satisfaction, and by acceding to the frustrating demands of reality. Out of this grows neurosis in that the pleasure-seeking impulses repressed by the Ego out of fear demand an outlet in some form. These substitutes comprise the gamut of neurotic symptoms.

A glance at what this reality consists of may illuminate the conflict. For a child, reality comprises the parents or those who stand in their places. If the parents are truly typical of our patriarchal authoritarian culture, they have their own inner conflicts and neurotic symptoms, mild or severe. Confronted by the natural pleasure demands of the child which are in direct opposition to their warped and rigid character structures, they tend to impose their own frustrated standards and compulsive morality patterns on the child. Confronted by such harsh realities, upon whom it depends for its own pleasure-seeking instincts and feelings and for protection's sake, the child adopts the neurotic standards of its reality, though only after a protracted battle. Reality wins, as it always must, because the odds are in its favor. Given the stresses and strains of everyday life, neurotic symptoms evolve from this disturbed character structure. Once the child's ego is crippled by having to turn a deaf ear to some of its own drives, its functional capacity to deal with later problems suffers accordingly. This restricts the range of ego activities. Substitutive fantasies and symptoms, in marked conflict with reality, are the outcome.

Freud has expressed somewhat the same idea, his formal language being different:

> "The purpose of the defensive mechanisms is to avert dangers. It cannot be disputed that they are successful; it is doubtful whether the ego can altogether do without them during its development, but it is also certain that they themselves may become dangerous. Not infrequently it turns out that the ego has paid too high a price for the services which these mechanisms render. The expenditure of energy necessary to maintain them and the ego-restrictions which they almost invariably entail prove a heavy burden on the psychical economy…the defensive mechanisms produce an ever-growing alienation from the external world and a permanent enfeeblement of the ego…" (3)

Reich's solution in *The Sexual Revolution* is to give free play to the child's movements towards sexual experimentation and satisfaction. All the laws of the land must be directed towards the protection of the child and the adolescent in their search for love and pleasure. By theory, this would avoid the circumscription of the ego and the necessitous development of neurotic gratifications. An ego thus inherently strong, because satisfied, would then be more capable of dealing naturally and decisively with the adult world and its complex problems without the need for compulsions, obsessions, phobias, etc.

The notion of rigidity in character development will be found to have highly significant meaning in that it functions purposefully to reduce the likelihood of anxiety states which might occur if libidinal needs arose. If they were indulged, threats to security from people in the environment might occur, provoking intolerable insecurity. The armor is developed in order to survive adequately, without dangerous inner needs and without external threats to continued safety. With rigidity goes the constant possibility of neurotic and psychosomatic symptoms. Unforeseen stresses and strains of everyday living serve to precipitate inner turmoil and its anti-biological sequelae. Leon Saul says:

> "This is the meaning of 'neurotic' in the broad sense; inappropriate ways of thinking, attitudes, moods or behavior patterns which arise from infantile motivations or their derivatives or reactions against them." (9)

As a patient persists in the dynamic process of therapy, some of the earliest character trends and formations emerge in stark clarity. One is then enabled to perceive vividly the motivations for the repression of affects through the development of the character armor. Often these traits are not at all what one might first have supposed them to be.

\*\*\*

Nellie, a borderline schizophrenic girl who originally presented only the essential hallmarks of a severely afflicted obsessional patient, seemed to be restraining great rage and anger. At the same time, whenever there was the slightest possibility of this rage being expressed in the office, she was overwhelmed by panic. As a positive transference slowly developed, the counterplay of rage and fear was clearly observed.

Months elapsed without making much headway. It was evident that though she could be brought close to tears, there was an involuntary mechanism which automatically, as it were, prevented her from crying. Only then did some of the underlying schizophrenic symptoms become apparent—cloudiness in the head, a woolliness of thinking, feelings of deadness and remoteness, depersonalization and negativism, together with a sense of utter chaos and confusion. It was not until close to the end of therapy that her loneliness, despair and hopelessness came to light. Having arisen early in childhood, they were wholly intolerable to her. Solely by repression and by the erection of the armored barricade to distort the truth was survival possible under her difficult circumstances.

Her parents were schizophrenogenic. They were over 40 when she was born, and as soon as she was able to understand she was told repeatedly that their whole lives revolved around her. But this did not mean that they wanted her to become a "spoiled brat."

Apparently, they did all they could to ensure her total subjugation. Time after time they told her that their sole happiness lay in her love for them. Once she broke down, feeling so alone and depressed, and weepingly confessed to her mother that she was very unhappy. Mother was shocked and disappointed. She told Nellie that she had everything in the world to make her happy, and she was showing the basest ingratitude which could only result in making both her parents miserable.

When parental squabbles occurred, one or the other would snap at her, telling her that before she was born they lived in paradise. Only her presence had brought dissension.

Father was bad-tempered, frugal, unfriendly and hypochondriacal. If the mother spent what he thought was an unnecessary nickel in the market, it became the occasion for an outburst of temper. Mother would complain bitterly to Nellie about her father's shortcomings. When the mother had aroused Nellie to berate her father for his churlishness and meanness, the mother would immediately become the mealy-mouthed peace-maker, telling Nellie that her father was not really so bad. He was a good provider and meant well. It was no wonder that she had not the slightest idea of there she stood with them at any time. This led to a distrust of her own emotions, and to a withdrawal from reality.

Following one of these scenes, the outcome of which would be a bilious attack lasting for three or four days, she would suffer from a deep sense of depression which her mother would dismiss lightly, suggesting that her unhappiness came from her warped imagination and was without reality. Inevitably she came to discount her feelings altogether, accepting her mother's distorted judgments. She developed a defensive blankness and emptiness which, as her character armor, was the only means by which she could deal with so chaotic an environment.

This is the character structure she presented upon first arriving for therapy. She was rigid and unbending in her early therapeutic sessions. One could watch her frantic efforts to conceal her anger and fear of reprisal. The loneliness and despair could hardly be guessed, so sketchy was her anamnesis at the outset. But once she had yielded to the latent need to cry, outpoured the bitter torrent of dependency and isolatedness which her parents had forced on her.

Character structure has a special significance for Reich. He has written some elaborate descriptions of the various types of structure. At first his descriptions were couched in the conventional terms of current psychoanalytical formulations—oral, anal, urethral and phallic character traits. Later, however, he essayed more trenchant descriptions of types in terms of nosological categories so that ultimately we find in his writings vivid portrayals of such fundamental character structures as hysterical, compulsive, passive-feminine, phallic-narcissistic, schizoid, and masochistic. These delineations are clinically verifiable, and extremely well-drawn. One orgonomist has told me that for all intents and purposes the followers of Reich employ only four of the above formulations so far as everyday clinical evaluation of their patients is concerned. Most patients are considered as having passive-feminine, narcissistic, compulsive or phallic-narcissistic structures. It seems advisable to give a short précis of Reich's descriptions of these types also described by Lowen in his 1958 book (7). In this way, though much abbreviated, the descriptions will have the air of the authenticity of the original formulations.

Since the general function of character, like body tension, is the defense of the organism against offending stimuli (from within and from without) and maintenance of psychic homeostasis, the compulsive character will be portrayed first. It so vividly demonstrates these two factors.

**1. Compulsive character.** There are fluid transitions from the well-defined compulsion symptom to the corresponding character attitudes. All of life must run according to a preconceived inviolable program, any deviation from which is felt as unpleasurable or with anxiety. Because this character trait predisposes to intensity and thoroughness, it facilitates "doing things." But because it also fears change, adaptation and newness are not compatible. Rarely will the great statesman be a compulsive; too much imagination and flexibility are required. Scientists, as a rule, are much more likely to have this trait. But since pedantry paralyzes speculation, pioneering discoveries become precluded. Circumstantial and ruminative thinking are other characteristics found in the compulsive. Pedantry, circumstantiality, meticulousness, tendency to rumination and thriftiness all derive classically from anal eroticism. When these reaction-formations have been unsuccessful, the result is extreme sloppiness, incapacity for dealing with money, collecting rubbish as well as more valuable possessions, and chaotic life-situations. Hostile and aggressive feelings are often directly gratified in such traits.

Indecision, doubt and distrust are yet other character traits, outwardly displayed as restraint and self-control—the hallmarks of affect-lameness. It is typical of the compulsion neurosis that the repression of genitality is followed by a regression to the earlier stage of anal interests and of aggression. During puberty there are fantasies of rape, feelings of emotional weakness and inferiority, together with the compensatory responses of ethical and aesthetic reaction-formations. Development becomes characterized by a progressive flattening of affective reactions which may impress the untrained observer as a particularly good social "adjustment," though the patient subjectively experiences a feeling of inner emptiness and lack of contact with people. The affect-block is one great spasm of the ego which makes use of somatic spastic conditions. All muscles of the body—but particularly those of the pelvis and pelvic floor, the shoulders and the face—are in a state of chronic tension. Hence the somewhat mask-like appearance of many compulsive characters and their physical awkwardness. There are two layers of repression in the compulsive character: superficially, the sadistic and anal impulses; more deeply, the phallic ones from which the repression occurred.

**2. Phallic-narcissistic character.** This character impresses the observer as self-confident, arrogant, elastic, vigorous and often impressive. The more neurotic the inner mechanism, the more obtrusive appear these modes of behavior. The physique is most often that which is called the athletic type, and the facial expression shows hard, sharp, masculine features. Their behavior is usually haughty, either cold and reserved or else derisively aggressive or "bristly." Sadistic traits are invariably found in their love relationships.

Such individuals usually believe attack is the best defense. Their narcissism expresses itself not in an infantile manner, but in the exaggerated display of self-confidence, dignity and superiority, despite that the basis of their character is no less infantile than that of others. In spite of their narcissistic preoccupation with themselves, they need people and are highly dependent on things and possessions. It is not by accident that this type is most frequently found among athletes, aviators, soldiers and engineers. They have aggressive and sadistic behavior. Analysis invariably discloses that this aggressive behavior represents a particular kind of defensive function.

They are highly virile and sexually potent, but their sexual activity rarely provides adequate energy discharge; that is to say, they are not orgastically potent. Sexual satisfaction is hardly possible for them. Basically they are contemptuous of the opposite sex and such men are highly desired by women because they *appear* to be so masculine.

All phallic-narcissistic characters have in common a fixation in which the anal-sadistic phase of development has been left while the genital object-libidinal position had not yet been attained. Under these circumstances, the penis is not in the service of love, but is an instrument of aggression and vengeance. The sexual act for such characters has the unconscious meaning of again and again proving to the woman how potent they are. Simultaneously it serves as the agent of their hostility. In women, the converse is true—the impulse being to destroy the male, of taking vengeance upon him, of castrating him during coitus, or making him appear ridiculous. This is in no way at variance with the strong sexual attraction which these strongly erotic characters exert on the other sex. The phallic character does not regress as does the compulsive or the hysterical type. He remains at the phallic stage and even exaggerates its manifestations in order to protect himself against a regression to passivity and anality. Character is determined not only by what it wards off, but by the impulses and manner in which the defense is effectuated. The combination of phallic narcissism, phallic sadism and simultaneous compensation of passive anal and homosexual strivings makes for the most energetic characters. Whether such a type turns into a creative genius, a highly successful business executive, or a large-scale criminal depends largely upon the social atmosphere and the fortuitous events of the environment.

**3. Passive-feminine character.** The hysterical character is also subsumed under this heading. Obvious sexual behavior, with specific bodily agility, is the most outstanding characteristic. The connection between female hysterical behavior on sexuality has long been known, and is evidenced by multiform coquetry in gait, gaze and speech. In men, there is softness and over-politeness, a feminine facial expression and feminine behavior, such traits appearing with more or less outspoken apprehensiveness.

Facial expression and gait are never hard and heavy, or self-confident and arrogant. The movements are soft, more or less rolling, and sexually provocative. Easy excitability seems to be the keynote. Compliance exists cheek by jowl with quick depreciation and groundless disparagement. The suggestibility of the hysterical character predisposes him to passive hypnosis, but also to flights of imagination. They can give rise easily to pathological lying owing to the difficulty of separating fantasy from reality. An extraordinary capacity to form sexual attachments of an infantile nature is also evident.

There is a fixation of the genital phase of infantile development with its incestuous background. Mouth as well as anus represent the female genital, while in others these retain their original pregenital function.

The feminine-passive character suffers from direct sexual tension. It may appear paradoxical, but it is a fact that here genital sexuality is directed against itself. The more apprehensive the total attitude, the more pronounced is the sexual behavior which serves the purpose of determining from which direction the expected dangers will arise.

There is little tendency to sublimation and intellectual achievement, with a much lesser tendency to reaction-formations than with other types due to the libido being neither discharged in sexual gratification nor being extensively anchored in the character armor. It is discharged largely in somatic innervations or in anxiety and fear. Sexual excitations do not lend themselves to anything but direct gratification. Their inhibition severely impairs the sublimation of other strivings which have become endowed with excessive libidinal energy. The general character armor is far less fixed or solid than in the compulsive character. The armoring is simply an apprehensive defense against the genital incest strivings.

Muscular tensions will be found massively in the pelvis and thighs, and in other areas to which the libido has become displaced.

**Freud's "death-instinct" and its concomitants.** Only the smallest minority of this type develop a masochist-perversion. The masochistic *attitude* shows not only in interpersonal relationships, but also in the inner life of the person. Typical character traits are the following: subjectively a chronic sensation of *suffering* (which appears objectively as a *tendency to complain)*, chronic tendencies to *self-damage and self-depreciation,* and a compulsion to torture others which makes the patient suffer no less than the object. All characters show a specifically *awkward, atactic behavior* in their manners and in their intercourse with others, often so marked as to give the impression of mental deficiency.

In a case described by Reich, there is a classical description of the neurotic sexual behavior and the characteristic beating fantasy in a young male. The main question to be asked: had a beating given him pleasure? Analysis showed unequivocally that he had anticipated something far worse. He had quickly turned on the stomach primarily to protect his genitals from his father, and *for this reason had experienced the blows on the buttocks as a great relief.* They were harmless compared to the anticipated injury to the genitals, and this relieved him of a good deal of anxiety. One must clearly comprehend this basic mechanism. *The penis had to be protected; rather suffer blows on the buttocks than have the penis injured.* The masochistic wish is a reaction-formation to the original fear of punishment. The beating fantasy thus anticipates in a milder form an expected heavier punishment. He approaches pleasurable activity like any other person, *but the fear of punishment interferes.*

Such character types often try to *provoke* the therapist with the typical masochistic silence. Reich's patient did it with infantile spite reactions. Its intent was to place the analyst—or his prototype, the parent—in a bad light, of provoking him into behavior which would rationally justify the reproach of "you don't love me!"

Behind this provocation there is a *deep disappointment in love.* It is directed especially against those objects who caused a disappointment; that is, objects which were loved intensely and who either actually disappointed or who did not sufficiently gratify the child's love. The actual disappointment in the masochistic character is intensified by a particularly high need for love which makes a real gratification impossible. This provocation also has a second purpose, namely to see how far the patient can go before the analyst would withdraw his love and proceed to punishment. It is a way of *demanding love,* of needing palpable proofs of love to reduce anxiety and inner tension. The masochistic torturing, the masochistic complaint, provocation and suffering all explain themselves on the basis of the frustration (fantasied or actual) of a demand for love which is so excessive that it cannot be gratified.

The masochistic behavior and the demand for love always increase in proportion to the unpleasurable tension, the prepotency to anxiety, or the danger of loss of love. It is typical of this type to avoid anxiety by wanting to be loved. Just as the complaints are a disguised demand for love and the provocation an attempt to force love, so is the total masochistic character an *unsuccessful attempt* to liberate himself from anxiety and unpleasure. It is not successful because he never really gets rid of the inner tension which constantly threatens to turn into anxiety. *The feeling of suffering, then, corresponds to the actual facts of a continuous prepotency to anxiety.* The essential element of the failure is, however, that the spite and the provocation are directed against the loved person from whom love is demanded. In this way, the fear of losing love is increased. The guilt feelings also increase instead of being decreased because it is the loved person who is being tortured. This explains the peculiar behavior of the masochist: the more he tries to get out of his situation of suffering, the more he gets entangled in it.

The excessive demand for love is based on *fear of being left alone* which the masochist experienced intensely in very early childhood. The fact that he so often gets lonely is the secondary result of the attitude. "See how miserable, alone and deserted I am." He cannot tolerate giving up an object (hence the masochistic sticking to a love object) any more than he can divest it of its protective role. He does not tolerate the loss of contact and tries to re-establish it in his inadequate way, that is, by showing himself miserable. The fear of being left alone is based directly on the fear which may arise when contact with the skin of the beloved person is lost.

The fear of being left alone sets in at a time when, unlike the previous oral and anal impulses, violent aggression and infantile sex curiosity met with severe rebuff from the beloved parents. The combination of skin eroticism, anality, and the fear of being left alone, counteracted by demanding bodily contact, are the specific masochistic mechanisms. It is axiomatic that he has always suffered severe frustrations of love; *but often the excessive demand may be so a result of over-coddling* (which could have been a parental reaction-formation to not wanting the child).

The sexual attitudes of the masochist are invariably distorted and perverted. Many have the delusion of having a small penis, and believe that anything connected directly or indirectly with sexuality is a mess and filthy. Men often feel envy towards a rival in the love situation, though this may be concealed by a passive-feminine attitude of over-politeness, deference and courtesy.

There is also evidence of repressed exhibitionism which results later in a severe inhibition in the general behavior. The exhibitionistic onset of the genital phase with immediate strict prohibition and repression of exhibitionistic impulses and complete inhibition of further genital development is another specific for this type. This type *cannot stand praise* and has a strong tendency to *self-depreciation*. The inhibition and repression of genital exhibition leads to a severe impairment of sublimation, activity and self-confidence in later life. This inhibition of exhibitionism goes so far as the development of contrary traits—*self-depreciation, in order not to stand out.* For these reasons, this type cannot be a leader, although he usually develops grandiose fantasies of heroism. His anal fixation makes him passive. This is complicated by the compulsion to *feel stupid or to make oneself appear stupid.* To exploit every inhibition for the purpose of self-depreciation is in full harmony with the masochistic character. To show oneself is connected with severe anxiety, so this type must make himself insignificant and humble in order to avoid this anxiety.

All this taken together causes a feeling of inner ataxy, often a painful embarrassment about appearance. The inhibition of the ability to show and demand love openly brings about all kinds of distorted expressions and makes a person stiff and unnatural. There is a very peculiar *spastic attitude,* not only in his psychic, but also in his genital apparatus which immediately inhibits any strong pleasure sensation and thus changes it into unpleasure. There is often a cramping of the musculature of the pelvic floor.

The masochist has an anal and urethral inhibition and anxiety which goes back to early infancy. It is later transferred to the genital function and provides the immediate basis for his excessive production of unpleasure. The customary toilet training (too early and too strict) leads to the fixation of anal pleasure; the associated idea of being beaten is definitely unpleasurable and at first anxiety-laden. It would be erroneous to say that the unpleasure of being beaten turns into pleasure. Rather, *the fear of being beaten prevents the development of pleasure.* This mechanism, acquired on an anal level, later is transferred to the genital.

During therapy, when genital pleasure becomes possible, there also develop "melting sensations." Such patients perceive these sensations, which normally are pleasurable orgastic sensations, as unpleasure and with anxiety. They fear that the penis might "melt away," or that the skin of the penis might dissolve as a result of that sensation, or even burst. This melting sensation of pre-orgastic pleasure is *itself* perceived as the anticipated threat. The anxiety which was acquired in connection with anal pleasure creates a psychic attitude which makes genital pleasure appear as injury and punishment. The masochist strives for a pleasure situation, but frustration, anxiety and fear of punishment interfere and cause the original goal to be obliterated or made unpleasurable. The patient avoids any increase in pleasure perception.

The masochistic character is used to the anal kind of pleasure which has a flat curve of excitation and has no peak; it is a "lukewarm" kind of pleasure. He transfers anal practice and the anal kind of pleasure experience to the genital apparatus which functions entirely differently. The intensive, sudden and steep increase of genital pleasure is not only unaccustomed, but for one used only to the mild anal pleasure it is apt to be terrifying. If to this is added an anticipation of punishment, all conditions are given for an immediate conversion of pleasure into unpleasure.

The masochistic attitude and fantasy stems from the unpleasurable reaction to the pleasurable sensation. It is an attempt to master the unpleasure through an attitude which is psychically formulated as "I'm so miserable—please love me!" The beating fantasy must enter because the demand for love also contains genital demands which force the patient to divert the punishment from the front to the rear. "Beat me—but don't castrate me!" Anality mobilizes the whole libidinal apparatus without, however, being capable of bringing about relaxation of the tension. The inhibition of genitality is not only a result of anxiety, but produces anxiety in turn. This increases the discrepancy between tension and discharge.

Mention should also be made of the common masochistic sex attitude of neurotic women, an attitude which by many analysts is erroneously considered the normal feminine attitude. This passive rape fantasy in the woman, however, serves no other purpose than that of allaying her guilt feelings. These neurotic women can engage in intercourse without guilt feelings only if—actually or in fantasy—they are raped, thus shifting the responsibility to the man. The formal resistance of many women in coitus has the same meaning.

One has to view with the greatest scepticism the success of the treatment of masochistic characters as long as one has not understood every detail of the character reactions, and therefore has not really broken through them. The characteristic symptoms of the masochist usually persist until it has become possible to eliminate the described disturbance of the pleasure mechanism. Once genital orgasm has been achieved the patient usually undergoes a rapid change.

*\*\*\**

The ultimate goals of all psychotherapy—whether verbal or nonverbal—are directed towards freeing the personality from rigid involuntary controls, enabling it to manipulate its environment satisfactorily and at the same time to express itself in such a dynamic manner that it will make some personally and socially gratifying impression upon that environment.

All of this is summated in Reich's concept of the "genital character." Frederick Perls has suggested that, perhaps, it is a somewhat idealistic concept, and to that extent unreal or fanciful. It resembles some of the commonly accepted notions of "normality" conceived of as an ideal goal not yet attained but to which we are striving. Certainly no absolute standard or arbitrary norm is implied here. Most psychiatrists today, while asserting the relative value of the concept of cultural normality, still lay down certain propositions or characteristics which might be considered as essential components of the concept of normality but which, while useful, are tainted by one defect or another.

For Reich, "homo normalis" is more or less equivalent to a biopathic personality, one afflicted with the emotional plague. Lindner does not speak of the normal person or the well-adjusted person. His special thesis relates to the dynamic development of the rebellious instinct in a whole person, the life-affirmative person. In the psychic profile he paints of such a cultural stereotype he insists that several characteristics be present, though feelings and affects are not considered at all significant. He suggests the following:

**1. Awareness.** The mature person will have a broad view of his hitherto unconscious motivations and thus no longer be a puppet of his own unconscious strivings. He will be a self-conscious person in the philosophical rather than the psycho-pathological sense of the term.

**2. Identity.** The average person suffers from innumerable but unconscious identifications with the powerful figures of his childhood. These he projects into his present-day environment. In the shuffle of these identifications, his own particular identity is lost. The adult should have separated himself from his past and arrived at a sane appreciation of his own value and worth as a conscious striving, mature person.

**3. Skepticism.** Each of these profile traits is, of course, dependent upon the preceding. As the person becomes more aware of himself and sloughs off these infantile identifications with others, the more intellectually curious he becomes and the more skeptical is he of authority *as* authority. I am reminded of an English poet who wrote, in effect, that he went to bed one night with faith and in the morning found her a harlot. He went to bed with doubt and in the morning found her a virgin.

**4. Responsibility.** By this factor is implied the willingness to permit children to learn by experience the consequences of their own behavior. He loathes the imposition of compulsive moral inhibitions upon those who know not what these mean.

Lindner extends the idea to the social level, too, believing that sympathy and empathy, together with instinctive needs, result in companionship and group activity. "Each man is every man's brother and keeper, part of an organic whole in which he is an individual as well as a geared-in unit." (5)

**5. Employment.** Lindner defines this as not merely being productive or even creative, but rather as having a "vocation consisting of the dedication of one's existence to evolution, to the lending of one's life consciously and conscientiously to the on-going parade." (5)

**6. Tension.** Semantics could be a distinct nuisance in this connection, but Lindner defines it specifically and acceptably as a "condition of alertness which recognizes the distance, the gap, between what is and what should be; and the state of internal restlessness or dissatisfaction or lack of contentment with 'things as they are,' together with the determination to participate in change." (5) Only in this connection does Lindner suggest the inclusion of emotional factors in his picture of the mature person. This lack of definite inclusion is the prime defect in his profile.

I doubt that Reich would be too outraged to see his concepts coupled with this brave profile of Lindner's. True, Reich had painted such a picture many years before this particular prescription for rebellion by Lindner. In many ways his scheme is far more complete and satisfactory. But time is of no concern to us here, nor who did what first. Instead we can construe this effort as a corroboration of the basic psychological principles that Reich so valiantly fought for.

Several years after his theoretical formulations regarding the character armor, Reich proceeded by way of experiment and experience to the concept of the muscular armor. He thought that the character armor shows itself to be *functionally identical* with muscular hypertension, the muscular armor. The concept of "functional identity" which he introduced meant nothing but the idea that muscular and character attitudes serve the same function in the psychic economy: they can influence and replace each other.

The significance of this formulation, unfortunately, has all too long been neglected. And the psychotherapeutic field in general has had to pay a high price for this neglect.

As the years elapsed, Reich modified some of the original concepts about the muscular armor which were largely psycho-analytical in nature, and elaborated them in terms differing considerably from conventional psychodynamics. The muscular armor derives in large measure not only from various types of early toilet training, table disciplines, play restrictions and sexual prudery, but more basically from our own attitudes towards birth itself. A powerful indictment of some of our current hospital practices which, only here and there, are being corrected and replaced by more humane approaches was included in one of Reich's books.

He said that in highly respected lying-in hospitals infants are not allowed to be at the mother's breast during the first 24 to 48 hours… The infants suffer and cry, a crime against the rules of hygiene! The newborn, just torn out from total contact with the warm uterus after nine uninterrupted months was suddenly transferred from an environment with the temperature of 37°C to a temperature of 18°C to 20°C, and is not permitted to contact its mother's body. It is against the rules of hospital administration, against culture and morality, a provocation of the Oedipus complex, a crime against propriety and custom, a life expression condemned by medicine, as represented by the academies of science and all the honorable doctors and officers of all universities where electrons and protons next to neutrons and positrons dance the St. Vitus dance of atomic explosives. Here, thought Reich, and nowhere else, are the bases implanted in the newborn for war. The newborn reacts to the cold at first with anxiety, then crying, and finally with contraction of its autonomic system, the first contraction of its life, if a dead uterus has not already damaged its organism.

The separation from the maternal body is the first major impetus to the development of muscular armoring. Ontogenetic events that follow merely confirm the need for the armor, which throughout the ensuing years grows in strength, density and rigidity. The result is that all the vitality of the organism becomes posited in the armoring itself. The person becomes a mere shell. Life, then, for that organism can only become empty of all value, meaningless and frustrating.

Non-verbal psychotherapy is directed exclusively against this shell. By considering another example we may get a further understanding of the dynamics of repression and the physiological processes involved. Repression in a child begins possibly as simple inhibition or suppression. The need to suppress anger is usually initiated by external stimuli, nearly always from a parent or a parent-surrogate or another sibling. The expression of anger elicits reprimand, threat of rejection, threat of punishment. Under these fear stimuli, suppression is mandatory. However, suppression is not only a psychological gesture, but of necessity must be accompanied by muscular gestures of one type or another. So the child begins to grit the jaws together, fists are clenched, neck and shoulders tensed, respiration short and jerky, abdominal muscles become rigid and stiff and thigh muscles sometimes hypertonic. Only by such muscular tensions can the powerful vegetative or emotional impulses be controlled. In order to maintain control and sustain suppression, these tensions need to be perpetuated. Relaxation becomes comparatively impossible, even during sleep. Many children during sleep show manifold jerky and hypertonic movements, certainly indicative of a physical state that is far from relaxed. As time proceeds, tension becomes a constant from the physiological point of view. The "pre-dormescent start" of many adults is ample corroboration of this fact.

The early rigors of unimaginative toilet training can also be considered in a broad manner to depict one way in which the muscular armor undergoes development. As a rule these disciplines are harshly imposed upon an infant before the neural possibility of discrete visceral performance or finely coordinated muscular activities has developed. Therefore, the attempt to control the anal and vesical sphincters prematurely, that is to keep them spastic until the "right" time and place is available, can only result in many unrelated groups of muscles also being made rigid and tense. The attempt to restrain the exit of urine, feces and gas in order to avoid parental displeasure must needs be accompanied by a considerable amount of hypertonus. Persisted in over a long period of time, as it usually is, obviously the muscular tension must become chronic and eventually involuntary. In contrast to the usual psychoanalytical statement that the lower gastro-intestinal tract and urinary apparatus become cathected with libido which becomes fixated there, the Reich nomenclature appears far more explicit and precise. One has only to watch a youngster prancing and dancing in the frantic attempt not to soil his garments to appreciate how he must struggle by means of muscular tension to "control" himself. It becomes a great deal easier to understand the whole functional concept of the muscular armor, whether it be interpreted in the familiar terms of Reich or the neuro-physiological interpretation of Guze (2), Hebb (4) and others. "For example, a subject restraining urine in the full bladder, moves the feet or legs. This is compensatory in that there is thus some completion of the sensory-motor cycle, albeit in an inappropriate channel. Here the drive (sensation) persists, although it is momentarily perhaps reduced," wrote Guze. (2)

This leads to another important feature of Reich's formulation about the armor. *Its function is to reduce the intensity of vegetative sensations.* Sensations are the evidence of vegetative excitation—plasmatic movements within the cell structure. And if the movement or plasmatic sensations are in the bowel or the bladder at the "wrong" or inappropriate time and place, there is the anticipation of trouble if they are heeded and acceded to. So the muscular tensions and compulsive behavior patterns have the direct function of blocking off these bodily sensations, and so of controlling autonomic function. The armor provides a necessary kind of control over bodily drives and feelings. It pushes the latter into the background, replacing them by compulsive acts which are protective and substitutive. Eventually this muscular control becomes so chronic and automatic that it cannot be discarded even when the individual wishes to do so. Many patients presenting psychosomatic complaints in the lower back and pelvis, for example, usually reveal a history of harsh toilet disciplines succeeded by varying types of elimination problems. The vegeto-therapeutic approach of inducing lower back and thigh movements almost routinely releases an enormous amount of rage and resentment. Adequately discharged, the patient may become aware of the vegetative sensations to which the tension has made him insensitive.

The muscular armor thus blocks off sensations as well as motor activities. It must not be thought that it applies merely to the one. The whole sensory-motor cycle is involved in the armoring process. The armoring is a generalized dystonia in that some muscles are needlessly relaxed, while others chronically are tensed.

Another area of ontogenetic development which contributes significantly to the formulation of the armor relates to early sexual prohibitions. It is now more or less common knowledge since Freud's great pioneering efforts that sexual interest and activity begin quite early in childhood. Known also is the social and parental antagonism to such phallic preoccupations, forcing the child to repress these drives and interests. Over and above what Freud and his colleagues have contributed to this theme, Reich emphasizes the notion logically enough that a great deal of effort and neuromuscular energy has to be extended by the child to prevent any overt demonstration of his sexual precocity.

It would not do for the parents to discover his masturbatory experiments or his experimental indulging in sexual curiosity and play with neighborhood children or siblings. Discovery carries with it the implied promise of threats and insinuations that are so grave that long before puberty rolls around most memory traces of such early experiences have been lost. Yet the tense pelvis, abdominal and other disseminated neuromuscular tensions offer eloquent testimony to their continued existence in this compensatory form.

A complex and highly developed set of muscular tensions points to the perpetuation of infantile sexuality in the armored area. Unacceptable feelings and vegetative excitations had to be blocked off by the formation of these tensions. Reich noted that children fight lasting and painful anxiety states accompanied by typical sensations in the "stomach" by breath-holding. They behave similarly when pleasurable sensations in the abdomen or in the genitals arise and they are afraid of them. Holding the breath and keeping the diaphragm contracted are among the earliest and most important mechanisms of blocking pleasure in the abdomen, or for nipping "belly anxiety" in the bud. The way in which our children accomplish this "blocking off of sensations in the belly" by way of respiration and abdominal pressure is typical and universal. Vegeto-therapeutic work swiftly penetrates to the very core of the defensive network of tensions, releasing both the blocked-off drives and the anxiety they have engendered.

Reich is highly critical of the current tendency to avoid dealing directly with the sexual problem. He is contemptuous of modern medicine which, to use his words, regards the sexual problem as a "potato too hot to handle." Much of his heaviest artillery has been directed against unwise parental handling of children's sexual curiosity and the denial of rational and biological sexual outlets for pubescents and adolescents. Despite all the recent findings pointing to the peak of sexual potentiality in the mid-adolescent period, our entire approach is to condemn as "delinquent" any adolescent who dares violate our prohibitions on this score. The cruel stifling of these early biological sallies into life leads to extensive characterological disturbances. And since these are widespread, indeed universal, they can only lead eventually to corrupt social institutions. Society shapes character, and of course individual character shapes society. There is a continuous "feedback" mechanism operating here. Sexual restriction in children and youngsters results in the forced development of compulsive character traits, surely the most prominent features of our particular society. The latter perpetuates psychic pathology in the form of "the emotional plague." The basic dynamic mechanisms in this social epidemic are repression, displacement, irradiation and projection.

The cure of the emotional plague—the fundamental solution to the character-muscular armor problem of individuals and society—is for Reich intrinsically a sexual matter. Some have called him a fanatic on this score, roundly condemning him for his uncompromising stand. Be that as it may, he rebelled against our pathological sexual attitudes which are both unnatural and stupid. Studies by Kinsey, Ellis and others have confirmed his views. Many of their recommendations for legal and social reform were long ago intrinsic parts of Reich's fundamental approach to psychotherapy and sociology. His attitude—basic, uncompromising, modern, as well as biologically oriented—was that extensive, painstaking and conscientious clinical investigation establishes the fact that one thing alone—the establishment of the sexual life of children, adolescents and adults—can eliminate from the world the character neuroses, and with the character neuroses the emotional plague in its various forms. In enunciating this dogma, he is largely confirmed by the findings of several anthropologists, Malinowski and Mead being two of the more outstanding.

Some day it is to be hoped that someone well qualified in the field of the social sciences will make a detailed study of Reich's contributions to sociology and juvenile delinquency. It is the latter which is a problem of serious import and controversy today.

The identity of psyche and soma—that dichotomy which some people attempt to eliminate merely by hyphenating the two words—is verifiable by clinical phenomena. Polygraphic and myographic studies point to the unity and integrity of the psychosomatic organism. Pulse rate, blood pressure, electrical conductivity of the skin, respiratory function, the movements of the entire gastro-intestinal tract from its circular muscles of the mouth to those of the anus, testify as involuntary witnesses to affective changes, and bear witness to the functional identity of the character-muscular armor.

Shagass and Malmo recently reported some significant myographic studies. In the setting of the therapeutic situation, psychodynamic themes relating to sex and hostility were investigated by literally miles of electromyographic tape recordings. As they themselves conservatively summarize their conclusions:

> "To date the E.M.G. method has been demonstrated as valid for two important aspects of objectivity study of the psychiatric interview. These include local muscle tension associated with particular conflictual themes brought out during interview and symptom-related muscle tension. There is also the suggestion from present findings that level of muscular tension may, in some cases, be related to mood, and to clinical improvement." (10)

This is a most cautious evaluation of their findings. I am concerned here only with the fact that the entire concept of psychosomatic unity and character-muscular armoring is confirmed by clinical findings, no matter how cautious the evaluation.

This being factual to Reich's perceptions, he has devoted a great deal of attention to the muscular armor. His clinical experience over many years has enabled him to describe its salient features with some degree of clarity. For the sake of convenience, he has divided the armor into sections or segments. His biological interests first rendered possible the conceptualization of segments. This has also occurred to Pottenger, whose book on visceral innervation concerns essentially the notion of the "segmental man." In his preface, Pottenger states that

> "this book attempts to bring an important phase of physiology to the physician. It is preeminently a discussion of *man as a segmental organism*. On the one hand, it describes visceral and somatic relationships to neurons which take origin in the various segments of the cord; and, on the other hand, it describes the reflexes which result from this association (6) (italics mine)

These segments fall into several functional rather than anatomical units. Unlike Pottenger, whose segments coincide with vertebral innervation, Reich stressed the notion of broad functional units. Admittedly it is an arbitrary division, but nonetheless a useful one. According to Reich, segmental structure of the armor means that it functions everywhere laterally like a ring... *Armor segments, then, comprise those organs and muscle groups which are in functional contact with each other, and can aid each other to participate in expressive movement.*

The following description of the armor is largely a resumé of Reich's dissertation on the armored segments found in the essay "The Expressive Language of the Living" in the third edition of *Character Analysis.*

**1. Ocular Ring.** This is the area well above, around and back of the eyes themselves, and includes the immobility of the muscles of the forehead and of the eyes, empty expression of the eyes, of protruding eyeballs, a mask-like expression or immobility of the cheeks on both sides of the nose. The emotional expressions of tenderness, crying, anger and grimacing of every kind are dependent on the mobility and flexibility of the ocular segment.

**2. Oral Ring.** This segment of the armor consists of the musculature of the mouth, chin, throat and the occipital muscles. Much cervical tension is related to those emotions expressed in tight lips, pursing the mouth, gritting the teeth and clenching the jaw. Many tensions in the lower segments cannot be released until those in the oral area have first been dissolved.

**3. Cervical Ring.** The deep cervical muscles are involved here, including the platysma myoides and the sterno-cleidomastoid, and the lower part of the trapezius. It also includes the larynx, trachea, the upper portion of the esophagus and part of the bronchial tree. These are invariably very sensitive and painful due to chronic tension and, when attacked, release hatred, fear and tears.

**4. Chest Ring.** Included here is the chest as a whole and the auxiliary muscles involved in respiration, apart from the diaphragm. Thus are included the intercostals, the pectorals, deltoids and those muscles on and between the shoulder blades. The arms and hands are considered to be extensions of the chest segment.

**5. Diaphragmatic Ring.** Here is considered the diaphragm and the organs directly under it, particularly the spleen, stomach and gall-bladder. The dissolution of the diaphragmatic armor is the central therapeutic task, as will be perceived a little later. Some therapists consider the cervical and diaphragmatic segments as being related. The tight diaphragm and the globus hystericus accompany one another as a rule.

**6. Abdominal Ring.** In this segment, the recti muscles, transverse abdominals, latissimus dorsi and the sacro-spinalis are often found chronically stiff and rigid. The psoas major is not directly accessible, but some of the movements and motor attitudes specifically affect it. The tight belly is perhaps one of the most commonly encountered armored phenomena and is pathognomic of severe neurosis.

**7. Pelvic Ring.** The armor of the pelvis comprises in most cases practically all the muscles and viscera of the pelvic basin. It is an essential Reich theorem that the viscera enclosed within a particular segment constitute integral parts of that segment. The lower extremities are considered integral parts of the pelvic segment. Release of tensions in the thigh unlocks the pelvic inhibitions in which case sexual excitations become capable of expressing themselves.

It is further characteristic of Reich's thinking that normal biological impulses become distorted and perverted by the armor in their attempt to gain outlet. Love becomes hatred, sex becomes perversion, self-regulation becomes morality. Healthy biological functioning under these circumstances becomes totally impossible. Drives dash themselves, as it were, against or in the surrounding armored tension and become "retroflected," to use the apt term of Frederick Perls. Reich explained that the lack of ability to experience natural orgastic gratification regularly leads to development of sadistic and other impulses. This phenomenon can be directly perceived on the treatment couch. As the softening-up process proceeds, the patient becomes more and more capable of feeling love, warmth and tenderness. Periodically, however, as he becomes aware of his own armored blocks which prevent this affective expression, blind fury and rage make themselves felt instead. Then remorse and guilt set in and, unless the therapist becomes aware of this process and helps the patient to negate it positively, the armoring process is employed once more.

A civilization or a culture comprised of armored persons is patently a sick organism. Its government, politics, religion, philosophy, art and all of its institutions are infected with the same pathological virus. It is Reich's contention that without a direct attack on the individual armoring process, all social progress is merely manipulation of the superficial social armor. Where individual reconstruction or reorganization of the personality through psychotherapy or vegetotherapy is not attempted, "adjustment" consists merely of adaptation to the pathological armoring process and the emotional plague. And in this case, the armor is still the armor, permitting the direct expression not of normal healthy drives, but of their diseased equivalents, the secondary drives. Reich has formulated a whole series of sociological concepts of supreme importance in our perilous times.

## BIBLIOGRAPHY

1. Cameron, D. Ewen. *General Psychotherapy.* New York, Grune & Stratton, 1950, p. 55.
2. Guze, Henry, "Compensatory Behavior as Completion of the Sensory-Motor Cycle," *Jnl. of Gen. Psych.* 1953, 83, p. 293.
3. Freud, Sigmund. "Analysis Terminable and Interminable," *Collected Papers Vol. V,* London, Hogarth Press, 1950, p. 531.
4. Hebb, D.O. *The Organization of Behavior.* New York, John Wiley, 1949.
5. Lindner, Robert. *Prescription for Rebellion.* New York, Rinehart, 1952. p. 252 *et seq.*
6. Pottenger, Francis Marion. *Symptoms of Visceral Disease.* St. Louis, Mosby Co., 1944.
7. Lowen, Alexander. *Physical Dynamics of Character Structure.* New York, Grune & Stratton, 1958.
8. Saul, Leon J. *Emotional Maturity.* New York, Lippincott, 1917. p. 100.
9. *Ibid,* p. 100.
10. Shagass, Charles & Malmo, Robert B. "Psychodynamic Themes and Localized Muscular Tension during Psychotherapy," *Psychosomatic Medicine,* XVI, 4, 1954.

# Chapter III

## Method I

"...in the psychical field, the biological factor is really the rock-bottom."
— Sigmund Freud

It was Reich's contention that neuromuscular tensions not only ensure successful repression of forbidden impulses, but that the functional group of muscles involved actually anchor or store the emotions themselves. His manner of stating this problem, however, has been thought to leave many problems unsolved. His elucidation of these problems is considered by physiologists and psychologists to be unsatisfactory. He does not elaborate on the physiological mechanisms or the psychodynamics of the anchoring of affects in taut muscles. Most scholars can hardly conceive muscles to store anything but glycogen, lactic acid and carbonic acid. Though most of Reich's clinical findings can easily be substantiated, some of his theoretical formulations are believed to be so out of harmony with current attitudes as to make them unacceptable.

When muscular tensions are worked upon and reduced by the active methods to be described, obscure reflexes are initiated which involve the central nervous system. These muscular probings must initiate a complex series of neural reflexes of which we know but little. *Rather than muscle, the brain is prodded to give up affects and memories which have long been stored there.* In all fairness to Reich, it should be added that it is equally obscure how memory—or anything else—can be stored in cerebral cells.

The fundamental basis of neuromuscular tension in voluntary muscle is a carefully struck balance between myotatic reflex centers in the spinal cord and the higher cerebral centers. In other words, there is a fine balance between impulses from upper and lower motor neurons. Labyrinthine and cervical muscle receptors also exert an influence upon this background of tonus in skeletal muscle. Finally, pathways from cerebellar, mid-brain and cerebral centers convey impulses along the final common path to produce exquisitely fine adjustments in the tonic state and to maintain normal distribution between antagonistic groups of muscles. It will become evident that the vegeto-therapeutic work temporarily disrupts this delicate interplay of tonic impulses. Whatever the degree of tonus or hypertonus in the skeletal muscles, its intensity and distribution is disturbed in one way or another by therapy. It is this disturbance of the existent distribution of tonus which results in the profound relaxation which most patients experience towards the close of any session.

Recent neurophysiological notions enable us to conceive of the brain, viscera and skeletal muscles as separate units of a highly complex "feedback" system. Under ordinary circumstances there is a completion of the sensory-motor cycle. If, however, the motor phase of the cycle cannot be normally completed because of personal or social factors, then substitutive or compensatory outlets will be found. The sensory phase of the cycle is perpetuated in terms of "feedback."

Guze wrote that, "It is the opinion of this writer that a circuit in the organism's brain would be brought into action particularly if the stimulus, externally or internally induced, could not be 'released' in terms of neuro-motor response." (6) This, perhaps, might be one of the simplest interpretations of the meaning and origin of the muscular armor. It comprises a potentiality or a habit-pattern of compensatory and substitutive responses that have become more or less permanently ingrained in the nervous system. The vegeto-therapeutic work on the chronically rigid muscular armor is to interrupt the conditioned responses and feedback mechanisms, resulting in their extinction, and permitting the freer expression of motor impulses without involuntary cortical substitution.

The classical definition of neurosis relates to a dynamic conflict between ego and id, between thinking and drive, between cortex and soma. The complex history of familial training, social pressures and moral injunctions plays a great part in the cortical set of configurations. As a result, intellectual preoccupations and socially acceptable behavior become preferable to feeling and body impulse. Sterility in personality and in life-spontaneity is the inevitable outcome.

In vegeto-therapy, one of the most fundamental aims must be to free the soma and its intrinsic drives from excessive cortical control and regulation, to free the id from the inhibitions of the ego and superego, at least temporarily, until a higher or more civilized kind of integration and reconciliation can be worked out. The intent is primarily to hinder the automatic inhibition of the cerebral cortex which would then release somatic drives and needs, whereby tension would be eliminated. *Tension, from the viewpoint of this thesis, is actual muscular control to prevent the eruption of such drives.* Such eruption, if permitted, produces anxiety. Only by the elimination of irrational cultural "controls" can anxiety be eradicated, permitting the satisfactory gratification of biological needs merely by their release from the constant vigilance of the superego. Their reactivation or release would force the necessity of the reorganization of a higher type of homeostasis.

These fundamental facts offer useful hints as to the practical ends of therapy. It circles around the notion that by grasping a significant factor in the patient's psychic economy we can manipulate it to our therapeutic advantage. Speransky, in another medical area, expressed a similar concept when he said: "It is clear that exact knowledge of all the details is not indispensable for useful interference in the course of a pathological process. It suffices sometimes to comprehend accurately the basic condition, the 'leading link,' and by grasping it to manipulate the whole chain."

In this instance, we are concerned with the patient's affect-lameness which we relate to the neuromuscular hypertonus. This is the basic clinical condition and the leading link. We must, therefore, use every technical device to shake him loose from his chronic employment of contactlessness. Consider for the moment the not unusual patient who can verbalize with some ease, whose intellectual grasp of his problem is keen, yet whose neurotic symptoms—visceral, psychological or behavioral—still persist. He can rarely be moved into any overt emotional catharsis. Despite his attention being directed persistently to the existence of irrational transference attitudes to the therapist, his emotional reactions to these perceptions remain unaltered.

The therapeutic devices described here are admirably suited to this type of patient who perpetually functions behind a façade. He is locked within the closed sphere of a tight and rigid personality armor and has no capacity, even when he ardently wishes it, to release his pent-up affects. So much "control" has been invested in the armor itself that the individual eventually loses the ability to voluntarily modify the automatic inhibitions established in early life. They have finally achieved an autonomy of their own. These controls are summarized in the concept "armor." *It is the armor that lives and functions at the expense of the individual.* There is no flexibility, no spontaneity, no freedom—only neurotic control. Out of this restraint grows bitterness and frustration and hatred. For this reason Reich believed "that in the rigid, chronic armoring of the human animal we have found the answer to the question of his so gigantically destructive hatred and his mechanistic as well as mystical thinking." (8)

\*\*\*

Altogether apart from personal experience in having undergone vegeto-therapy, my authority for the following description of the technique is derived from three extraordinarily lucid pieces of writing from the pen of Reich.

1. *The Function of the Orgasm,* p. 266 *et seq.*
2. *Character Analysis* (3rd edition), p. 357 *et seq.*
3. *The Cancer Biopathy,* p. 154 *et seq.*

There are many profound observations and much clinical data in these works. A ripe and mature wisdom is depicted here, ready to be drawn upon usefully by the open-minded therapist.

The goal of vegeto-therapy is the eliciting of the orgasm reflex. The basic principle of the technique for eliciting the reflex is:

1. Find the places and mechanisms of the inhibitions preventing unitary character of the orgasm reflex.

2. Intensify involuntary inhibitory mechanisms and the involuntary impulses, such as the forward movement of the pelvis, which is then capable of inducing the total vegetative reflex.

The language of this simple set of directions may not appear significant at first sight. Prior to having undergone therapy, I myself had read these words a number of times without understanding the full significance of the method. *Muscular blocks and psychic tensions are functionally identical;* this is the backbone of the entire system, The therapeutic attack on the neurosis can be started at either end of the organismic scale. However, most of the tensions and inhibitions are usually so well concealed that they may not appear at all clearly to cursory inspection. A method has to be developed for intensifying and exaggerating the latent blocks so that they may be brought into the purview of both the patient and the therapist. Once some awareness of them has been established, something can be done to alleviate the muscular tension together with the corresponding character inhibition.

The manner in which this is usually done goes something like this: the male patient strips down to shorts; if a female, to basic underwear of brassiere and briefs. If the brassiere is too tight, this will have to be discarded. Embarrassment is not to be repressed. This, too, is an emotional response of a kind and as such must be encouraged to emerge.

The patient lies down on the couch on his back and is instructed to bring the knees up, planting the feet firmly on the couch, near the buttocks, with feet and knees several inches apart. The elbows are crooked at the side with the hands open and flat on the couch, shoulders pulled down. The head lies on the couch without a pillow so the muscles of the neck and shoulders can fall into a relaxed position. The mouth is kept open, with the jaw permitted to drop. All of this at first sight sounds easy. More often than not, however, it meets with considerable resistance from the patient—sometimes overtly, but more often covertly. Some will not and cannot keep the mouth open. Others may feel they need a pillow under the head to avoid developing a stiff neck, though this wish is not acceded to. It is the frankly sexual implication of the working position which evokes criticism and open hostility most of the time. This resistance emanates more commonly from hysterical women and some homosexual men.

Recent discussion has also revealed that some professionals have to be included amongst those from whom objections will be made about the partial nudity. These people seem to be as neurotically "modest" about body exposure as is an occasional patient. One, a self-admittedly prudish educator, suggested that the patient wear a light hospital gown or that a sheet be draped over the body. In this way modesty may be respected.

This attitude misses the point of the procedure entirely. Such therapists propose immediately to make concessions to the patient's guilt about his body. They fail to realize that this partial nudity plunges the hesitant patient into direct contact with an important phase of his neurotic problem. Stripping off the clothes may be analogous to stripping off the armor. This is altogether apart from the fact that any additional covering may interfere with the therapist's inspection of the patient's muscular problems to begin with, and the patient's response to therapy as it proceeds.

The exhibitionist who theoretically may enjoy exposing himself to the therapist's gaze will find scant comfort on the couch. Though he will be conscious of the therapist's inspection, and thus glory in his narcissistic role, his pleasure is bound to be short-lived. The dynamic effect of therapy rapidly breaks into the neurotic egocentricity, releasing affects that are concealed by the blatant exhibitionism.

Therapy will be needed by the psychologist and psychiatrist as well in order to overcome their own body guilts. Merely because one has medical or doctoral qualifications does not, in itself, eradicate the neurotic feelings that are characteristic of our culture, There is little difference between the layman and the professional so far as these factors are concerned. Couch work elicits this fact immediately and without much difficulty.

This working position in vegeto-therapy is similar to that described by Todd in her book on body mechanics. She suggests its use primarily to develop kinesthesia. It was her contention that by placing the body in generally unusual positions and noting the changes in body feelings that such positions produce, one might find a better balance for one's bodily forces. The instructions are to lie on the back on the floor, with knees bent and drawn up, feet resting on the floor, arms folded over the chest—which is only a slight deviation from the vegeto-therapeutic work position. There the arms are placed by the side of the patient, flat on the couch, with elbows extended or crooked. In this position gravity works through the body from front to back, instead of from head to foot, so that weight falls in a different relationship to each vertebra of the spine. The pull upon chronically strained muscles is thus lessened and it is consequently easier to release tension than when the body is in the customary position.

In this position "the diaphragm may adjust its rhythms to longitudinal breathing instead of wide, full breathing." The latter kind of breathing merely extends the ribs laterally. In this way, strains are put on the diaphragm—which it has been said is the organ of, or the gateway to, the emotions. And it is this latter set of strains and tensions we wish largely to eliminate.

Once the position has been assumed, the patient is instructed to breathe as easily as possible. Above all, he is to pay special attention to producing a full exhalation with a soft signing sound—with the mouth open. The sound resembles "ah-h-h-h-h"—a long exhalation. It is difficult to describe in words, much easier to demonstrate. The sound itself should be a short one, passing easily into the soft sound of the exhalation of the breath. Making this sighing or moaning sound is embarrassing to some patients and initially provokes some resistance.

During vegeto-therapy the conjunction of respiration with different sounds is constantly enjoined and utilized. This should be elaborated on to avoid possible misinterpretation with the suspicion that mystical concepts are being enunciated. There is no mysticism here at all. It is a known fact that, although emotional *capacity* is inborn and unlearned, the *form* taken by the emotions is the product of early conditioning and acculturation. Whatever form of emotional expression the child is exposed to during the formative years of life, this form becomes incorporated into the child's character-structure, identification playing a prominent psychodynamic role. In this emotional expression, gestures and sounds are perceived as intrinsic to the emotion, are perceived as *belonging* to it. Some people cry silently as though with enormous reservations. Others sob from deep down inside with no shame attaching to the sounds they make. Obviously there is sound associated with all such affective demonstrations which the child cannot help but observe and notice. This also applies to laughing and outbursts of anger. Sounds may carry with them the meaning of, for example, having heard a sick parent cry and moan. Or they may embody the significance of an early sickness, when as a child there was moaning and crying from pain and discomfort.

In other words, sounds become associated with basic emotional responses. So far as the affect-lame person is concerned, the possibility of labile emotional reactions is locked up within his cement-like armored structure. A direct line of attack is usually impossible. However, if the therapist can take advantage of this conditioned association of sounds, sensations, gestures and emotions, it might be possible to evoke out of the locked darkness of the personality those affects which are directly connected with the patient's neurosis. First the stiff bonds of character-structure are loosened by hyperventilation and by dissolving the tensions in the several muscular segments. This accomplished, then can begin the slow and sometimes arduous process of teaching the patient to emit sounds of one kind or another to the accompaniment of different breathing techniques. These latter are so designed to affect different parts of the respiratory system to further the softening-up process and to release the pent-up emotions.

It only requires some little experimental work with a patient here and there to become wholly convinced of the veracity of these associations.

Reich described the most important means of bringing about the orgasm reflex as a breathing technique which developed almost by itself in the course of the work.

It is difficult to determine with any degree of accuracy the historical or clinical events that originally made Reich emphasize the therapeutic significance of breathing as the fundamental basis of vegeto-therapy. But there is little doubt that it was a stroke of sheer genius. One has only to study sympathetically some of the material amassed in the last several years about hyperventilation to realize it is a useful therapeutic device. If a patient is chronically affect-lame, and if the evidence indicates that when subjected to hyperventilation even the most stable person becomes emotionally demonstrative, then it is clear that these two sets of facts require to be placed in juxtaposition. Even the most heavily armored person can be made to abreact vigorously with hyperventilation. No matter what other elements are comprised in vegeto-therapy, this fact is basic.

The following quotation from a piece of research writing by Bela Mittelman amply corroborates this thesis. The results of hyperventilation have been likened to cerebral anoxia and the latter can be experimentally produced by exposing subjects to atmospheres containing oxygen under lower concentration and pressure than usual.

> "Effects of Low-Oxygen Atmospheres.
>
> "Seventeen medical students who breathed an atmosphere of 13 percent oxygen (corresponding to an altitude of 12,400 feet) for three hours revealed marked changes in affective behavior, *with the impairment of emotional control...*
>
> "Psychoneurotic patients after inhalation of the low oxygen mixture revealed an even more marked *lack of emotional restraint,* with feelings of exaggerated self-esteem and sexual preoccupations...
>
> "Forty college students with careful personality studies, including Rorschach test, were exposed to 9.3% oxygen (corresponding to an altitude of 18,500 feet) for about one hour. The following statistically significant relationship was found between tolerance for low oxygen and personality types without overt psychoneurosis: *Individuals who are rigid, anxious, not very dependent on themselves and inhibited in their responses react poorly to the high altitude situation.* Individuals who are outgoing but do not have sufficient inner balance also experience difficulties, although not to the same degree as the highly inhibited group. Individuals well integrated with respect to the use of their inner resources and responsive to external stimulation react best of all."
> (7) (italics mine)

The italicized sections above constitute the best objective proof of my contention that hyperventilation induces non-specific abreaction even in rigid, highly neurotic subjects. It does so because the cortex, by this means, becomes temporarily inactivated or dissociated. It is a neurological axiom that the

> "*neocortex inhibits effective behavior.* When removed in a cat, that animal becomes placid and exceptionally affectionate. Removing certain parts of the mesocortex and archicortex, apparently association areas, has a similar effect. Removing other parts has the opposite ef-

fect: The animal becomes furious. The old nose-brain (rhinencephalon) certainly does much more in animals than mediate the sense of smell." (1) (italics mine)

A few preliminary respirations suffice to reveal extraordinary defects in breathing in the average patient and to indicate massive tensions in the thoracic cage. As a rule the patient is simply unconscious of these tensions. He has lived with them for so long that they feel a normal part of his equipment and his everyday living. Many will breathe with their bellies, with very little movement in the higher chest. Others will breathe with the lower ribs. This portion of the chest may expand laterally but not vertically, or vice versa. Others show inability to produce clavicular breathing at all. Encouragement to breathe more fully in this, that or the other area is often unavailing. Mild artificial respiration may be attempted to facilitate a more complete activity, though great care is needed. Broken ribs do not comprise an integral part of therapy!

The lower ribs may be squeezed during exhalation to improve the depth of exhalation and to increase the mobility of the chest. Pressure may be exerted on each side of the sternum, or laterally on the lower ribs to deepen respiration. A hand may be placed immediately under each clavicle, with pressure exerted downwards on the chest to aid in the total expulsion of air. Hunched up shoulders are pulled down. Shoulders bent forwards are pressed backwards.

These are usually severe problems. A great deal of time and effort may be required to correct these chronic conditions.

Emphasis is placed on improving the quality of exhalation, the main theory being that with exhalation complete, the inhalation will take care of itself. Difficulty is usually encountered here. The patient with years of fear behind him has learned to exhale jerkily, by short steps as it were, in order to control eruptions of anxiety, mild or severe, as the case may be. This conditioning problem is dealt with by a combination of breathing techniques and sound. There are too many possible combinations of these to warrant full description. But the fact remains that sighing sounds, moans and shouts made in conjunction with different breathing techniques result in the relaxation of various areas of the respiratory apparatus. Reich asked his patients to "follow through" with their breathing, to "get into swing."

If one asks the patient to breathe deeply, he usually forces the air in and out in a compulsive manner... After five to ten breaths, respiration usually becomes deeper and the first inhibitions make their appearance. (12)

Reich further remarked that there is no neurotic individual who does not show tension in the abdomen. The respiratory disturbances in neurotics are the result of abdominal tensions. Imagine that one is frightened or anticipates great danger. Instinctively, one draws in the breath and remains in this attitude. As one cannot do this for long, one will soon breathe out again. However, expiration will be incomplete and shallow. The breath does not flow out completely in one breath, but in fractions, in steps, as it were. In a state of anxious anticipation, one instinctively draws the shoulders forward and remains in a rigid attitude; sometimes the shoulders are pulled upward. In fright, one involuntarily breathes in as, for instance, in drowning where this very inspiration leads to death; the diaphragm contracts and compresses the solar plexus from above. Considerable attention should be paid to this formulation as it is all too often overlooked.

Reich thought that the inhibition of respiration was the physiological mechanism of the suppression and repression of emotion, and consequently, *the basic mechanism of the neurosis in general.* If a smaller amount of energy is created in the organism, the vegetative impulses are less intense and consequently easier to master. The inhibition of respiration has the function of reducing the production of energy in the organism, and thus, of reducing the production of anxiety.

Part, therefore, of the purpose of this non-verbal psychotherapy is to re-awaken these powerful body sensations—powerful, that is, prior to their suppression early in life through the development of muscular tension in the trunk. This was the motive for calling the method "vegeto-therapy"—inasmuch as it is dedicated to a re-activation of the vegetative or autonomic functions, to re-activating the "feel" of the body. Most adults have long since lost all vital recall or contact with their own body feelings in any dynamic sense.

This, too, provides a clue to the content and goal of this kind of psychotherapy. Far less emphasis is placed on the recovery, *per se,* of infantile memories and painful early events, as in psychoanalysis.

*What is sought after is the recovery of the innate capacity to feel, the ability which was lost in childhood as a result of repressing feelings related to painful events.* Merely recovering a memory does not of itself bring back the feeling implicit in that experience. The opposite in much more likely to be true. Retrain the patient to re-experience emotion; then it becomes possible to remember, if necessary, earlier occasions when similar emotions were felt. *It is the organismic sensitivity and feeling which are sought after, emotions and sensations upon which the whole personality is structured, not merely a sterile memory devoid of inner content.*

This inner content is best recovered by encouraging a full and complete exhalation in which both the thorax and abdomen function freely. As a technique, it bears little or no relationship to ordinary breathing exercises or any kind of gymnastics. In fact they are antipodal. Despite the fact that various so-called "exercises" are employed, the aim of therapy is certainly not the development of muscles, but of flexibility—not strength, but suppleness, coordination and motility. When these characteristics are established on a sound biological level, natural organismic function cannot be far off. It would not be out of place to emphasize here that the entire burden of Reich's work is on this one notion—naturalness. This simple word, with all its dynamic implications, is the basis of the therapeutic goal, the naturalness of a healthy human animal. The athlete in this respect is certainly no better off than his sedentary brother.

Among my patients were two young men who, before therapy, took up "body building." They had frequent workouts in the gymnasium with track-work, swimming, weight-lifting, etc. The most palpable result of all this training was a tremendous muscular development. It served only to obscure their inadequacy and fear. The task of dissolving their compulsive muscle-bound condition was herculean. Therapy might have pursued a smoother course without these over-developed muscles. Even their breathing was inadequate, so spastic and hypertrophied were their chest muscles. In any event, only personal experience in the therapy itself will indicate how diametrically antipodal it is to such things as stereotyped "setting-up exercises" or physical culture work. It is a dynamic therapy which does its work on the character.

More recently, a man who had been a professional boxer was referred to me. He had a splendid physique and finely developed set of muscles. A three-mile run every day was about the only thing that would alleviate classical anxiety tension symptoms. Yet, inspection on the couch revealed his breathing to be altogether unsatisfactory. To inhale, he had to employ his neck and shoulders, while to exhale he had to squeeze his belly. He was muscle-bound, and his constant work-outs did nothing but aggravate his existent muscular tensions.

\*\*\*

While the patient breathes fully in the manner prescribed, the therapist probes with his fingers into the neck, the ribs, the abdomen, seeking above all to relax tense musculature. This is where the need for almost total nudity during the session arises. Only with near-nudity may one clearly perceive areas of relative fixation or tension and handle them easily without the interference of tight clothing. The fingers probe into the epigastrium gently, then going deeper and deeper. Gradually, in some instances over many sessions, the whole belly wall softens up in a remarkable way. By itself this process induces a profound feeling of relaxation, which invariably enhances the respiration. The recti muscles and the obliques are palpated. This is reminiscent of a massage technique utilized by Georg Groddeck—often called the father of psychosomatic medicine. As I understand it, he would occasionally grab one of the recti muscles between the thumb and forefinger and give it a decided tweak. This caused a spasmodic contraction, followed by a physiological relaxation of the muscle. Many a former Groddeck patient has spoken of the considerable pain engendered by this manipulation and described the screams of pain the doctor would force from them. Often the skin would be bruised due to the rupture of underlying capillaries—but it did produce relaxation.

Palpation and probing may do little at first to relax the muscle, so chronically tense it has become. Yet there are many occasions when such gentle probing rapidly creates emotional distress. It may be vague and indeterminate at first, but within a few minutes an occasional hyperventilated patient may be sobbing vigorously without the least understanding of his motive. This is in line with the general terms of the therapy to first permit the eruption of latent affects. Memories can be recovered easily and spontaneously—with the development of profound insights as a result—after the emotional tension has been discharged. The upwelling of tears may be preceded by other physiological manifestations. They help the patient to release massive quantities of tension on the somatic level first of all, where apparently it can most readily and easily be handled.

Reich observed that the loosening of the rigid muscular attitudes resulted in peculiar somatic responses: involuntary trembling, jerking of muscles, sensations of hot and cold, various paresthesias such as itching, crawling, prickling sensations, goose-flesh, etc., as well as anxiety, anger and pleasure. This is a very simple description of the experiential backbone of the system. The average therapist using conventional methods can hardly conceive of the accuracy of Reich's clinical observations.

I have sometimes thought that the patient who has experienced other forms of psychotherapy prior to undergoing vegeto-therapy is in many ways better prepared for these weird physiological manifestations than is the person who comes to this therapy "cold." Yet, paradoxically enough, this is not wholly true. The well-educated person, intellectually arrogant and familiar with technical literature, has all too often merely strengthened, though unwittingly, one part of his character armor. It is a significant contribution of Reich that the whole thinking apparatus may be appropriated as it were by the armor and turned from reality testing in the direction of self-defense. Anna Freud has also elaborated upon the notion that, in the adolescent, for example, the intellect undergoes tremendous development hand-in-hand with the ability to fantasize at the expense of the sexual and emotional life which has undergone considerable repression. The resulting affect-lameness and massive rationalizations are so extensive and so permeate all the organismic functions that to crack through this all but impenetrable ego-system requires time and sincere effort. All the resources of the patient are involuntarily directed against both the therapist and the therapy. In such instances, non-verbal psychotherapy is a distinct advantage—the patient is not given the opportunity to use that particular set of defenses. Verbalization is reduced to a minimum, if not actually forbidden, and he is forced backwards upon his own somatic and biological functioning.

As these peculiar bio-energetic sensations develop in the unprepared patient, considerable panic is often evoked. The therapist should consequently *make haste slowly* and spend some time orienting the patient to the intent of this particular form of therapy. At least the basic theorem should be clearly explained to the patient—that as the muscular tensions are broken down, relaxation will, of course, follow. But as this relaxation develops, some body feelings or emotions will erupt, breaking through the now-softened muscular armor, primarily in the form of multiform physical sensations.

Reich, in referring to this, observed that the emotions are specific functions of living protoplasm—in contrast to the nonliving—which responds to stimuli with *"movement,"* or "motion"—"emotion." From the functional identity of emotion and plasmatic movement it follows that even the most primitive protoplasms have sensations. The sensations can be seen directly in response to stimuli. The kind of reaction naturally corresponds to the kind of stimulus. These basic emotional reactions of plasmatic flakes are not different from the reactions of highly-developed organisms. Again, it is imperative to indicate that this idea—the identity of body sensations and emotions—lies at the foundation of all Reich's thinking.

***

I do not believe that this particular type of therapy is a panacea for all neurotic and psychosomatic ills, nor that it will eliminate the need for other systems of psychotherapy. I do not believe in "cure-alls." I do suggest, however, that vegeto-therapy has a well-defined sphere of usefulness and it should be restricted to that sphere. For those patients who are affect-lame and highly blocked, it reigns supreme. In conversion hysteria—where function is blocked in the classical motor, sensory, visceral and cerebral areas—in the hypochondrias, compulsions, severe obsessions, etc., it should also prove invaluable. At the same time I contend that some conventional therapy is strongly indicated as an ancillary process. The distressing physical and emotional reactions that occasionally emerge as the character-muscular armor is attacked and dissolved give rise to considerable panic on the part of some patients. They may wish to bolt from therapy. When they experience the tingling sensations which augur the breakthrough of the bio-physical energy or vegetative excitations, alarm is engendered. The spasms, spontaneous myoclonisms and paresthesias that also develop may likewise create apprehension. The transference relationship has to be fostered, understood and interpreted to keep the sensitive patient in therapy. This end can best be accomplished by a broad psychotherapeutic frame of reference in which any method and any approach can be used when it is specifically required and called for. Fanaticism has no place in any kind of psychotherapy. When it is found, it suggests the urgent need of therapeutic personality restructuring for the therapist.

Conventional psychotherapy is still the therapy of choice in the acute anxiety states, counseling of superficial conflicts on the current level, and so forth. All methods have to be fitted into a broad frame of reference. They have to be perceived as integral parts of a whole. Perhaps the broad, eclectic therapeutic framework once enunciated by Wolberg (9) could serve this purpose admirably. It is a wise, liberal and comprehensive survey of most of the accepted technical methods. It is based upon extensive experience by the author in both teaching and clinical practice.

Whether vegeto-therapy is of value where the so-called functional psychoses are concerned, I am not able to say at this time. The therapeutic experiments I have undertaken for short periods of time with a few latent schizophrenics were abortive. It is not only that adequate contact cannot be made with them by this set of technical devices, but their fear is so vast that, like frightened deer, they bolt and withdraw upon sensing anything unusual about the therapist's approach or about their own feelings and sensations. But some valuable data may be obtained with regard to the magnitude of the muscular armoring and the extraordinary discrepancy or lack of coordination between thoracic and abdominal movements during respiration and their dynamic relationship to psychotherapy.

Even after reading Reich's brilliantly provocative paper on the treatment of a catatonic type of schizophrenia, I am far from optimistic. But there is ample room for experiment and research. It is my fervent hope that the technique will be appropriated by the psychiatric field and, on the basis of this tentative neurological approach, be experimented with to ascertain more accurately the clinical areas where it can best be employed. Hospitals and other centers with facilities for research and experiment are the obvious organizations to which this thesis is submitted, because it is from them now that we have to look for corroboration and critical analysis of this therapeutic discipline.

When doing non-verbal therapy there should be many occasions when the patient may be encouraged to verbalize his inner conflicts and difficulties, insofar as they have been exacerbated by the therapy. Some of my colleagues have evolved a technique in which one session per week is spent on non-verbal therapy, while in another periodical session the verbalization of the patient's reactions to, and understanding of, previous active sessions is verbalized. There are times when just a word or two from the therapist towards the close of an active session may evoke vivid emotional responses. Non-verbal therapy had brought them, as it were, near to the surface, but verbal communication was requisite to release them in open abreaction. Reich himself appeared to have had an appreciation of this, for he observed that once the power of muscular vegeto-therapy has been experienced, one is tempted to give up character-analytic work in its favor. But experience soon teaches one that it is not permissible to exclude one form of work at the expense of the other.

The efficacy of periodical or alternating sessions of verbal with non-verbal therapy is quite evident in practice. Every now and again a verbal session appears to give the patient sufficient insight as to facilitate great advances on the non-verbal level. Sometimes a discussion about the transference—started off by "What do you feel about me?" or "What do you feel about the therapy?"—leads to such illuminating areas that the previous release of psychosomatic tensions is provocative of massive personality changes. The opposite is also true. The patient may have become so blocked that discussions prove sterile. After a series of non-verbal sessions, a return to the transference discussion then produces gems of clarity and sharp insight and character transformation. Free association is often rendered far more productive when preceded by some minutes of active vegeto-therapeutic muscular release. I cannot believe that there should be a sharp dichotomy between verbal and non-verbal methods. They must accompany each other as parts of a single process.

Reich has described at great length his earlier method of closely observing the patient undergoing analysis in the attempt to single out some major character trait that serves as the active, though not necessarily conscious, focus of resistance. During therapy, this one major trait is concentrated upon at all times, almost to the exclusion of all else until, by the reductive method, it is analyzed out of existence, as it were, or down to its roots when it yields up the forbidden affects which it shields and absorbs.

Frohman, following his training with Stekel, employed a similar idea with regard to what he calls the "psychic signature." The similarity extends only to the theory, not to the operational method of handling it. Signatures, wrote Frohman,

> "are the specific behavior responses as uniquely characteristic of each human being as his signature. Because they are as consistent and individual as fingerprints, they are also described as 'psychic imprints.' The patient discloses his dominant psychic signature virtually from the onset of a psychological investigation and it reappears many times during the ensuing interviews as the *leitmotiv* of his emotional history. A psychic signature may be one or a combination of the traits on the following list, which gives only a portion of the many aberrations of behavior which are considered neurotic manifestations when unduly consistent and intensified."

He then gives a long list of character traits which includes arrogance, contempt, doubt, envy, evasion, hostility, laziness, masochism, pessimism, sadism, scorn, self-depreciation, shiftlessness, suspicion, unrestrained enthusiasm and many others. (3)

The attack on the predominant psychic signature is an integral part of vegeto-therapy. It has evolved from the same empirical roots as did character analysis. The vegeto-therapist attempts to ferret out the major character trait of the patient and to discover how it is employed as the primary defensive weapon. He then directs his attention to that functional group of muscles that appears chronically rigid and which appears to be related to the neurotic character-trait.

For example, the haughty patient may hold his head erect—too erect—with an impassive and immobile face, tense neck and shoulder muscles. The belligerent patient's lower jaw may jut forward, bull-dog fashion; the upper lip may be largely immobile. The sullen patient may show a tight belly with a rigid back, the shoulders being pulled downwards and hunched forward. The fearful patient may show the blank face and dead, glassy eyes, and so on indefinitely.

To round out the clinical picture, it must be mentioned that the muscular armor is not always characterized by tension. Sometimes one will encounter a patient who is soft, flabby and even "rubbery." These vehemently deny the possibility of having a muscular armor. The fact remains, however, that their atony is usually the end product of long periods of muscular tension. As a result, chronic muscular fatigue has set in with atony. The "rubbery" patient has apparently developed a fine capacity to relax. There appear at first sight to be no tensions. He will roll easily with a push against the shoulders or pelvis while in the work position. Appearances nonetheless are deceptive. The apparent relaxation is merely a façade and is superficial. The "rubberiness" is a particular defense—a defense against resiliency. The anamnesis will inevitably depict a psychosomatic status far removed from resiliency and flexibility. Therapy will, after a while, highlight many areas of deadness.

Fenichel confirmed this finding when he wrote, "Motor inhibitions are not necessarily manifested by hypertonic phenomena but may also appear as a limp and hypotonic muscular slackness which excludes the possibility of speedy and precise functioning." (2)

The obese patient also represents a difficult clinical problem. The evidence is that such patients overeat as a means of allaying anxiety. In this instance anxiety is experienced as vegetative excitations in and around the diaphragm. The large masses of fat help to desensitize the patient to his body sensations. Palpation of muscular tension becomes rather difficult because of the obesity. Moreover, their perseverance in therapy of any kind is low. I suggest that compulsive dietary measures and some counseling should initially be used to bring the patient down to a workable weight. When active therapy is at last embarked upon, it is likely to liberate a great deal of anxiety. More counseling may be required to help the patient develop some insight into his problem. With the dynamic eruption of affects, he may be tempted to revert back to his former eating techniques to cope with them.

These different types of armoring are difficult to handle. Fractional therapy may be more effective than any prolonged intensive form. A few months of active therapy followed by an equal period of vacation from therapy—with this cycle repeated many times—may augur better for ultimate success. Rarely has the obese patient the stamina or necessary perseverance to complete the therapeutic regimen without interruption.

In all instances, however, once therapy is instituted and some affects are worked off, these different types tend to react as do the others. Twitchings, rigidities, myoclonisms and paresthesias develop in due course, Eventually they come to experience with immediacy their own body sensations. At all times the therapist must be prepared for the discharge of massive quantities of anxiety. Occasionally, medication may be required to enable some patients to allay the excessive affect and so to permit them to proceed with therapy. The passage of time will certainly disclose the underlying character traits of which they are so fearful and which they barricaded beneath these peculiar armored formations.

Both the muscular armor and the neurotic character trait are worked upon and attacked *ad nauseam* until the patient is capable of giving them up, permitting the repressed affects to emerge and be re-experienced. It is a methodical, deliberate and precise technique for opening up the patient's resistances or muscular defense mechanisms against his instinctual impulses and feelings, and permitting him to experience the almost-forgotten luxury of his own autonomic excitations. So long as the neurotic character traits exist, so long also will they block off specific biological excitations. As their somatic bases are dissolved through relaxation and emotional discharge, the neurotic character traits break down and in their place the dreaded excitations emerge. It was for this reason that Reich wrote that the character armor and the muscular armor are functionally identical and subserve the same organismic purpose. He found that whenever he dissolved specific muscular inhibition or tension, one of the three basic biological excitations made its appearance: *anxiety, anger* or *sexual excitation.*

\*\*\*

Though the critic inexperienced in and unfamiliar with this therapy may question Reich's clinical findings, I reaffirm that they are altogether factual. Before one can suggest that these claims are silly and unscientific, one should have experienced a course in vegetotherapy. Only then, after having felt anxiety emerge when a throat-block is released, for example, can one appreciate Reich's verisimilitude. Hyperventilation alone will sometimes elicit many of these responses, as the literature already indicates. But when the technical devices just described are added to hyperventilation, even the most hardened and "cold" compulsive patient is bound to respond with these "biological excitations."

"Between the ages of 10 and 20 years, when restraint and self-control are imposed as marks of acceptable social behavior," wrote Gillilan in a neurological text, "the diversion of emotion and the expression of certain stresses is more than ever directed within the individual and of necessity is not outwardly expressed, but it is expressed in disordered autonomic function. As in all conditioned reflexes, once a particular mode of emotional expression has been set up, it is facilitated by repeated stimuli and soon becomes integrated into the behavior pattern and personality of the individual." (4)

It is not claimed that these clinical phenomena always occur as soon as the first session is started. On the contrary, very few overt results may occur for some time with the heavily armored patient. Gradually, however, as he becomes acclimated to the routine of therapy, and as some of the more chronic tensions become slowly resolved by the relaxing process, more and more of these psychosomatic reactions occur. In the presence of severe emotional and muscular blocks, other vigorous procedures have to be instituted. It is in this connection, perhaps, that some of the malignant criticisms of this form of therapy have had their origin.

One occasionally finds a patient whose shoulder muscles are rigid and highly sensitive to the touch. If the therapist firmly grips each trapezium between thumb and forefinger and vigorously maintains this pressure, the patient is likely to resist or push the therapist's hand away. He must be told to refrain from doing this and to express his displeasure or pain by pounding the couch and yelling as loudly as possible. The character structure of the patient reveals itself quite clearly at this juncture. Some will yell vociferously or let off a few feeble peeps, perhaps bursting into tears shortly afterwards. One here and there will resist vigorously, or open the mouth in a futile manner, finding himself incapable of screaming or yelling. One patient, under these circumstances, would raise both hands to the face, as if to cover the mouth to stifle a scream, even jamming both hands into the mouth.

Reich's findings were that the abdominal tension has the function of exerting a pressure on the solar plexus, and without exception, neurotic individuals display a tonic contracture of the diaphragm. Almost all patients remember suppressing these abdominal sensations as children, particularly when they felt anger or anxiety. They learned spontaneously to achieve this suppression by way of holding their breath and pulling in their abdomen.

Reich found that pressing with two fingers about an inch below the sternum (without frightening the patient), one soon notices a reflex-like tension or a constant resistance. *The abdominal content is being protected.*

Another technical device employing this concept is to administer a light, but firm, tap with the first two fingers on the epigastrium just below the ensiform cartilage or somewhere on the belly while the patient unsuspectingly proceeds on his way with full respirations. Actually, it is not painful. However, there is the element of surprise together with the light shock. After the patient has protectively doubled up to protect the belly and has been tactically forced to relinquish control by yelling, one of several phenomena usually occur after a few moments of easy breathing. First a gentle, light quivering begins. Just where depends entirely on the structure of the patient. It may begin in the knees or shoulders. Then the abdominal recti muscles may spasmodically convulse, jerking the chest and pelvis together in a curious motion reminiscent of post-orgastic movements. Finally, the nostrils may be seen to dilate, the eyelids grow reddened, the lips and chin quiver, and ordinarily tears begin to flow. The sobbing is at first easy and light, gradually deepening into deep convulsive sobbing in which the entire organism participates.

*Every single event in therapy is directed towards one thing and one thing only—heightening the patient's emotional capacity so that all of him can feel.* A great many of these devices appear to call for hurting the patient physically by pinching, squeezing and tapping taut muscles. *The bodily discomfort which is felt becomes the sensory medium for inducing an unfamiliar emotional state.* At times, after an intense period of active work, a few words from the therapist summarizing the patient's character structure may succeed in accomplishing similar ends. It is the eruption of such feelings that cracks the rigidity of the armor. It becomes threatened as soon as the patient can be brought to function on a feeling level. If discomfort of a few seconds' duration can accomplish this more directly than dozens of hours of verbal analysis, its value need not be questioned.

## Bibliography

1. Cobb, Stanley. *Emotions and Clinical Medicine.* New York, Norton Co., 1950, p. 65.

2. Fenichel, Otto. *The Psychoanalytic Theory of Neurosis.* New York, Norton Co., 1945, p. 180.

3. Frohman, Bertrand. *Brief Psychotherapy.* Philadelphia, Lea & Febiger, 1949. p. 26.

4. Gillilan, L.A. *Clinical Aspects of the Autonomic Nervous System.* Boston, Little Brown & Co., 1954. p. 15.

5. Gillilan, L.A. *ibid.* p. 14.

6. Guze, Henry. "Compensatory Behavior as Completion of the Sensory-Motor Cycle." *Jnl. of Gen. Psych.,* 1953, 83: 293.

7. Mittelman, Bela. "Psychosomatics," *Encyclopedia of Psychology* (Ed. by P.L. Harriman). New York, Citadel Press, 1946, p. 695.

8. Speransky, A.D. *A Basis for a Theory of Medicine.* New York, International Press, 1934, p. 348.

9. Wolberg, Lewis. *The Technique of Psychotherapy.* New York, Grune & Stratton, 1954.

# Chapter IV

## Method II

> "Recognition of the importance of the patient's *feelings* during the analytic hour cannot be overestimated in the dynamics of any school."
> — Ruth L. Munroe

Reich has developed a variety of adjuvant techniques to relax tense muscles and evoke latent emotional responses. These can be summarized under a few headings, though it must not be assumed that these comprise the totality of the method. It is astonishingly rich in content and highly flexible in form. Once the neurological implications are fully grasped, innumerable changes can be rung on these very simple themes in order to achieve the final goal of emotional release, organismic re-structuring and reintegration.

> A good physical examination should be insisted upon as a preliminary—with every patient. This is not merely to rule out the presence of organic pathology and thus, negatively, to establish the existence of a neurosis. Its purpose should be to evaluate the assets and liabilities of the patient on as many functional levels as possible. The therapist should have access to all the data about the patient he is about to conduct through therapy. In the event of palpable pathology, it might also be advisable to work in close contact with the patient's own physician.

The problem of which particular somatic area to deal with first in order to dissolve the armored tension is not as obscure or as arbitrary as it might seem at first. The therapist may of course rely upon ordinary inspection and observation to reveal the most prominent area of tension. Secondly, palpation will indicate to the touch just those groups of muscles that are stiff and rigid and which need loosening up. Finally, as the softening up process continues, the therapist can rely upon the forced respiration and hyperventilation to accentuate and increase the latent tensions in any area.

One of the most significant products of hyperventilation is the induction of tremors, spasticities, myoclonisms and tetanies of varying degrees and intensities. These should serve as reliable guides to the procedures to be followed. Those areas intensified spastically are those to be loosened up and dissolved. For this reason, there should be no haste in having the patient flit from one so-called "exercise" to another. Enough time should be permitted following each gesture to permit the appearance of somatic symptoms, or for concealed affects to emerge. It tends to eliminate the natural tendency to speculate intellectually as to what should be the next step to follow. No matter how intuitive the therapist, or how successfully he may identify with the patient's problems, nothing actually replaces the keenness of clinical observation and perception. The grosser indications of the presence of hypertonicity are the inevitable sequelae of the physiological effects of hypocapnia. As the grosser areas become softened up and abreacted by vegeto-therapy, the more concealed areas become revealed and can then be more adequately dealt with.

In addition to these clinical indications, Reich's major recommendation still remains. He conceived the primary obstacle to the development of the so-called "genital personality" and the "orgasm reflex" to be muscular blocks to vegetative motility in the pelvic area. These become reinforced during the years of early growth by auxiliary blocks and tonicities in yet other areas. As the more recent and non-genital blocks are dissolved by the therapeutic process, permitting the abreaction of repressed affects, the major pelvic block becomes more accessible to therapy. He laid down the rule, therefore, that muscular tensions farthest removed from the pelvis should be dealt with first. In other words, the muscular armorings of the face, arms, shoulders, legs and feet should be loosened up first of all.

Many vegeto-therapists pay immediate attention to the chest and abdomen, attempting to procure the maximum mobility of these areas at the outset. After many sessions have elapsed, when these areas show evidence of emotional discharge, then the tensions in the face and neck, legs and feet are systematically attacked. Regardless of which procedure the therapist follows, he should still rely upon the particular organ sensations and muscular spasms experienced by the patient as hyperventilation initiates its physiological effects. These still function as the most reliable guide to the next therapeutic step to be taken.

***

The adjuvant techniques can best be described in relation to the armor segments which they are intended to release. This should not be too literally interpreted or rigidly pursued because many of these technical gestures and exercises actually affect more than the particular body segment being employed.

**First Segment: The Ocular Ring.** One very important part of the technique concerns the facial armor. Many patients have "dead pans." Gillilan wrote, "Civilization is restraint of emotional expression; the cultivation of the 'great American poker face' is a sign of genteel breeding. All of this produces a highly refined society with a minimum of friction and maximum of outward agreeableness, but the price of the inhibition and emotional restraint is reflected in the types of complaints encountered in modern medical practice." (2) If this is genteel breeding and civilization, many of us believe we have paid far too high a price for them.

As the therapy proceeds on its inexorable way, patients inevitably come to feel that their faces are stiff and expressionless. Much work has to be directed towards softening the facial expression, loosening up the facial muscles and attempting to release the emotions that such "flat" expressions conceal. Reich has laid down the proposition that although the central problem in the neurosis is the genital block, the attack on the armor usually begins at that point which is most distant from the pelvis. Thus the work on the face comes to have a special significance for the vegeto-therapist.

It is not difficult to divine the motives for this. Early in life children learn that parents are able to discover "what they have been up to" by looking at their faces and especially at their eyes. By way of self-protection, they have to learn to drain their eyes of meaning, blanketing the muscles of facial expression with an empty, defensive deadness. In this way they can conceal that they are "looking daggers" at people or "throwing them a dirty look." One woman with a particularly blank and expressionless face recalled her father angrily telling her as a little girl to "wipe that look off your face; and don't give me any more of those dirty looks."

George, whose facies were blank except for bulging eyeballs, recalled that as a boy he would sit in front of a mirror in his locked bedroom, masturbating. While so doing he would leer into the mirror, making ugly faces—fantasying that he was thus insulting his father whom he hated. He had developed consummate skill in "making faces," but once out of his bedroom would be haunted by fear that his hateful fantasies had somehow left an indelible impression upon his face that could be perceived by father. The next step, then, was to struggle to register absolutely nothing on his face. He almost succeeded—save for the fear in his bulging eyes.

As time goes on, this attitude becomes chronic and involuntary and the protective devices become mirrored in fixed facial attitudes and involuntary muscular gestures. This becomes part of what Reich has called "the expressive language of the living"—that organ language which the therapist strives so hard to understand and penetrate.

To counter this, one method often employed is to have the patient open his eyes wide, furrowing the forehead with every inhalation and to close the eyes tightly while exhaling. If the patient has been well-ventilated beforehand, dozens of repetitions of this device will initiate light tremors in the thighs and leave the forehead feeling alive and vibrant. It may come to feel stiff as the hyperventilation proceeds, but later this relaxes. One emotion that this may stir up is fear. In fact, some difficulty may be experienced with a few patients who may refuse to proceed because, in some way, they divine the feelings that it may evoke.

Another approach to be attempted when the patient is well-ventilated is to turn his head slightly so that he can look directly into the eyes of the therapist who leans over to be nearer the patient. No comment is uttered, save perhaps that the patient should continue breathing as fully as possible, gazing meanwhile at the therapist's eyes. Resistance may develop as once more the patient realizes that, to continue looking, he may cry. Others, however, will look and in the event that a warm, positive transference has developed, will perceive only warmth, tenderness and friendliness in the therapist and thus permit the tears to flow. One patient, highly critical and suspicious, became angry at the procedure and said: "What am I supposed to do—or feel? This is silly! You look just like an old owl staring at me." It was months before he softened up sufficiently to permit feelings of love and warmth to emerge. This emergence was impossible until the tears had washed out much of the compulsive protective hardness from his character.

If the therapist has really understood the general terms of the technique as already laid down, he should be able to develop his own particular approaches to softening the expression of the eyes and releasing latent affects.

In this connection, mention must be made of Ellsworth Baker's book *Man in the Trap* which definitely needs to be part of one's collection of basic Reichian texts. Considerable attention is there given to the problem of releasing tension in the ocular segment.

In the same sense, David Boadella's book *Wilhelm Reich—The Evolution of his Work* is a most important one, covering more or less the whole range of Reich's work in a factual and objective manner.

**Second Segment: The Oral Ring.** If the therapist has succeeded in divining the patient's major emotional problem, or let us say, has become conscious of the patient's psychic signature, he may ask the patient to make facial gestures corresponding to that feeling. For example, he may be asked: "If you hated me, what kind of face would you make?" Or, "If you were angry, in what way would you contort the muscles of your face?" Whatever the gesture, if the patient's controls have been loosened sufficiently by the complete respiratory effort, he will experience either some tingling in the area or some corresponding emotion.

Some of the breathing may be performed with the tongue pushed out. The patient should be instructed to push the tongue out sufficiently so that it rests visibly upon the lower lip. Some of the coarser tensions within the mouth itself, at the base of the tongue, or in the throat are affected by this procedure. If the abdomen is strongly tonic, nausea may set in spontaneously without any prompting from the therapist. Gagging may then be instituted to relieve the epigastric hypertonus.

Palpation may reveal powerful tensions at the angle of the jaw and observation may show that the patient grits his jaws commonly. When asked, he may confirm this and confess to bruxism. A direct assault on the masseters may be attempted, or the patient may be asked to bite hard on a thick fold of a small turkish towel. Much muscular and emotional tension can be abreacted most successfully in these ways. Sometimes considerable trembling and involuntary quivering sets up afterwards in the jaw and face as though premonitory of the gestures involved in crying. One can actually watch the chin set up a fine tremor, or the circular labial muscles pucker up as though pulled by a draw string. These oral manifestations are fairly common. They indicate an energy fixation in the oral area which can often be reduced by crying, biting or abreacting in other ways.

These responses can be further facilitated by asking the patient to open his mouth as wide as he possibly can and to continue breathing vigorously until the muscles of the jaw ache. In most instances a physiological relaxation occurs. Or, as the quivering and tremor develops, the patient may be asked to simulate it voluntarily and deliberately, breathing all the while. Affects invariably break through in a wholly unforeseen and unpredictable manner.

This segment can also be worked upon during the last phases of the session, when the patient is relaxing and attempting to heighten his awareness of somesthetic perceptions. He may be instructed to close the mouth and, while breathing easily through the nose, hum nasally during the exhalation. Usually this renders the energy sensations much more vivid and strong, particularly in the sinuses, throat, thorax and diaphragm.

**Third Segment: The Cervical Ring.** Ordinary manipulation of anatomical structures is quite useful here. The hyoid bone can be gently moved from side to side; the therapist may be surprised at the rigidity of this area in many instances. The sterno-cleidomastoid muscles can be gently manipulated from the attachment at the sternum gradually moving upwards to just behind the ear.

Vigorous manipulation is not necessary. An occasional patient will begin to weep before actually being hurt. These muscles on some patients stand out rigidly. Reich has labelled these as "anger muscles"—a good description. Working these muscles loose, even with gentle manipulations, will evoke fury which the patient should be encouraged to discharge. All of this should eventuate in tears.

The gag technique is extremely valuable in relieving the block in the cervical segment. The cervical block can usually be detected by listening to the patient's voice; the speech and a foggy breathing tone invariably reveal some evidence of laryngeal tension. Once this is detected, the above are some of the measures to be employed.

With asthmatic patients and others with a similar block in the upper respiratory tract, a shrill crowing inspiration may be used effectively. It resembles the forced inhalation through a constricted throat commonly heard in sobbing as well as in *laryngismus stridulus.* Frequently it will precipitate heightened tonus in the tracheo-laryngeal area and the patient will cough, splutter and gag. Not too many of these "croaks" should be done; a half a dozen of them followed by a number of ordinary inhalations is ample and then the cycle may be repeated. In the chronic asthmatic patient a full-fledged attack of dyspnoea can often be precipitated by the croaking. Gagging may break into this tension, relieving the tight diaphragm and throat. Hyperventilation alone may induce difficult breathing in the asthmatic patient, but any one of the methods described here should make rapid inroads into the attack.

In this gesture, the diaphragm should be pulled in by the patient while crowing. Here most patients will discover how little control they have of their muscles. Usually they protrude the diaphragm instead of tucking the stomach up under the ribs. As the patient becomes more adept in this gesture—listening to the clarity of the exhalation sound it produces will prove his adeptness—he can be instructed to carry the gesture a little further. Three or four croaks should be made one after another. The sound resembles the jerky rapid series of inhalations through the mouth made by a sobbing person. If one watches the latter, it will be seen that the diaphragm and belly vibrate or flutter with each crow. The patient should be instructed to attempt the same. Done slowly at first, the patient crows and pulls in the epigastrium, releases it and crows again while pulling in the epigastrium, and crows again. After the series of three or four croaks, he should be instructed to breath out silently and completely. Many sessions may be required before he is able to do this *as if* sobbing, but with success he will have paved the way for the emergence of many affects.

One variation is to inhale with a croak and then immediately to shout with a quick push of the belly which is then relaxed while the exhalation is completed. A great deal of practice is required on the couch to operate these gestures successfully and easily. But the effort and time spent will be worthwhile.

The goal is not only to relieve the asthmatic of his dyspnea or to achieve flexibility or muscular activity, but to enable him to make contact through actual experience with the dissociated emotions which are responsible for the respiratory difficulty. *The inhibition of respiration,* as Reich pointed out, *is the basic mechanism for the perpetuation of the neurosis.* It is one thing to tell the patient that the asthma is a physiological substitute for the crying related to infantile loneliness. It is quite another for a piece of insight to dawn while engaged in couch work, conveying the emotional experience of asthma. When he is brought near to tears and tightens the diaphragm at the critical moment to stop its sobbing flutter and swallows desperately to choke back the lump in the throat and very soon begins to wheeze and hears and feels the rales in his throat and chest, then he will know the meaning of asthma. This is true for many other symptoms presented by other patients.

No mechanical relaxation of any muscle will change the character structure of the patient. Only the affective release of the dynamic implication of the tension will produce anything worthwhile in the long run.

Another set of motor activities is initiated by asking the patient to jut his chin forward in a Mussolini-like gesture. This results in the forced tension of the fibers of the platysma myoides. He is then instructed to growl ferociously while slowly bringing the head forward until it digs into the chest. As soon as the head touches the chest, he is to throw his head backwards on the couch and breath easily and softly. This should be repeated a number of times with several normal breaths between each gesture. One of the dynamic effects of this attitude is to eventually relax the occipito-atlanteal muscles, the whole of the larynx and all the muscles in front of the neck. More important, it may succeed in evoking rage and violent aggressive feelings. When these feelings emerge, the patient comes to understand his motives for the chronically stiff neck.

During the eruption of this aggressiveness it may be noticed that he is clenching or gritting his teeth—or muttering vile imprecations between these clenched teeth. The masseter muscles will be perceived to protrude noticeably on the side of the jaws. These can be relaxed with some manual manipulation. The vegeto-therapist digs unashamedly into these tight muscles with his thumbs. Screams of pain followed by tears are the invariable sequelae to these procedures to provoke the more complete emergence of hostility.

In connection with this work on the muscles controlling facial expression, some therapists keep a small hand-mirror near the couch on a side table where it can be reached quickly, As the loosening-up process continues on the muscles of the forehead, cheeks, mouth, chin and jaw, there is often a remarkable change in facial expression. Some therapists believe the mirror to be of enormous value so the patient may perceive what the therapist perceives. The patient who cannot believe that he is full of hate, spite and anger, or who cannot realize that the major motivating factor in his life is the grossest kind of fear, may find himself recognizing this emotion registered on his own face when the mirror is placed before him. At other times the mirror may indicate to him relaxation of the lines and furrows around the mouth and nostrils, giving a softer, gentle appearance to the face. Or, after a siege of crying from deep down in the belly, the eyes show a considerable softening. Glimpses of emotion in this manner sometimes provide a considerable amount of insight which the patient can use constructively.

Once, when I held the mirror in front of a young man whose face was contorted with blind rage, he was so appalled by what he saw that at once he broke down and cried.

Occasionally, the softening-up process on the muscles of the neck, belly or thighs brings about facial expressions which might be useful for the patient to perceive. The manipulation of the sterno-cleidomastoid often contorts the face not merely with cyanosis and pain, but with rage and hate, and it is valuable for the patient to see for himself what others may see. It is particularly useful for the patient who previously has been so affect-lame and "poker-faced" that he believed he was without feeling.

**Fourth Segment: The Chest Ring.** Most of the breathing exercises already described are designed to loosen the thoracic muscles. The therapist must closely observe just where the muscular blocks are located in this segment and direct the patient's attention to those blocks. If the sub-clavicular muscles are rigid, these can be worked over by pressing down on the chest with the palms of the hands during exhalation. The chest can be pressed down with both the therapist's hands, preventing the patient from taking a deep breath. While he is pressed down in this manner, he is urged to shout. Naturally the shouting is feeble, as there is little air and room for the diaphragm to move. But it does result in a stretching of the diaphragm and of the costal muscles. And sooner or later it results in the discharge of affects—with the inevitable trembling, tearfulness and sobbing. The vigorous inhalation that follows will be perceived to be fuller than before. If this does not suffice, then the thumbs may be used to dig into the intercostal muscles all over the upper segment of the chest until a physiological relaxation occurs or until crying itself brings with it the surcease of chest tension. The muscles between the lower ribs likewise may be found to be immobile; here the chest may be perceived to flare out like an hourglass. Once more, one hand on each side of these lower ribs can press inwards during exhalation to deepen the exhalation and force the muscles to give up their tension. Pressure with the thumbs here is invariably painful, eliciting tears or angry protest in the form of shouting and yelling.

> Shouting discharges muscular tension in the throat, chest, diaphragm and belly, thus permitting the free exit of affects—only one of which is tears. I recall one female patient with erythrophobia whom I treated shortly after I began to use vegeto-therapy. She stubbornly refused to shout even while realizing the utter irrationality of her refusal. She confessed that at times she would

> lose her temper with her two teen-aged daughters and scream wildly at them when they goaded her beyond her endurance. Despite her anxiety and refusals, I pushed her into screaming. After six sessions, she dropped out of therapy. Since that time, I have developed a healthy respect for a patient's defenses. A patient can progress just so rapidly and no more, and this the therapist must recognize and evaluate. He must not be misled by the patient's desire for quick results; this is a common sentiment with very little reality behind it to give it justification. Nor must he be unduly influenced by the patient's complaint about financial difficulties which may restrict the number of sessions he can afford. This could force the therapist to attempt to get results quickly. If he does push too hard, the patient experiences great anxiety and may quit therapy. "Make haste slowly" is wise counsel here, as well as the advice given to me while I was undergoing therapy—strive for minimal rather than maximal responses at each session.

When the patient exhales, he may be asked to raise his arms imploringly upwards and lower them upon the chest when breathing in. It is to be a gesture of a beseeching or yearning nature with emphasis on the muscular phase of reaching. The shoulders should be aided in leaving the couch. Sometimes in the comparatively flexible patient the pelvis will move up at the same time. The entire gesture may be evocative of the orgasm reflex. Sometimes the skyward reaching throws the pectoral and shoulder muscles into spasm and clonisms, but physiological relaxation soon follows. A little later, clonisms and athetoid motions may occur in the arms, shoulders and chest which thus become markedly loosened up preparatory to the coordinated spontaneous movements of the orgasm reflex. The quality of respiration naturally becomes enormously improved. Sometimes the patient will spontaneously comment about how easy and full and pleasurable breathing has become. An occasional patient may break into tears, a gentle weeping, with soft, tender and yielding feelings as he speaks of the hitherto unknown pleasure in this type of long and easy respiration.

Before the crying begins, the muscular attitude may evoke very disturbing feelings which heighten the patient's recognition of his contactlessness and isolation. One patient remarked after performing this gesture, "I feel an emptiness in and across my chest." Another became aware of a deep misery which he must have carried within him for years. A third remarked that he felt his heart was broken. These and other feelings are characteristic of the response provoked by this gesture.

**Fifth Segment: The Diaphragmatic Ring.** Here again, most of the breathing work is directly connected with eradicating the diaphragmatic tensions. Occasionally pressing with thumb and second finger into the epigastrium will soften the tension here to improve the depth and quality of respiration. Many of the technical devices related above will automatically aid the diaphragm in letting go and permitting the emergence of vegetative excitations. Innumerable variations may be rung on these respiratory techniques designed to achieve different ends with varying types of patients. There is a vigorous respiration confined solely to the upper chest, with no accompanying vocalization, rapidly inducing vertigo, which is one of the most important operational tools employed in this therapy. This procedure attempts to keep the chest raised in the chronic inspiratory attitude, thus intensifying the already-latent tension. It swiftly exaggerates the muscular inhibitions in the chest as well as in the diaphragm so that after a few minutes the patient may complain of generalized body sensations.

A great deal of previous therapy is required before the patient can be instructed to push the belly out forcibly during the exhalation and emit a loud but deep shout with some of the component sounds made as if straining at stool. The effect of this is to stretch the tight diaphragm where curious sensations may soon be felt. Another later variation of this, when more dexterity has been acquired, is to push or flick the belly out very gently with an easy exhalation. A short signing sound from deep in the belly is emitted during the light push. It may sound simple, but much softening of the diaphragm is necessary before the average person is coordinated enough to succeed in an easy unstrained movement. It results in softening the diaphragm still further to bring about the "falling anxiety" which serves as a prelude to a sudden warm flush and the orgasm reflex. Sometimes, in lieu of the above, patients experience a tremendous sense of hunger as the diaphragm relaxes. The interpretation is often made that in this organ sensation there is concealed yearning and longing for affection which had been repressed and armored. The eternally hungry obese person rarely understands that his unsatisfied craving for food is a substitutive longing for love.

Many of these methods for softening the diaphragm also release tension in the entire abdominal and pelvic areas. Though Reich considers these as separate segments, they are integrally related. One method is to instruct the patient to throw the pelvis off the couch smartly while bellowing a loud and open shout. Usually the patient is so rigid that more than the pelvis itself is thrust off the couch. Much training is required before merely the pelvic segment achieves the motility that is sought after. Anyway, the specific movement results in the release of a great quantity of chronic neuro-muscular tension. As the patient breathes easily after several movements, trembling may occur in the thighs, chest and diaphragm, or elsewhere, with perhaps the emergence of tears. Once crying develops, there is a tremendous emotional softening, so that the patient who complained previously of hardness, coldness and emptiness, begins to experience emotional warmth, tenderness and even love. As one looks at the eyes of a patient as these feelings emerge, a lovely softness and warmth is apparent there.

These and similar technical methods tend to release chronic diaphragmatic and abdominal tensions. They permit a wider range of diaphragmatic excursions. Once the diaphragmatic tension is relieved, the schizoid division between "higher" and "lower" is also removed. There is a free flow of vegetative excitations throughout the organism—feelings and their related sensations. One patient described this schizoid split of which she became aware through these devices in these words: "My head and bottom seem somehow disconnected; there's a break in the middle—as though one doesn't control the other any more. They feel as if they are miles apart. It frightens me! My head feels funny! And funny things are going on in my bottom!"

**Sixth Segment: The Abdominal Ring.** Most of the work intended to dissolve tensions in the abdomen has already been described in a preceding section. Breathing plays an important part here, especially the long expiration without squeezing. The full exhalation is made possible by so much of the other work, some of which may render the patient rather breathless at first, so that as he gradually becomes quiet the breathing becomes deeper more or less automatically. The gentle probing into the belly area during respiration also aids in softening up the spastic tissues.

> If an occasional patient appears to be ticklish to palpation, imploring the therapist to desist, it becomes imperative to the therapeutic process to deliberately tickle him until he laughs hysterically, breaks down and cries, or protests in the form of bodily wiggling or a vigorous temper tantrum. Any one of such responses will be discovered to have dissipated much of the hypersensitivity of the skin. At least it will represent a specific set of challenges to his defenses. For almost immediately after, there occur some of the neurophysiological phenomena already indicated.

I have already described one of the major tools for dealing with rigid muscular attitudes in this segment—the unexpected tap on the abdomen. It is a highly efficient tool. Like gagging, one develops a very healthy respect for it. In the later stages of therapy it may be but little used. A few pushings out of the belly by the patient when exhaling usually suffice to start extensive clonisms and tremors and those involuntary bodily movements which become the orgasm reflex. Only then is the patient capable of appreciating the phrase "belly feelings" and the notion of excitations welling up from the genital area.

**Seventh Segment: The Pelvic Ring.** It should be recalled that the pelvis and the lower extremities are classified together as belonging to the same segment. As tensions are released in the legs, usually the pelvis relaxes also. For this reason a great deal of the work revolves around dissolving rigidities in the thighs and legs. For example, as the patient lies on the couch breathing away, with knees raised as already described, the therapist may push the knee nearest to him and repeat the push every few seconds. Some patients will roll right over as if relaxed; most of the time they roll too easily with the push, not permitting the latent tonus in the heavy thigh muscles to be affected by the gesture. Others will gently resist the push, but the therapist continues to "needle" the patient as it were. Slowly, almost imperceptibly, the patient becomes more and more annoyed when, instead of merely resisting the movement, he may shove against the therapist's hand. It is to be continued until open hostility breaks through, when the patient may attempt to kick the therapist.

At this point it might help if the therapist moves to the foot of the couch and holds a thick pillow in front of him. The patient is instructed to kick this pillow just as hard as he can, one foot at a time, while shouting.

The intention is to loosen up the musculature of the thighs and pelvis where a trembling or quivering may occur. Various affects may also break through. The gesture helps to release the tension in this body area and to elicit the sought after emotional reactions. I have known patients to break down and cry after having kicked the pillow and shouted but a few times.

When the session is well under way and dizziness and vasoconstriction have begun, the patient may be instructed to raise the pelvis gently off the couch to the accompaniment of every exhalation. This sounds simple, but in many instances this gesture is impossible to perform. The belly, pelvis and thighs seem glued solidly together in single mass of tension, so that separate movements of any one of these parts cannot occur. It may require much persistent practice on the couch before some patients can accomplish this. Such massive tension was originally induced to block off sexual excitations.

Many patients will recall masturbating as youngsters, trying not only to keep their respiration calm and unhurried, but also to keep the pelvis from moving. Rapid breathing would be a dead give-away if someone came into the bedroom, and if the pelvis moved the bedclothes might be disturbed and rumpled—a sure clue to their "misbehavior."

Once some ease in performing the gesture has been obtained, these feelings emerge and with them some of the original anxiety. This gesture is considered to be one of the most important in the therapist's armamentarium. It predisposes to those pelvic myoclonisms which presage the orgasm reflex.

Under ordinary circumstances, the belly begins to soften and the knees may tremble with much of the neuromuscular tension shaken off. In the event that this response does not readily occur, the thigh adductors should be examined. These so-called "chastity muscles" have long been unconsciously used to block off a wide variety of feelings, mostly sexual in nature. The "dead pelvis" is perhaps the most commonly encountered phenomenon in this area. By "dead" is meant a chronically tense somatic area where, after a period of hyperventilation, active gestures and manipulation, no sensations or feelings arise. Persistent therapy may render these areas throbbing with life and energy. For some patients this experience is highly disturbing.

A variation of the above-described gesture is to have one or both knees *drop* heavily apart on every exhalation, bringing them slowly together upon inhalation. Tension soon builds up in the inner thigh where neurotic controls break down and the relaxing tremor begins. This tremor may extend upwards to the pelvis which may begin to bob spasmodically up and down. Once the tremble begins, the breakdown of involuntary tension becomes possible. Sometimes a vigorous manipulation of the thigh adductors may be required—no instructions are needed for the patient to yell the pain out. One patient covered his genitals with both hands frantically as he screamed during the pinching of these muscles. Yet later he confessed that the manipulation itself was not very painful. He had merely become horribly frightened. In other words, the pinching of the thigh adductors evoked the latent fear of castration. No verbal orientation was required for this patient to appreciate the concept of genital anxiety.

*\*\**

Betty, a 25-year-old compulsive, felt unalloyed panic when the inner thigh was pinched twice during a session. Hysterically she began to pull her own hair, covering her mouth to stifle the piercing nature of her scream. Almost immediately she began to verbalize, as though hallucinated, a hitherto repressed trauma which occurred when she was only eight or nine years old. As was her custom, she had gone upstairs in the apartment house where she lived to visit a neighbor who had always given her candy or cookies. Unfortunately the neighbor was out shopping. A 55-year-old male boarder invited her in anyway to wait for the return of the lady. Betty entered, unsuspecting of any untoward event. As he talked to her on the sofa, he edged closer and closer, very soon trying to touch her genitals. To prevent his hand from touching her vulva, she stiffened her thighs, but his approach so paralyzed her with fear that she could neither scream nor struggle away from his grasp.

In his excitement he impatiently pinched her thighs to make her open them. The pain made Betty scream loudly in terror and she dashed for the door. The experience tormented her for many days and nights. So distant was her relationship with her parents, she was unable to tell them about the molestation lest she be beaten. When I pinched her thigh adductors, the scream successfully evoked not merely a sterile recall but a memory heavily laden with emotion that had been completely repressed to that moment.

Sometimes one may ask the patient to turn over and lie face downwards on the couch. He is then instructed to lift the hips—and only the hips—and thrust them into the couch as energetically as possible, giving a loud shout simultaneously. As the patient attempts this gesture it may again be noticed that thighs, pelvis and the lumbo-dorsal area are so rigid that they operate as a mass. The gesture is intended to break into this rigidity, permitting each part to move separately, with its own movements and flexibilities.

One advantage of this gesture is that it assists in the discharge of hostility from the pelvic area. All too often, sexual feelings and anger have become closely knit together. Many patients have told me that as children, when they were frustrated by their parents, they would go to the bathroom and masturbate furiously, with murderous fantasies. Not only is this factual, but every psychoanalyst knows the enormous hostility engendered by the close personal contact of the marital relationship. The familial squabbles provide outlet for a mere fraction of this chronic irritability. Varying degrees of impotency and frigidity offer other avenues for venting the spitefulness that so often develops. As the hostility is discharged through the hard thrust, pelvis muscles relax, permitting the patient to experience the bio-energetic sensations rising to various parts of his body. Sometimes fear of these genital feelings emerge. More often, tenderness, warmth and loving emotions come to be experienced as this hostility is discharged.

Yet another advantage is that while the patient relaxes after the above gesture, other groups of muscles on the back can be palpated for evidence of tension. Wherever tight cords are found along the spine, between the shoulder blades, or on the shoulders, some manipulation should be employed to loosen them for the release of affects. In particular, the muscular area around the lower two or three dorsal vertebrae and the upper lumbars should be singled out for attention. First, the crurae of the diaphragm are inserted anteriorly here; also the powerful *latissimus dorsi* has its insertion in the same area. Finally, the *psoas major* has its origin here also. All in all, with the origins and insertions of these three sets of muscles, the area has a profound significance. By means of the *latissimus dorsi* the shoulders are pulled downwards and backwards which in turn pushes out the chest. When the diaphragm is spastic, the whole chest is elevated in the chronic respiratory attitude. And by means of the *psoas major,* the posterior wall of the abdomen and the small of the back are kept rigid, thus facilitating the task of maintaining the tensions to keep vegetative excitations subdued and repressed. I have often dug with knuckles of both hands into this very tense area, twisting and thrusting into the rigid spinal muscles. Relaxation here induces an easing up of the whole respiratory process. Many patients will react to this part of the therapy *as if* they were in great pain. Later they admit that the pain was minimal. The vigor of their response was dictated out of fear, since they felt that some one of their hitherto involuntary "control centers" was being attacked.

***

Again and again I have indicated how different gestures tend to evoke tears, anger, fear or love, As some of the trembling and shaking subside, these emotions gradually make their appearance. Occasions arise when a gesture originally relating to the arms, belly, chest or even legs will elicit spontaneous movements in the pelvis. Almost any gesture to dissolve an inhibition in any segment may encourage these spontaneous pelvic motions that are plainly copulatory movements. Strangely enough, as the muscles of the face and neck are softened, these pelvic movements may arise without prompting in some few specially pre-disposed patients. Pre-disposed, that is, by virtue of their own particular problems, their past history, and the peculiar type of armoring which they have developed.

Then the pelvis seems to take on an independent life of its own in a manner comparable to that in which tics may appear on the face or jerky movements arise in shoulders or thighs. It may move up and down, or from side to side, in a rhythmic motion. At first there may be no feeling, nor even a marked sensation. It may start off with some mild tremors or clonisms of the thigh adductors which rock the pelvis. It is expected that, sooner or later, the muscular automatisms and clonisms will be initiated. Being involuntary and induced by hyperventilation, they may resolve themselves into the rhythmic movements of the orgasm reflex and break down the incoordinations and remaining muscular blocks. No one is more surprised than the patient who lifts his head from the couch to peer down to see his hips moving and waggling in this strange way. As time proceeds and he becomes accustomed without alarm to this type of motion, learning how to permit a complex series of coordinated movements to occur, organ sensations of the most exquisite kind emerge. Patients can only describe these as "sweet," "ecstatic," "yielding," "exquisitely soft," "loving surrender," etc. The patient may recall that at one time, much earlier in life, these sexual sensations occasioned him much distress and anxiety because of training and environmental pressures. And to keep them suppressed, manifold tensions were required for survival's sake. Some distress and anxiety may arise anew as the pelvis breaks loose from the armoring, but as the patient is reassured, these soon disappear and he learns to surrender to his own somatic feelings and vegetative excitations.

It is axiomatic to this therapy that all bodily functions should yield pleasurable sensations. In fact, these must be considered the criterion of good health. Armor development forces awareness of such somatic sensations into the background where they are soon lost to consciousness. As the therapeutic war of attrition attenuates the armoring process, there is a gradual emergence of awareness of the ever-presence of these delightful body feelings.

It becomes patent then that therapy does not contribute these sensations *de novo* to the organism, but has merely enabled the patient to shed some of his chronic psychosomatic defenses and to feel what has always been present from the earliest days of his life. If one goal of psychotherapy has been defined as making conscious that which has hitherto been unconscious, then this definition is amply justified by what occurs to the patient on the couch in the course of vegetotherapy. Sometimes all the patient has to do, regardless of where he may be, is to exhale fully a few times, become cognizant of the ensuing muscular and visceral relaxation, and then the awareness of the pleasurable—almost ecstatic—body sensations arises. This awareness serves thereafter as the sole and impregnable rock of inner security from which all ego activity emerges, as the criterion by which all behavioral manifestations are evaluated. Whatever does not jibe with this basic awareness has to be avoided and discarded; otherwise tension, anxiety and sickness are the inevitable resultants.

After thirty or forty minutes of the session's work has been devoted to various motor activities and vigorous respiration, it is customary to have the patient lower his legs and stretch out on the couch. He is instructed to keep his mouth slightly open and to breathe softly, easily and fully. After a few minutes, depending entirely upon the patient and upon the stage of therapy he has reached, quiverings and twitchings of different groups of muscles set in. No effort on the part of the patient or therapist is indicated. They are spontaneous and involuntary in every sense. They may be light—though I have seen massive myoclonisms which resembled, if anything, a grand-mal convulsion. The twitchings tend to occur in specific isolated areas which, until then, have been excessively tense and spastic.

In one patient the legs may twitch; in another, the shoulder and chest muscles, while in yet a third, the expressive muscles of the face may grimace grotesquely. Other patients may experience tinglings and pulsations in different areas. Still others may become involved in feelings and emotions which have slowly emerged from the dark, hitherto unknown hinterland of the visceral unconscious where muscular tensions had kept them for so long imprisoned. In all instances, what is experienced and perceived should be noted and observed by the therapist. They are preparatory to the final goal of therapy—the orgasm reflex.

***

From the testimony of his writings, as well as the evidence presented by both favorable and unfavorable critics, it is clear that there is no need to question Reich's skill as a clinician. The multiform psychosomatic phenomena that Reich describes as occurring during therapy are factual. Anyone choosing to experiment with this therapy (even if only in a trivial way) must soon become wholly convinced of Reich's accuracy and verisimilitude. It is necessary now to delineate some of the clinical phenomena that arise and to explain them in terms of standard and accepted therapeutic and neuro-physiological findings. It must be emphasized that this outline represents only a bare skeleton as it were, of a complete and intricate scheme. Further reference should be made to the several writings of Reich where a mass of significant material will be found and which has had to be ignored here. But the inquisitive therapist will find such an examination of supreme value.

The manifold phenomena occurring during couchwork can be classified under several headings. I should like to describe them briefly in the order in which they tend to occur in the great majority of cases. Naturally it must be understood that some patients evince few of these neurophysiological reactions. Others will manifest all of them in profusion. Most react in the manner to be described.

1. As the patient proceeds with forced respiration aided by the therapist, there soon occurs a considerable flushing of the face with a feeling of warmth suffusing the body as a whole. More or less quickly, this is followed by a sense of light-headedness accompanied by a well-defined dizziness. The patient usually relaxes at this point, relinquishing the intensity of his respiratory efforts. He tends to

become sluggish. If he is encouraged and assisted to proceed just beyond this, with a few minutes more devoted to deep exhalations, the dizziness and the flushing vanish.

2. Pallor and blanching of the skin follow. More often than not the feet feel very cold. If not, the hands, chin or some other area of the body feel cool. As the patient becomes aware of the impending chill, fearfulness and anxiety may arise. Reassurance on the part of the therapist may be necessary to help him proceed. At this juncture, some patients tend to become schizoid, withdrawing to a high degree of inaccessibility. They need to be prodded gently out of this retreat.

3. Quite casually, there often occurs at this period a little trembling. It may be light, but as the breathing continues it may develop into a vigorous quivering. The lips may be the first area to show these tremors. Or else it may arise in the chin, the shoulders or the pectorals; the belly may shake quite noticeably. Then the trembling tends to spread—perhaps to the knees and thighs, becoming generalized shortly thereafter throughout the body. There are times when an ever-deepening series of profound yawns herald the onset of the tremors and each succeeding yawn provokes this condition still further.

4. Sporadic tics are likely to appear in the muscles of the face, neck or shoulders. If, later, these are touched very gently, stroked or lightly manipulated—though they should be permitted to operate unchecked for a little while—they vanish. In their stead, curious sensations of energy streamings or various emotions begin to be felt. These tics may presage the development of clonisms—heavy jerks and spasms. As these gain headway, considerable pleasure may also be experienced, especially when a profound relaxation is felt after their cessation.

5. Most patients, however, experience them with fear—evidences of what Reich called "the falling anxiety." Anger and rage may well up, or the patient may begin to weep. The crying may be dictated either by fear or by anger. But whatever the autonomic manifestations, feelings of one kind or another begin to emerge in the lame personality that once had an abhorrence for feelings.

6. The weeping usually begins in a very gentle way, with the feeling that the whimpering may soon pass into a heavy sobbing.

There is a curious quality about this weeping. As a rule it does not resemble the weeping of an adult. It stems from a deep emotional level, resembling much more than anything else I know the brokenhearted anguish of a child. Once the well-springs are tapped, the weeping may continue for long periods without cessation and without the therapist having to press the patient for action. Holding the patient close as one might hold an unhappy child during the crying spell may permit the freer expression of the weeping and facilitate development of positive transference feelings.

7. In lieu of weeping, the group of more heavily armored patients dramatically develops a variety of overt neurotic symptoms. Bouts of sneezing reminiscent of hay-fever and coryza attacks, asthmatic episodes, violent occurrences of diffused itching, creeping and similar paresthesias are common precursors of the weeping. When crying is not permitted to break through immediately because of pride, fear or shame, it is not uncommon for these symptoms to persist until the next session. Insomnia and an indescribable sadness may also be present to signify the anxiety experienced over the impending eruption of such feelings. Vegeto-therapy succeeds in evoking the latent tears when, again dramatically, the neurotic symptoms vanish completely. However, these symptoms may persist for weeks or months as the case may be, depending on the magnitude of the inhibitory block.

8. It should be noted that the patient who weeps all too readily from the start of therapy is usually the frustrated, hysterical person whose desires have been thwarted, who cannot get his own way, or wishes to make another feel sorry by this show of tears. It has been used before, over and over again, as a substitute for a direct show of hostility. These patients under therapy have to be taught deliberately to block their weepiness in order to permit the emergence of another set of feelings. As already intimated, this is usually hostility of a violent kind—spitefulness repressed years before because of fear of rejection or other forms of punishment.

9. Dynamically related to this is laughing. I have seen patients chuckle at this stage for no apparent reason and pass into a heavy abdominal laughter which may continue for the rest of the session, persisting no matter what the therapist may do. He should do nothing about it except encourage its expression, because an occasional

patient may feel silly about such irrational laughter and attempt to curb it. It is as much to be welcomed as any other muscular-emotional response.

Meanwhile, the therapist would do well to observe closely the somatic and muscular events involved in the process of precipitous laughter. They bear many resemblances to those involved in the orgastic reflex itself. During later sessions, the patient may develop insight and realize that this laughter was wholly defensive.

10. Similarly, some patients go through phases when the whole session is devoted spontaneously to yawn after yawn, hiccoughs, belching and flatulence and other expulsive devices for the passage of gas. They may experience gastric distress and nausea, followed by retching and vomiting. These phenomena often puzzle such patients. The fact remains, however, that the release of abdominal and thoracic tension is startling and indescribable as these physiological activities proceed. Only later can they recognize in these occurrences the body-wish to cry despite their own affect-lameness.

11. When most of these phenomena have subsided, the patient, supine on the couch, is instructed to breathe normally through gently parted lips. No effort is required for deep exhalation. While relaxing, he is asked to note whatever physical sensations he feels and report them as they appear. Perhaps the most common reports are of a gentle tingling, a mild pins-and-needles sensation, or a buzzing, as others describe it, in the fingers or in the toes. He is requested to watch these more closely while breathing easily. Gradually after a number of sessions—though not in response to inadvertent suggestion—these become stronger and appear to become more extensive. Carpal and pedal spasms occasionally appear with these tingling sensations. Several patients have described the sensations as if they were connected to an instrument delivering a strong galvanic current. In due time these sensations spread all over the body. Where and when they do not, there are blocks in the form of gross muscular tensions impeding their progress. These tensions can be attacked and relaxed in subsequent therapeutic sessions.

12. With the spread of these sensations, a metamorphosis of the tingling is reported. It is now felt as a deep inner vibration—later as a well-defined streaming or pulsation. It is invariably described as

pleasant and relaxing; some more sensitive and perceptive patients use such words as "melting," "sweet" and "yielding." Tender emotions are felt, so that the patient can often speak for the first tine in his life, perhaps, of love and warmth and basic human contact. Such descriptions augur well for the personality reorganization under way.

One has only to read superficially some of the comparatively recent monographs on the subject of hyperventilation to achieve a vivid realization that the phenomena described above are central nervous system manifestations. An enormous literature has developed around the topic of hyperventilation, much of it having its origin in connection with aviation medicine and research.

In Reich's day—at least, when he turned his attention to the extraordinary phenomena that resulted from his breathing techniques— little of this was known. In the bibliography of Altschule's book of 1953, some eighty-nine direct references to hyperventilation are listed. (l) And this is only a small sampling of the work that has already been done.

## Bibliography

1. Altachule, Mark D. *Bodily Physiology in Mental and Emotional Disorders*. New York, Grune & Stratton, 1953. p. 78 *et seq.*
2. Gillilan, L.A. *Clinical Aspects of the Autonomic Nervous System.* Boston, Little Brown & Co., 1954. p. 14.

# Chapter V

## Theory

"The brain...becomes an enchanted loom where millions of flashing shuttles weave a dissolving pattern, always a meaningful pattern, though never an abiding one..."
— Sir Charles Sherrington

The essence of Reich's respiratory approach to the treatment of psychoneurosis is simplicity itself. On the basis of hyperventilation, a large number of neurophysiological phenomena occur, phenomena that were skillfully employed by Reich to restructure the neurotic personality. He placed considerable emphasis on breathing as the basic operational tool of therapy by insisting that:

1. Every neurotic breathes inadequately.
2. This is caused by abdominal and diaphragmatic tension.
3. The motivating factor in the above is fear of emotional expression. The muscular tension anchors affects.
4. Respiration generates enormous metabolic energy. If this energy production can be reduced, then there is less energy available for instinctual and emotional processes.
5. Therapy must reverse the process—and so, for Reich, it starts with the re-education of the patient to breath easily and fully. It must be noted here—said Groddeck in more or less the same connection—that respiration provides and releases an incredible amount of energy. One only needs to hold the breath for a few seconds to be convinced of this. Groddeck also said that breathing also is the major motivating force of the circulation of body fluids which we have been considering. (6)

The use of this respiratory tool in therapy results in:

1. Relaxation of belly and chest.

2. More adequate and effort-free respiration.
3. Higher metabolic production of energy.
4. Appearance of repressed emotions and the ability to function on a feeling level.
5. Improved biological activity.

Clinically, this is valid. About these deductions there can be very little question. Curiously enough, there is nothing in any of the several writings of Reich to indicate that he had formulated any theory about respiration differing from the above. Even Frederick Perls, who overtly acknowledges his indebtedness to Reich, though differing from him on some theoretical and clinical grounds, adheres closely to Reich's original theory. At no time has either suspected that perhaps the dynamic factor in the use of breathing as an operational tool in therapy is hyperventilation. Hyperventilation is largely responsible for the wide variety of clinical changes that may be observed. For example, the following is fairly typical of the viewpoint so often expressed by Perls in his major book:

> *"Anxiety is the experience of breathing difficulty during any blocked excitement...* It occurs in neurosis as an emergency measure produced by the conflict between strong excitement and fearful self-control... In our society no 'strong' person wishes to reveal fear by panting or gasping, and this establishes the close connection between fear and anxiety." (11)

Almost *in toto,* this is the Reichian viewpoint. But I call attention to the fact that as far as therapy is concerned, neither author formulates a theory except on the proposition that if breathing difficulties occur in blocked excitement, full breathing should release both anxiety and excitement. The much more practical neurophysiological theory answers a far larger number of hitherto obscure questions.

\*\*\*

**Hyperventilation.** Most authorities indicate that *hyperventilation induces a condition of hypocapnia resembling intoxication.* A partial loss of control, a depressing of some of the inhibitory centers and less critical evaluation of biological activity are some of the simpler signs and symptoms of cerebral intoxication. These are precisely those signs of dissociation arising as the result of hyperventilation. From intoxication of the cortex with oxygen, a pseudo-pathological condition follows that in many ways resembles a mild delirium. Delirium means literally "out of the groove." *When hyperventilated, the patient is out of the common groove of restrained responses and behaves characteristically in a less critical, less controlled and less inhibited manner than he otherwise would.* It indicates a temporary derangement of the normal metabolism of the brain, due to blowing off of carbon dioxide.

The so-called "hyperventilation syndrome" recently reported by Lewis (8) among others, describes in great detail the symptoms that develop as a result of overbreathing. He observes that while the etiology is not always psychogenic, emotional manifestations are almost always evident as a result. He classifies the physiological symptoms under several headings: central neurovascular, peripheral neurovascular, muscular, respiratory, cardiac, gastro-intestinal, psychic and general. These he attributes to the resultant hypocapnia and alkalosis which alters the internal environment of the brain. In hyperventilation induced spontaneously amongst anxiety neurotics, the "shakes" and the "trembles" comprise outstanding symptoms responsible for alarm. Many a physician has been called out of bed in the small hours of morning to treat such reactions—most of the time with tranquilizers. Non-verbal psychotherapy apparently induces all the symptoms of this syndrome without, however, inducing a bona-fide pathological state as we shall see.

The flushing, dizziness and subsequent blanching that occur during couch-work are readily explainable in terms of hyper-ventilation. In fact, Best and Taylor have observed that

> "probably the first subjective observations of the student will be dizziness and faintness resulting from some relaxation of his efforts... In this last group of cases (the majority) that one may find the cold clammy skin, pale cyanosis and thready pulse... There is evidence of vasoconstriction of the peripheral vessels, and vasodilation of the vessels in the splanchnic area has been observed during surgical operations. Good evidence of circulatory disturbance exists in the coldness of the extremities. The condition is suggestive of shock." (2)

Schimmenti (16) has observed that in respiratory alkalosis "cold clammy hands and feet are an important sign. At times the extremities may be cyanotic... Numbness and tingling in the extremities may be unilateral and cause the patient to fear a stroke." Fenn, Rahn, Otis and Chadwick (3) confirm the above, and provide additional facts that are noteworthy. They state that "if this dizziness can be tolerated for a short time, it disappears." Gibbs *et al.* (5) explain the disappearance of the dizziness on the basis of homeostasis. At first there may be insufficient cerebral vasoconstriction to compensate for the reduction in carbon dioxide during hyperventilation. When homeostatic mechanisms are adequate, sufficient cerebral vasoconstriction occurs, and the oxygen is distributed under pressure again.

Fenn *et al.* continue:

> "If the acapnia comes on more slowly, the dizziness may not appear at all and the first symptom will then be tingling in the fingers or toes... Thereafter the only symptoms of acapnia may be a slight tremor or unsteadiness or a deficient mental performance... Along with the tingling there may be cold sensations in the legs and thighs or a feeling of tightness as if the tone of muscles was increased, or as if the muscles were about to go into tetany. Some individuals experience tingling in the chest or face and one of our subjects becomes unable to talk intelligibly because of spasms of the facial muscles. Another of our subjects on two occasions has practically become unconscious from acapnia, failing to respond to signals and making glaring errors in his manipulations. He does not actually faint, but simply sits upright, apparently normal but quite unresponsive... Tremor of the hands is a common symptom of acapnia which is clearly evident in the handwriting." (4)

Another clinical finding which further highlights the significance of this thesis is a considerable degree of mental confusion which the patient evidences after several minutes of hyperventilation on the treatment couch. Sometimes, when the patient is asked to perform a simple gesture, he may display a considerable talent for confusing the specific terms of instruction. For example, he may be asked to raise the pelvis gently with each exhalation. So often have I found many of them raising the pelvis vigorously or with sharp jerks to the accompaniment of the inhalation instead of the exhalation. Or, when I ask them to lift the arms in a yearning gesture in rhythm with the exhalation, again some will do this with the inhalation instead. Many forget what they are doing. Some appear distinctly puzzled—even confused. This bewilderment may persist despite the number of clear explanations and directions given. Schizoid and withdrawal trends may also appear. There is thus a temporary suspension of what Head identified as "vigilance." This phenomenon is no cause for alarm. By the close of the session, with the alleviation of the hypocapnic condition and the return of the cortex to its previous state of normality, these and other mental symptoms vanish completely.

It seems to me to warrant emphasis that all the manifold symptoms earlier enumerated are central nervous system phenomena. The symptoms of tetany; paralysis of arms, hands and legs; sensations of numbness of chest, abdomen, head, or fingers; paresthesias of different kinds; spasms, clonisms, athetoid movements and so forth occur on the basis of simple hyperventilation—and so are neurological and physiological phenomena. They occur as some of the cortical controls—severe and chronic—become abrogated by cerebral anoxia to permit other types of lower nervous system activity.

Lewis observes that "faintness, dizziness and blackout spells serve a protective function by stopping the overbreathing and so prevent tetany." (8)

Morgan also offers the explanation that,

> "Hyperventilation does not significantly increase the amount of oxygen in the blood because the red corpuscles which carry the blood's oxygen are already near their saturation points. What hyperventilation does do, however, is raise the rate at which carbon dioxide leaves the blood and is exhaled; *removing carbon dioxide raises pH and therefore tends to raise the excitability of the brain."* (9) (italics mine)

This thesis of the altered pH of the blood is further elaborated by Shock: "Alkalinity of the blood may also be markedly increased by loss of carbon dioxide brought about by increased respiration." (Shock and Hastings, 1935). The increase in neuromuscular excitability found under such circumstances may easily be experienced by the reader if he will exhale forcibly about 30 times a minute for one or two minutes. The dizziness, the feeling of muscular tenseness about the mouth, and the contracture of the fingers are all physiological results of the increased alkalinity which has been produced by the excessive loss of carbon dioxide through the lungs. Experimental studies show as the results of hyperventilation diminished sensory acuity (Gellhorn and Spiesman, 1935a, 1935b), increased sensory latent periods, decreased sensitivity to pain, decreased speed in mental calculations, idiosyncrasy of response to association words (Gellhorn and Kraines, 1937) and even amnesia. *Since loss of $CO_2$ produces vasoconstriction of the blood vessels of the brain* (Gobb and Fremont-Smith, 1931); (Wolf and Lennox, 1930), *it is believed that many of these mental effects* of carbon dioxide loss *should be attributed to cerebral anoxia* (Gellhorn, 1936). "This hypothesis is supported by the increased mental performance possible under low oxygen tension when small amounts of carbon dioxide (5%) are added to the inspired air. The added carbon dioxide produces a vasodilatation in the brain with increased blood flow and greater delivery of oxygen." (17) (italics mine)

The dizziness and light-headedness resulting from forced respiration are among the major objectives to be worked towards at the outset of therapy. It is almost the indispensable prerequisite if success in non-verbal psychotherapy is to be achieved. Some patients will become dizzy quite readily. Others are highly recalcitrant. In some strange manner, they overtly resist the onset of dizziness for some time no matter how vigorous and intensive their breathing. Constitutional factors must play a very large part here. Whether these factors, exaggerated in this manner, are the pathological expression of the whole process of armoring is difficult to say. It might be more convenient to assume they are emotionally blocked, highly compulsive people for whom fear of any kind or degree is a grossly intolerable state. From the earliest years of their lives, they have learned to armor themselves heavily against it.

As one watches the patient's active behavior on the couch in response to the breathing, to the emotional attitudes, and to the muscular manipulation, his specific character structure becomes quite apparent. In some there will be an increase in tension—either focal or general—to block the emergence of feelings and sensations. Others will wriggle and move without rhyme or reason, an escape into motor activity. Hysterical reactions are perceptible in yet others. Comparatively few will be found able to enjoy or experience objectively the body feelings that make their appearance. In short, this specific response is characteristic of the person, and is an index to the nature of the character structure.

Many patients respond to the onset of dizziness with alarm. The usual response is to quit breathing for several seconds. Obviously this apnea is normal enough from the physiological viewpoint, though this more or less prolonged pause defeats the purpose of therapy. Actual shock reactions, moreover, must be strictly avoided.

Others toss their heads from side to side in quite evident alarm. Still others will raise their hands to their heads, shaking or knocking the temporal area, as though to throw off the dizziness, while others become schizoid, withdrawing so thoroughly that when spoken to they offer no evidence at all that they have heard anything. In all cases underlying and basic character trends appear in all their stark nakedness. It is reminiscent of the adage *in vino veritas.* In this instance, the intoxicant happens to be oxygen, but the state of intoxication is not too different from that induced by alcohol. Hysterical, fearful, schizoid, paranoid, homosexual or compulsive traits of character become apparent quickly after the induction of the initial lightheaded state brought on by forced respiration.

For this reason I suggest that hyperventilation can be used as a diagnostic tool in psychiatry. Usually an incipient or arrested schizophrenia will show up vividly after a few minutes of hyperventilation. The patient may become so withdrawn as to be inaccessible. He may be spoken to, but will give no response at all, so catatonic has he become. Tapping the abdomen firmly may elicit a cry of pain and terminate the tendency to withdraw. Often the diagnostic clarification of a severe obsessional state from an arrested incipient schizophrenia is extremely difficult, but they can be differentiated by this means.

All patients when hyperventilating need reassurance that the therapist has fully anticipated whatever is happening. Occasionally the alarm is so excessive that the patient does not heed the calming words uttered by the therapist. Here, then, more vigorous measures need to be taken by the therapist to utilize advantageously the confused state of semi-shock or intoxication experienced by the patient. Even this state is useful as indicating, perhaps, that the patient's first lines of defense may not be operating at their normal full efficiency. We might even use symbolic terms and say that temporarily his superego has been dissolved in oxygen. If he is manipulated aright, some of his repressed feelings nay be elicited in full force.

The therapist has to be on guard lest shock intervene. For this reason, pulse rate and pressure should be palpated at frequent intervals. Embarrassment of the heart or a major disturbance of the circulatory system are hardly desirable symptoms. In this therapy, a considerable strain or burden is put on the therapist who must not be caught off guard for a moment. In many ways, the therapist is as active during each session as is the patient. "On the *qui vive*" is his watchword. The therapy is as effective for the therapist as for the patient.

Conversion hysteria illustrates the usefulness of the hyperventilation approach as one phase of a psychotherapeutic process. When the patient is so utterly blocked that verbal communication is devoted wholly to defensiveness and evasion, discussions elicit very little. Ordinarily such patients are dismissed after a trial period as not suited to psychoanalysis. Hyperventilation breaks the Gordian knot. It opens up the patient's defensive system sufficiently to permit intensive psychotherapeutic work. The following case illustrates this viewpoint.

(It should be noted that this type of case history is not particularly encouraged amongst orgonomists. If the patient seems inclined to discuss the historical events of his life during a session or as a result of the dynamic process of any specific reduction of chronic muscular tension with an affective release, well and good. It may assist his understanding of his character structure and his individual type of muscular armoring. But, generally speaking, it is the patient's physical status here and now which is the primary consideration. The orgonomic description of a patient is less in terms of previous memories or conventional diagnostic labels than an account of how the therapist perceives the patient on the couch. It is a description of character traits and their dynamic armoring in diffuse muscular tensions involving the armored segments of the body. The total body and psychological (defensive) attitudes of the patient under treatment are the dominant contents of the history or descriptive process.)

Joan is about twenty-nine years old, has a good athletic physique, is pretty but hysterical in character structure. She had been somewhat unsatisfactorily married for about four years. There are sexual difficulties. As she expressed it, "I can take it or leave it." She picks irritably at her easy-going, good-natured husband even though realizing this is irrational behavior. During the four years of her married life she has undergone surgery twice, first for an appendectomy and later for a cholecystectomy. The original symptoms were vertigo, gastric tension with "butterflies," pain in the chest but particularly over the left breast and shoulder, tachycardia with an occasional skipped systole. Apparently her physician had not been rendered familiar with Altschule's warning that

> "many physicians have learned through experience that unsatisfactory results are usually obtained when a poorly functioning gall bladder is removed in a patient who complains only of indigestion, without colic, fever or jaundice. In many such instances the dyspepsia is owing to neurosis, the diseased gall bladder having little influence on the symptoms... The finding of a chronically diseased but clinically quiescent gall bladder may divert attention from the true nature of the disorder with the result that an unnecessary operation may be performed." (1)

Eventually he referred her to a neuro-psychiatrist. For twelve weeks, twice weekly, she was a highly resistant patient, defensively forcing him to prove to her that her symptoms were psychogenic. She remained wholly unconvinced and, despite the prescription of a tranquilizer, terminated therapy to go "doctor shopping." After I had a couple of sessions devoted to information gathering, a tentative diagnosis of conversion hysteria was established. In view of her provoking defensive tactics with the previous psychiatrist, non-verbal psychotherapy was forthwith instituted. The immediate intention was to try to convert the neurosis into an acute anxiety state which might be more amenable to treatment.

Upon inspection it became abundantly clear that the pelvis and thighs were rigid almost to the point of immobility, the belly was only moderately tense despite the two surgeries, but the chest was involuntarily raised in the chronic inspiratory position. The ribs appeared to be almost wholly fixated. The facial muscles were fairly mobile, though blank, and the eyes were alive and expressive. One interesting event occurred in the first active session, behavior which was to be repeated in every subsequent session. No more than five to ten minutes of hyperventilation reduced her to tears. Then the chest would move freely with rapid disappearance of the tension and pain.

However, she would not willingly permit this and struggled with every ounce of determination to suppress the crying. Her defensive measure then became apparent. Respiration became markedly shallow, superficial and clavicular. The diaphragm made only short, jerky excursions and tension built up in the epigastrium. The throat muscles tightened almost to a stricture and the chest was raised as before in the chronic inspiratory attitude, as if she knew that by so doing the sobs could be suppressed. Only sterner measures sufficed to break though her muscular block to evoke the deeper crying. She still fought, but when the sobbing eventually broke through her restraint, she would follow through—when the chest and belly walls would relax and respiration once again became easy, smooth and profound. The symptoms spontaneously disappeared—at least temporarily.

Her history provided the motives of this lack of insight and this great resistance to therapy. There were two younger brothers about whom she was uncommunicative. The most significant fact emerging from the history was that her father was an alcoholic. Her attitudes were indeterminate towards him. All she would verbalize through her scotoma was that she never knew from day to day as she walked home from school whether he would be sober or not, so that she always hesitated before inviting girl friends home. A great deal of caution developed for she feared the precipitation of a scene by the inebriated father, embarrassing both her and her girl friends. This defensiveness became incorporated into her character structure. In school she was a fair student, moderately interested in different subjects, but she made very little effort to apply herself. She made friends without difficulty and during high school dated often and readily.

Hers was a Catholic family. She was given religious training in parochial school, took communion, went to confession faithfully, and attended church services regularly.

After graduation from high school she worked in large department stores and offices, developing into a competent secretary. She had dates, went to parties, theaters and shows, and managed to have a good time. There were occasional somatic symptoms occasioned by anxiety, but she did not recognize them as such at the time and medicated herself as many people do. For a headache she took aspirin. For indigestion, a patent medicine. For the occasional cold, antihistamines. When menstrual cramps occurred she would stay home for a day, use a hot-water bottle and take aspirin. For the occasional round of insomnia, when she was apparently disturbed by her father's drinking and by the fact that she was not yet married, she would take a Nembutal.

When she was about twenty-four, she met a man of another religion altogether antagonistic to her own and she fell in love. They never discussed religion and their respective churches. There were a couple of scenes at home when she had invited Bill in for a nightcap to meet her parents. There was the inevitable drunken scene initiated by father in his habitual evening drunken state. Bill was not scared off by these scenes.

They became more intimate as time went on and Joan became pregnant. They decided to elope. A formal church wedding was out of the question since neither of them dared risk the inevitable disapproval of their respective families from whom they anticipated only opposition and resentment. Upon their return home, the folks quickly recovered from the shock of the undesired marriage and persuaded Joan to go through a church ceremony. A couple of weeks afterwards she decided upon an abortion, believing that both she and Bill ought to work for a year before raising a family. Answering a direct question from me, she stated emphatically that she felt no sense of guilt about either the marriage with Bill or the abortion. Paradoxically, she volunteered the information that she had not been to church or to confession since her marriage. This is characteristic of the patient—an extraordinarily low degree of awareness of possible guilt feelings, the psychodynamics of repression and denial being outstanding features.

From this time forward marital difficulties developed, mostly because she objected to Bill having one night out each week with the boys for poker, bowling, etc., since he was also kept out one or two nights a week in connection with his work. She became hostile and resentful. It was then that she began to nag at him and pester him with criticisms of his behavior at home. As an anodyne to boredom while Bill was away at night, she enrolled in an adult education program at a local high school. Here she was enticed into an arts and crafts class, where she soon struck up several warm friendships. One of the teachers was attracted to her and a sexual relationship ensued, about which she felt no overt guilt until much later.

At about this time some of her early symptoms became crucial. Occasional attacks of dizziness, cold hands and gastric distress would intervene, for which her family physician prescribed sundry medications. When the symptoms persisted and grew worse, complete physical checkups were inaugurated. These were done by her own doctor, and at later dates by two internists, a cardiologist, a gastroenterologist and, finally, by the psychiatrist already mentioned. Throughout all of this, the conviction dominated her thinking that her symptoms had grown out of various physical pathologies. Any attempt to orient her to the notion that fear, hostility and guilt reactions were related to her problem fell on deaf ears. She was so utterly resistant to the theme that getting her to verbalize her emotional problems in relation to difficult life-situations was utterly impossible, There *had* to be a somatic origin for her symptoms,

It was this that impelled me to institute vegeto-therapy and to avoid any verbal discussion about her problems. In light of her history it became patent why tears occurred after a short run of hyperventilation and why she resisted insight into its significance. If she credited the tears with meaning, she might have to face up to her shame and fear of her father's drunken and irrational behavior, her justifiable resentment over the humiliation he had heaped upon her and her family, and the vindictive feelings which she could not and dared not tolerate because of her rigid religious training. All of this became crystallized in the marriage. The marriage relationship with its manifold implications of guilt and revenge merely forced her to recapitulate latent responses from years earlier. Adaptation to this renewed stress placed too much strain on an organism barely capable of handling it, so that a much-needed escape into sickness was the outcome. Sickness enabled her to cope with a desperate family situation without having to admit to emotions that were wholly unacceptable to her, emotions that a poorly trained and inadequate ego had earlier pushed aside and blocked off.

***

**Central Nervous System.** Changes in blood chemistry produced by hyperventilation exert, as we have seen, a profound influence on cerebral function. "Slight increases in alkalinity," states Shock, "tend to increase motor reactivity to stimuli particularly at the reflex level, but to decrease functions involving higher levels of the central nervous system." (17) Responsiveness of the cerebral cortex is markedly diminished in hyperventilation. It is the accepted viewpoint that motor activity seems to originate from the lower cerebral centers, and that one role of the cortex represents an inhibition and deviation of primary impulses. The cortex splits the primitive motor impulse into several phases producing a retardation, if not total blocking, of the response through lengthening of the time between perception and reaction. In non-verbal therapy a temporary severance of the lower centers from the educated inhibition of the neopallium is attempted so that later, when reintegration does occur, it will be on a different basis. The function of the cortex must be to give intelligent direction to impulse and affect, not to block them off entirely. It was Pavlov's contention that "the subcortex is the source of energy for the whole higher nervous activity and that the cortex plays the role of regulator for this blind strength, delicately guiding and controlling it." (10)

Thompson and Nielson believe that instincts are inherited neuronal patterns of behavior, crudely present in the human infant at birth, but subject to development and expansion, anatomically and physiologically, with the growth of the individual. "The instincts which are present at birth have their neuronal patterns in the diencephalon. Those which require knowledge must await myelinization before they can express themselves; those which require gonadal development must await puberty" (19) Furthermore, "emotion results from facilitation or from frustration of an instinctive drive. An emotion is expressed in the activity of the vegetative nervous system through the hypothalamus and is felt throughout the body as glandular activity and muscular activity. Each emotion, therefore, is closely associated with an instinct. With each drive there is expectancy (anticipation) and with each conclusion there is pleasure or displeasure." (20) Finally, they state that "undirected emotion is based entirely on engrammes in the brain stem but that all directed emotion depends on engramme patterns extending to the cerebral cortex." (21)

This places the burden of the entire therapy on a firm neurological basis. It is an attempt to free the diencephalon and brain stem from unnecessary cortical interference, primarily the product of acculturation.

Some vegeto-therapists to whom I have spoken about the possibility of a neurophysiological interpretation are altogether hostile and reject outright the acceptability of such a thesis. Possibly Reich himself would not and could not accept it. He wrote that the "highest" developmental product, the brain, together with the nervous apparatus of the spinal cord, is the "director" of the whole organism. Mechanists assume a center from which all impulses are sent out to move the organs. Every muscle has, connected by its respective nerves, its own center in the brain or in the thalamus. *From where the brain itself receives its assignments remains a riddle...* He also thought that since the mechanist does not understand the living, he must take flight into mysticism, so all mechanistic world pictures are always mystical and *must* be mystical. Mechanistic thinking itself is clearly modeled after the structure of the social patriarchy when the master is the brain, the telegraph wires the nerves, and the executing subjects the organs. And behind the brain "works God," or "reason" or "purpose." The situation in natural-scientific comprehension still remains as hopelessly confused as before. (15)

And yet he has elsewhere expressed a simple attitude which might be construed that, in spite of everything, he is fundamentally sympathetic to the neurological viewpoint. He stated that *it is possible the schizophrenic attack or process is locally anchored just as are other symptoms such as anorexia or headache or cardiac anxiety,* possibly the base of the brain (the region of the crossing of the optic nerve), or possibly schizophrenia is a true "brain disease," induced by some specific type of emotional upheaval with a local contraction of special parts of the brain due to severe anxiety.

Reich thought that many symptoms in schizophrenia seemed to confirm the validity of this assumption. The typical schizophrenic look in the eyes; the degenerative processes in the brain found in old schizophrenics (secondary degenerative changes in tissues) is due to chronic anxious contraction of the vascular system; reports from so many schizophrenics that they felt as if veiled or "flattened" on the forehead at the outbreak of the disease. (13)

Regarding his attitude to neurophysiology, he further stated that the brain would have to be regarded as an organ like others within the total functioning of the organism, as a special *"transmitter"* of total plasma functions, and *not as the source of motor impulses.* There are many species without any brain who function fully as far as living functions are concerned; and we know from experiment that brainless dogs continue to function, even if severely impaired by surgery. (14)

In this connection it should be recorded also that he believes that many of the pleasant body sensations occurring after the biological shrinking or vasoconstriction has subsided during the therapy session are related to the expansion of the autonomic nervous system. I have already indicated Reich's contention that visceral nerve fibers may contract and expand; they are not fixed stationary structures. Contraction goes with anxiety—"away from the world, toward the self." Expansion goes with pleasure and vasodilation—"away from the self, towards the world." Expansion, pleasure and free-moving vegetative excitations are related phenomena. I must reiterate that patients report these well-defined body sensations as couch experiences. There is evidence that perhaps his early inferences are not so far removed from fact, as suggested by Pfeiffer:

> "Until recently most investigators assumed that nerve fibres occupy fixed positions, or at least moved only as they grew. But new studies (at the University of Texas) indicate that brain tissue is far more active. As you read this sentence, fibers in your head are swaying like seaweed swept by tides. Tentacles of protoplasm are slowly moving forward, retreating, swelling and shrinking, waving from side to side." (12)

There is one other set of highly suggestive findings in this connection. W. Grey Walter described some fascinating experiments with electro-encephalography which are of inestimable value to this thesis.

"In 1948 we found that the information contained in EEG records could be greatly increased by subjecting the brain to rhythmic stimulation, particularly by the flickering of a powerful light in the eyes, open or closed. Early experiments of this sort had been done by shining a light through a rotating wheel with wide spokes, but the results had been inconsistent. One trouble was that as the frequency of the flicker was increased by turning the wheel faster, so the duration of each flash became shorter. Furthermore, to obtain a bright enough flash, very strong lights had to be used, and these tended to burn the retina. At the end of the war, easy and accurate flicker was attained by employing an electronic stroboscope which can be calibrated in fractions of a cycle per second, with a very short, brilliant flash, the duration of which does not vary with the frequency.

"It was found, as expected, that each flash of light evoked in the brain a characteristic electrical response. Experiments on the cortical response to light stimuli had become familiar before the war. But, now with the fresh technique, strange patterns, new and significant, emerged from the swift scribbling of the pens in all channels of the EEG.

"The flash rate could be changed quickly by turning a knob, and at certain frequencies the rhythmic series of flashes appeared to be breaking down some of the physiological barriers between different regions of the brain. This meant that the stimulus of the flicker received in the visual projection area of the cortex was breaking bounds; its ripples were overflowing into other areas." (19)

"...In order to compare the clinically epileptic responses with those of normals, we examined several hundred 'control' subjects—school children, students, various groups of adults. In three or four percent of these, carefully adjusted flicker evoked responses indistinguishable from those previously regarded as 'diagnostic' of clinical epilepsy. When these responses appeared, the subjects would exclaim at the 'strange feelings,' the faintness or swimming of the head; some became unresponsive or unconscious for a few moments; *in some the limbs jerked in rhythm with the flashes of light."* (20) (italics mine)

"...The greatest variety of mental experiences are described, not by any means all of them unpleasant. Some have seen profuse patterns of many colors, sometimes stable, sometimes moving; one of the first patterns we saw ourselves, the whirling spiral, recurs quite often and this is may have a peculiar mechanical significance as will be suggested later. Simple sensations in other than the visual mode are experienced. *Some describe feelings of swaying, of jumping, even of spinning and dizziness. Some people feel a tingling and prickling of the skin... All sorts of emotions are experienced;* fatigue, confusion, fear, disgust, anger, pleasure. Sometimes the sense of time is lost or disturbed." (21) (italics mine)

"...The more vivid and bizarre the experience of he subject, the farther from the visual areas are the evoked responses, and the more peculiar their form and geometry." (22)

The direct implication here is that sensory stimuli can irradiate from their normal physiological foci in the cortex to affect or activate other cortical and diencephalic areas. This results, as Walter has observed, in the perception of other sensations, psychomotor activities and a wide range of emotional responses. The interesting and important fact is that Walter's subjects experienced similar neurophysiological responses as do patients undergoing non-verbal psychotherapy. It appears, then, that by intoxicating the cortex with oxygen, vegeto-therapy does temporarily derange the normal physiological barriers between the component parts of the central nervous system. Neural thresholds are lowered. This disassociation permits the freeing of some lower centers which have been unduly inhibited by the cortex as a result of familial training, learning and conditioning. This temporary release upsets the previously acquired neurotic equilibrium which, over the long years before, had become soundly established. This situation now requires the integration of a new kind of equilibrium. Under the guidance of the skilled therapist, this homeostasis is to be on a more rational, healthy and organismic basis, to permit a freer play of emotions and instincts hitherto blocked off and repressed. It is to permit the active conjunction of thinking and feeling in a unified psychobiological process.

## Bibliography

1. Altschule, Mark D. *Bodily Physiology in Mental and Emotional Disorders.* New York, Grune and Stratton, 1953. p. 103, *et seq.*
2. Best, C.E. and Taylor, N.B. *The Physiological Basis of Medical Practise.* Baltimore, Williams & Wilkins, 1950. p. 414.
3. Fenn, W.E., Rahn, H., Otis, A.B., and Chadwick, L.E. "Physiological Observations in Hyperventilation." *Jnl. Applied Psych:* 1:11, May 1949, p. 773.
4. *ibid.* p. 736.
5. Gibbs, E.L. *et al.* "Regulation of Cerebral Carbon Dioxide." *Arch. Neural. Psych.* 47: 879–880, Chicago, 1942.
6. Groddeck, Georg. *Exploring the Unconscious.* London, Daniels & Co., 1938, p. 52–53.
7. Heath, Robert. *Studies in Schizophrenia.* Mass., Harvard University Press, 1955.
8. Lewis, Bernard I. "The Hyperventilation Syndrome." *Annals of Internal Medicine,* 38: 918–927, 1953.
9. Morgan, Clifford T. *Physiological Psychology,* New York, McGraw-Hill, 1933, p. 351.
10. Pavlov, I.P. *Conditioned Reflexes and Psychiatry.* New York, Int. Pub. 1941, p. 57.
11. Perls, Frederick, *et al. Gestalt Therapy.* New York, Julian Press, 1951. p. 128.
12. Pfeiffer, John. *The Human Brain.* New York, Harper Bros. 1955, p. 2.
13. Schimmenti, John M. "Hyperventilation Syndrome in Women." *Modern Medicine,* May 15, 1954, p. 142.
14. Nathan W. Shock. "Physiological Factors in Behavior." *Personality and the Behavior Disorders,* Vol. 1. (ed. J. McV Hunt). New York, Ronald Press, 1944. p. 592.

15. Speransky, A.D. *A Basis for a Theory of Medicine.* New York, Int. Press, 1933.
16. Thompson, George and Nielsen, J.M. *Engrammes of Psychiatry.* Springfield, Ill., Thomas., 1947, p. 39.
17. *ibid.,* p. 41.
18. *ibid.,* p. 43.
19. Walter, W. Grey. *The Living Brain.* New York, Norton, 1953. p. 91.
20. *ibid.,* p. 97.
21. *ibid.,* p. 106.
22. *ibid.,* p. 111.

# Chapter VI

## Tetany

"The clonic fit is the expression of a dilemma."
— Trygve Braatøy

**Vascular changes.** The marked sensation of coolness which gradually and invariably arises is evidently related to neurovascular disturbances of the peripheral circulatory system—to vasoconstriction. Reference has already been made to the observation of Best and Taylor that in a wide variety of experimental cases a cold clammy skin and pale cyanosis develops as a result of the hyperventilation. Hypocapnia and alkalosis induce the vasoconstriction.

Amongst the orgonomists, however, there is a somewhat different interpretation of this simple neurological and physiological fact. In the first place, one of Reich's contentions is that this vasoconstriction represents a temporary retraction or shrinking of the sutonomic nerve fibers. It is claimed that nerves are not rigid structures but are flexible, capable of contracting and expanding as with all living tissue. The retraction and shrinking is motivated by fear—"away from the world and into the self." Apparently the neurotic ego is incapable of tolerating certain affects in the early phases of therapy and retreats from them. But the affect-lame patient does not have the conscious awareness of the disturbing affects to be retreated from. Therefore, the involuntary somatic response serves as an index to the true state of the internal environment. *The conditioned cortex may lie; the body is incapable of doing so.*

An occasional patient sweats so copiously on the couch that the sheet is soaking wet.

Fenn *et al.* observe that "The exact mechanism by which the undesirable effects of excessive hyperventilation (numbness, tingling, tetany, etc.) are produced is unknown, but it would seem that the fundamental disturbance is an increased alkalinity of the blood and tissues." (5)

Lewis believes that peripheral and peri-oral paresthesias "are not of central origin but result from the local neurovascular changes." (7) Many of these phenomena are similar to those known to occur in anxiety states when the subject is convulsed with outright fear.

With continued hyperventilation, vasoconstriction and shrinking become more widespread. With it the coolness becomes more well-defined until the patient perceptibly begins to tremble. Sooner or later, regardless of which part or extremity begins to tremble first, the entire organism becomes involved. This massive trembling and shivering has little to do with the actual temperature of the room. I have seen patients tremble in a warm office in midsummer as if they had just emerged from a large walk-in meat freezer. Only after repeated sessions are some patients willing to concede to the admission of fear, almost of panic.

It is noteworthy that *in those somatic areas where previously there had been excessive muscular tension, there now appears a peculiar exaggeration of the trembling.* It is as though *the trembling has the involuntary function of shaking the muscle loose from chronic tension.* I cannot overemphasize the importance of this finding. *It is an autonomic form of abreaction of inhibitions.* In some instances the shaking and trembling may become so gross and coarse as almost to simulate a grand mal convulsion. At first patients fear these events, even when the trembling is very fine and slight. A few may fear these tremors on the basis of earlier experiences. A sibling or close family friend may have had chorea or Parkinson's, the neuromuscular movements of which have become associated with the present therapeutic phenomena. Or, as a child, one patient may have seen someone seized by a grand mal convulsion and experienced all the horror and awe that usually accompanies such manifestations for the layman. All of this is carried over into the therapeutic situation where reassurance that no harm will befall them under the circumstances of therapy may be necessary.

These massive tremors and shakings are also reminiscent of the total muscular activity of the child in expressing its needs and wants. This activity is non-discreet and generalized before coordination due to myelination has occurred. Perhaps the myoclonic spasms being discussed here are not only evidence of sub-cortical motor activity breaking loose form cortical control, but also represent a psychic regression.

Norman, about 45 years old when he came to therapy, had been severely affect-lame most of his remembered life. Instead of having feelings of different kinds, he recalled only innumerable physical symptoms and tensions of a disturbing kind. His adolescence was marked by utter loneliness and masturbatory guilt. He led a rich fantasy life, but a wholly uneventful reality life. An occasional encounter with a prostitute was characterized by impotence and total frustration. In his early thirties, as he gained greater control over his sensitive feelings, casual sexual encounters with shop girls and business women gave similar results. Eventually he was introduced through a business associate to a girl with whom he found himself capable of erective potency. Within three weeks he married her. Before a month had passed, he was a victim of headaches, indigestion, insomnia and a distressing restlessness. Throughout his life he had been particularly intolerant of hostile feelings, which were by the time of his marriage wholly repressed. As a result of the minor irritations which would occasionally occur through the intimacies of the marital situation, he would develop spasmodic acrial tensions, a rigid thoracic musculature, leg cramps and obscure abdominal pains. Progress in therapy was very slow—considerable effort being devoted to softening up first the abdomen and then the chest.

One day, during the last third of the therapeutic hour as he was relaxing, Norman was asked as usual to watch his own body feelings and organ sensations. After a while he reported a build up of considerable tension in the shoulders and neck, and along the length of the spinal gutter. Within a few minutes more he was in the violent throes of what appeared to be a full-fledged grand mal convulsion. There was only this difference: there was no frothing of saliva, no champing of the jaws, nor any loss of consciousness. He was perfectly aware of these polymorphous phenomena occurring, but could do nothing about them.

It was this temporary helplessness that at first scared him. He needed reassurance in order to permit the continuance of these physiological phenomena. It is largely in this connection that a solid positive transference needs to be established, so that in such critical moments a word of reassurance will be completely effective. These massive clonisms are productive of a profound discharge of muscular tension, while the relaxation that ensues is comparable to nothing else—for the patient feels alive in every part of his body. Each cell is *felt* as a living sensitive organism.

As he grew accustomed to these clonisms and learned to describe his feelings and sensations while he was being thrown around in a vigorous manner, he became aware of an ever-increasing sense of inner release and freedom from emotional strain and somatic tension. It took many sessions for him to work through this phase of therapy to where anxiety could be more easily discharged by tears, by the verbal expression of anger against his mother for her perpetual critical attitudes towards him and his father, and in other forms of somatic manifestation.

The comparison of these vigorous myoclonisms and tremblings to a grand-mal convulsion is hardly a legitimate one. Yet, for those who are unfamiliar with the terms of this therapy it may serve to permit some comprehension. It was asserted by Gibbs that "from an electroencephalographic point of view, epilepsy is an irritative reaction to injury or to a developmental defect. The epileptic seizure is only the external manifestation of *an explosive release of energy within the brain."* (6) (italics mine) Gibbs adds that, contrary to popular belief, epileptic seizures are not invariably accompanied by loss of consciousness. His observations are in general agreement with the neurological phenomena induced by the vegeto-therapeutic work. Therapy not only relaxes the tense musculature which comprise the armor—and parenthetically it may again be affirmed that tension and inhibition are equivalent—but it releases long-repressed emotions.

In addition to these findings, there is another result which Reich directed attention to long ago. These affects contain an explosive quantum of energy. In their therapeutic discharge, there is an extraordinary release of energy which is not only responsible for the clonisms and spasms, but which may be the causative factor behind the definite sensations of electricity, tingling, energy pulsations and vegetative excitations. The brain has to be considered as a powerful generator of energy, and when it is subjected to hyperventilation, glucose metabolism is accelerated so that vast amounts of energy are released over and above its normal output.

Furthermore the discussion of these phenomena recalls an earlier psychotherapeutic finding. Some of Stekel's early hypotheses about epilepsy are worthy of mention here. It was his contention that the epileptic convulsion, when not etiologically related to brain lesions or foci of irritation, is a substitute for a sexual act. He claimed that it is an orgastic experience which has previously been condemned by the conscience. The endopsychic conflict is productive of severe anxiety. This intolerable anxiety is allayed by repudiation and repression.

His theory propounds further that the convulsion is a substitute for a criminal act of some kind. The implication is that the sexual act and an act of criminal violence are not only linked together, but are in fact identical, thus providing the hidden motivation for total repression. In the epileptic convulsion, Stekel believed that there is a vicarious indulgence in both the forbidden sexual and criminal acts, accompanied simultaneously by a self-induced punitive measure for permitting this indulgence to occur. (10)

Reich has also expressed the view that the spasms and myoclonisms represent split-off components or fragments of the orgasm reflex. It is as if the body struggled for release in the only way open for it to do so.

Were enough cases observed and later analyzed, it might be found that these patients who harbor excessive aggressive impulses and whose personality is so defective socially as to be incapable of adequate sexual discharge are those who find emotional discharge easier through the muscular spasms and clonisms. My experience tends to confirm this idea.

Similar spasms and convulsive phenomena have been observed by Meduna during the administration of his carbon dioxide inhalation therapy. He calls them "adverse motor seizures," counseling against their induction on the ground that too much anxiety is evoked, scaring the patient from the continuance of therapy. However, the fact remains that when anxiety and motor activity are initiated by hyperventilation there is a far better tolerance than when carbon dioxide inhalation with narcosis is the initiator. It indicates that hyperventilation with its sequelae of alkalosis and vasoconstriction has had an extensive effect upon the cerebrum, gently lowing neural thresholds and temporarily breaking down the hitherto well-defined barriers of demarcation between one cortical center and another.

Another important evidence of neurovascular changes is a symptom called dermagraphia. After hyperventilation, the skin becomes extraordinarily sensitive to trivial stimuli.

Biological organization and psychical activity may not ordinarily be considered identical, but nowadays it is customary to regard them as different functions of the organism-as-a-whole. The skin is a very important component of this psychosomatic unity. It represents, as it were, the outer walls of a sanctuary, guarding that which is within and excluding that which is without. At the same time it serves a very delicate role as mediator in both functions.

Confronted originally by the dermographic lines and markings, I became so intrigued that I would occasionally trace out on a patient's abdomen a series of geometric figures and symbols. Later, when I realized the neural import of these cutaneous responses, they came to be regarded as indexes to the degree of activation of the autonomic chain and to activate further peripheral neurodermal responses in the patient.

I came to think figuratively of the skin as representing the keys of a piano and the brain as the hidden set of strings. By means of striking the keys, the strings can be stirred in to musical activity. Much of the vegeto-therapeutic work consists, not so much in the production of the dermographisms which, of course, are only incidental, but in the vegetative and energy sensations related to them and, even more important, in the eliciting of emotional responses through them.

It is important to remember that the skin and the nervous system evolve, *in utero,* from the same layer of embryonic tissue, the ectoderm. Originating from the same tissue, the connection between skin and nervous system persists throughout the lifetime. This is a basic neurological fact that is usefully employed here.

There is an illuminating paper by Montagu concerning the sensory influences of the skin which is worthy of consideration in this connection. His discussion concerns manifold changes in mammalian behavior when the skin of the young, for example, is licked or stroked.

> "If the newborn animal is for some reason not licked, particularly in the perineal region, it is likely to die of failure of the gastrointestinal system or genitourinary system to function... Rats, mice, rabbits and those mammals depending upon the mother for sustenance in the early days of life apparently have to be taught to defecate and urinate... The unstimulated hand-fed young die with an occlusion of the ureter and distended bladder... On the basis of the physiological relations already briefly indicated it seems that under similar conditions stimulation of the respiratory centers and apparatus could be achieved by subjecting the non-breathing baby to immersion in hot and cold baths... It is the cutaneous stimulation which activates the autonomic—which in turn acts upon the respiratory centers and viscera. The effect of a sudden cold shower upon the respiratory system is too well-known to require stressing here" (8)

Montagu also wrote:

> "Love has been defined as the harmony of two souls and the contact of two epidermis... Cutaneous contact between infant and mother is obviously of some organismic value to the infant...and cutaneous contact would seem to be the language which for some time the infant best understands... Human beings do not lick their young...breast-feeding brings the infant into close physical contact with the mother, resulting in much labial and facial tactile stimulation in cultures where infant and mother wear clothes, or total body stimulation where infant and mother habitually remain nude... Hand-shaking, nose-rubbing, kissing, putting one's arm around another person, holding hands, walking arm-in-arm, nuzzling and the like, are evidences of affection or friendliness."

This discussion becomes wholly intelligible during a vegeto-therapeutic session. After hyperventilation has been induced, a large variety of neuro-cutaneous effects can be achieved in profusion by pointing a fan-blower at the skin. If the patient feels hot and flushed, the cool air from the blower tends to precipitate the fine tremors and quiverings, betokening the shaking loose of neuromuscular tension and the emergence of a variety of sought-after affects. Or, should vasoconstriction have ensued and the patient fearfully experiences the sensation of coolness, warm air from the blower will produce feelings of tingling, vibration and pulsation and other paresthesias of which Reich has spoken extensively. These are, of course, evidence mainly of peripheral vasomotor activity. They may occur so massively that they are bound to induce an extraordinary array of sensations as normal physiological accompaniments. Sensations, according to both Reich and Montagu, go hand in glove with emotions.

Similar phenomena arise when, during the latter third of a session while the patient is relaxing, one gently strokes or touches the patient's skin. It does not make much difference where—this depends upon the patient and the site of his muscular tensions. But usually the costal arch, or the medial surface of the thighs is very sensitive to the lightest, gossamer touch. If one strokes gently the sides of the jaw, or runs a finger ever so lightly around the peri-oral region, a wide variety of emotional reactions may be elicited. These responses are those constantly sought after. Patients describe the physical sensations in terms of cold shivers, chills, thrills, goose-pimples. These are perceptible to the therapist. Often they serve to initiate a copious discharge of whimpering or prolonged tearfulness, muscular quivering or, more rarely, the orgasm reflex itself. One patient described some of these sensations in these words: "It feels as heavy as a heartbeat all over my body," or, "I buzz all over," or, "Cold shivers go all the way around me, then dart up my spine," or, "I just have to shudder all over," or, "When you touch my feet, I feel tingling rise from my behind to my chest."

Occasionally this most gentle of touches evokes white lines on the skin. These dermographic reactions occur not as a result of heavy pressure at all. Only the lightest stroking with a feather-like touch is required. The white skin-tracings appear in a few seconds; oft-times they will persist for as long as five or ten minutes.

Not only are peripheral vascular reactions involved here, but there is a vigorous reaction of the sympathetic fibers (2) as well as a histamine-like reaction by the tissue to the dermographic stimulus. Gastrin and histamine are indistinguishable chemically which perhaps may account for some of the gastro-intestinal symptoms— belching, eructations, nausea, flatulence—occurring during phases of therapy. Lewis believes that most of these latter symptoms are better accounted for by aerophagia which commonly attends hyperventilation. Nonetheless, Best and Taylor state that the fully conscious organism is not so sensitive to histamine as is the anesthetized. This may confirm the thesis that vegeto-therapy tends to intoxicate or anesthetize the cerebral cortex. This state renders the patient more sensitive to histamine—as well as to his own feelings.

**Tetany.** If hyperventilation is persisted, the sensations of tingling sometimes transform themselves into actual tetanies. At first the patient may merely remark that he feels rather stiff and tense. But as one watches without interfering with the process, the hands stiffen up so that carpal as well as pedal rigidity is apparent and a full-blown tetany has occurred. These events are found as the normal sequelae of cerebral anoxia. "Tetany varies from a slight stiffness of the muscles to well-marked contractures," observe Best and Taylor. "In the hand the most common attitude is ulnar flexion with relative extension of the radial side and some flexion of the wrists." (1) This, incidentally, has been specifically noted by Meduna in relation to his carbon dioxide therapy. Any shift of the blood pH produces similar affects.

Best and Taylor further state: "Tetany in the face can often be detected at a distance by a peculiar appearance of the eyes associated with a contraction of the surrounding muscles, particularly the inner part of the under lid. The involvement of deeper muscles can be brought out in the alterations of speech; occasionally, the orbicular muscles of the mouth are considerably affected. A few subjects will note particular contractions of the abdominal muscles and in the legs." The reference to contractions of the abdominal muscles is particularly significant since, when these occur, they give evidence to the falling anxiety and later they herald the onset of the orgasm reflex. Specific knowledge on the part of the therapist based upon personal experience is requisite here in order to facilitate the reflex.

Non-verbal therapy encourages these tetanic responses. They represent the breakthrough of diencephalic impulses temporarily liberated from chronic cortical inhibition. *Everything is directed to inducing loss of control. This is the* sine qua non *of therapy. And of course this loss of neurotic composure is what patients fear most.*

Apprehensively, some believe that if they do lose control, they will "fly to pieces," "be shattered into a thousand fragments," or "go stark raving mad."

These muscular automatisms are so important in my opinion that they should not be lightly glossed over. They are fairly common and are manifold. Their variety is almost limitless. There is a large percentage of patients who, as a direct sequel of hyperventilation, develop some strange oral symptoms in the course of a session. For example, not only may tetany of the hands, arms and legs occur as already indicated above, but the patient may gradually become aware of:

a. A slowly developing dryness of the mouth and lips.
b. Some tingling of the roof and floor of the palate, tongue and lips.
c. A gradual stiffening of the whole labial area.
d. Complete tetany of the mouth with grotesquely protruding lips.
e. Inability to speak coherently.

Since these symptoms occur gradually, the patient may be inclined momentarily to discount their significance. They crystallize slowly out of vague physical sensations which at first he ignores. He may consider the buccal dryness as *nothing but* the sequel of breathing with the open mouth. As time proceeds, and the full peri-oral phase of tetany sets in, a great deal of alarm thereupon arises. He may need some considerable reassuring in order to proceed still further, especially when he finds his mouth and tongue so stiff and paralyzed that he can speak with but difficulty. Before the speech becomes completely incoherent, some will express great fears of impending paralysis in the mouth, arms or legs. Others who have heard of cerebral vascular incidents will begin to worry about the possibility of a stroke. For the sake of reassurance he need only know that these phenomena dissipate within a few minutes or before the hour's session is concluded.

Reich's theorem here is that free plasmatic pulsation has in the past become arrested by an armored block in the buccal area. This latter is now being heavily charged with atmospheric orgone as part of the attack on the armor. And it is the concentration of the orgone here which will break down the muscular blockage. If one observes carefully, it almost appears *as if* this investiture of the mouth with energy, which purses it up and puckers it, is akin to the action of the mouth when sucking or crying. This kind of response probably occurs in those patients for whom crying is difficult, if not impossible. No matter how they are aided in other ways, there is a tremendous reluctance to weep. "Keep a stiff upper lip," the saying goes. As the tetany attacks the mouth area, again and again, session after session, the mouth loses its rigidity and becomes mobile and free once more. The emotional release of crying may then become a distinct possibility.

Freeing the vegetative excitation from its fixation in the muscular tensions of the head, neck, throat, etc., is the indispensable prerequisite of dissolving oral fixations in general. Neither the recollection of oral experiences nor the discussion of genital anxiety can take its place. This is the characteristic Reichian viewpoint. Without it, memory might be obtained, but not the corresponding excitations. These are usually concealed in unobtrusive types of behavior which seem to be natural to the patient. The mechanisms of the displacements and fixations of the vegetative energies may be hidden in the following: a weak voice, little movement of the mouth in talking, a slightly mask-like facial expression, a facial expression resembling a suckling infant, an unobtrusive wrinkling of the forehead, drooping eyelids, a tension in the scalp, a latent hypersensitivity of the larynx, a hasty jerky way of talking, seemingly incidental sounds or movements in talking, a certain way of holding the head to one side, of shaking it, etc. Fear of genital contact does not make its appearance as long as these symptoms in the head and neck regions have not been uncovered and eliminated.

Some psychoanalytical concepts, together with the terms of neurology, help to make these phenomena more intelligible as part of the necessary process of therapy. Analysts speak of an oral phase of genetic development when the mouth was an important sensory and erotic organ. Whether due to fear, frustration or other motives throughout the years, the mouth for some people remains emotionally an important part of their personalities. It has become heavily cathected with libido. That they are not aware of this fixation and its importance to them is of no significance at this time. As a result of vegeto-therapy, with its partial and temporary elimination of cortical inhibition, the mouth breaks loose from the previous cortical control. It is now able to "work through" the energy fixation which occurred many years earlier as a result of direct stimulation from its cerebral projection area.

Justification of this viewpoint is found in a detailed discussion by Cobb. He considers the behavior of some experimentally decorticated animals reported by Bard, Ransom, Fulton, etc. In many instances these animals, whose motor behavior was released by ablation of some cerebral structures, indulged in the most curious kind of behavior—all of which we can summarize by one word—oral! The following is a sample of their description of the oral behavior of a partially decorticated cat:

> "She had excessive licking movements... She would begin to lick her fur if stroked. Almost any object with which she came in contact would be licked: the floor, her paw, another cat... When licking a dish, if the rim came in between her teeth, she would bit it viciously... For two periods of about a week each, she was very irritable and reacted to striking and handling with explosions of rage—biting, scratching, hissing and crying out... Before autopsy, stimulation experiments were carried out and it was found that electrical stimulation of the anterior commissure cause movements related to smelling and eating. The animal puckered up her nose, moved her vibrissae and made licking and chewing movements." (4)

This seems to indicate that a specific sub-cortical area of the cerebrum is involved in the oral and other behavior of the decorticated cats as well as the patients undergoing non-verbal psychotherapy. Many experimental evidences are at hand to corroborate the general terms of this thesis—*that hyperventilation intoxicates the cortex, dissociating from its former rigid control the visceral brain and all the somatic areas they serve.* These latter, though subtly affecting the cortex, are very largely blocked by it in their multiform activities. The therapy temporarily lifts the block.

To return, however, to the discussion of the heightened tonicity induced by hyperventilation, it has already been noted that some patients develop rigidities and stiffness in the arms and hands.

Generally speaking no pain is experienced as the patient gradually becomes aware of the whole arm from finger to shoulder developing a rigidity as though *rigor mortis* had set in. Once in a while, however, there will be discomfort and ache accompanying this phenomenon. Then the therapist must attempt to dissolve the rigidity by manipulating the arm—bending it at the shoulder, elbow and wrist again and again, trying to work free the immobilized joints. It may take many minutes to do this. If there is a marked degree of spasticity and rigidity in the limb, with perceptible cyanosis and blanching, and if the pain is of such severity that the patient can hardly tolerate even the gentle manipulation required to loosen up the tonic area, I have found that placing a brown paper bag on the patient's head, enabling him to breathe back some of his own carbon dioxide, achieves relaxation.

The tetany induced by hyperventilation is due to the increased pH of the blood, brought about by blowing off carbon dioxide in the forced respiration. Therefore the administration of a few inhalations of carbon dioxide from the paper bag reverses the blood pH. Then the acute and severe stage of the tetany is enormously relieved and, after a short rest or respite from his therapeutic labors, the patient can proceed with whatever other phases of the work are called for.

Altogether apart from moving the limb or muscle or the use of the brown bag to terminate a painful tetanic episode, the conventional vegeto-therapeutic thesis must not be overlooked. Abreaction will terminate the tetany rapidly. A few sharp pinches of the sternocleidomastoid or the trapezium will induce enough response to provoke screaming with anger and pounding the couch with fists or feet. Under these circumstances there is free bodily movement, induced by massive sympathetico-adrenal discharge. Work on the thigh adductors or the sharp tap on the epigastrium will accomplish the same end. In other words, there is no cause for alarm when the patient complains of the pain produced by tetany. It is self-terminating if the therapy that induced it is also used to bring it to a close. Some corroboration is implicit here that rigidity is frozen emotion. Release the emotion and the frozen stiffness disappears.

When the muscular hypertonus finally subsides by one device or another, a profound state of muscular relaxation ensues. If the patient can be persuaded to tolerate the tension and is encouraged to overbreathe for just a little longer, as a rule the homeostatic mechanisms return to operation and the tetany spontaneously disappears. Within a few minutes, proprioceptive and somesthetic perceptions are clearly realized in that area. Sensations of energy streaming and pulsation are vividly experienced as enlivening the entire area that only recently felt stiff and dead.

The legs also commonly become tetanic. Occasionally the stiffening seems to start slowly and imperceptibly at the knees, spreading upwards along the medial aspects of the thighs to the pelvis and downwards to the ankles and feet. Regardless of the physiological mechanisms operating, there is no doubt that one of the psychological factors producing this situation is a profound fear of the fine tremor which has been felt in that area. If sexual energies have been bound up in the thighs and pelvis, the shaking and tetany will force relaxation of the inhibition and so release the feared sexual impulses. Not much of this may be immediately recognized by the patient, but after the area has relaxed and sexuality released, this explanation may be spontaneously offered by the patient. He will feel vegetative excitations rising from the pelvis in the form of tingling, prickling, surgings of energy and pulsations.

Some of the gestures are intended deliberately to facilitate this discharge. Having patients drop their knees to the side during exhalation and bring them back to the center with inhalation often helps. As the thighs stiffen up, I will often gently push one thigh, that nearest me. Again and again I will push, at intervals of a few seconds, continuing this for as long as five minutes, until eventually myoclonisms arise. When they do, the termination of the tetany is in sight. Before this occurs the patient may have worked himself into a violent state of anger. "Stop pushing me around!" Kicking will discharge the anger satisfactorily.

Less commonly the chest becomes involved. But when it does, it presents symptoms comparable to the tight hysterical band around the chest or head or elsewhere experienced by some conversion and anxiety patients. Sometimes it is perceived as a heavy weight pressing down on the chest, making respiration tedious at best and difficult at worst. Some anxiety, of course, is elicited by these events. It is as though after hyperventilation has progressed, the patient becomes significantly aware of what perhaps had been existing for many years, the massive armored tension in that area. Prior to this moment, it is possible he was quite unconscious of the armoring. The hyperventilation tetany impresses one true state of events upon his awareness. He sees what armoring really means. This realization is arrived at without the therapist's verbal intervention or interpretation. All of this is in accord with one of Reich's fundamental dictums—*intensify the inhibiting tensions first of all.*

At times the rigidity attacks the facial muscles. A common expression of patients in attempting to describe this kind of tetany is that "if I smiled or so much as moved a single muscle on my face, it would crack." "It feels stiff and dead and numb and expressionless." "Gosh, I never knew I had such a poker face!"

The muscular automatisms and fibrillations occurring during the vegeto-therapeutic session could readily be interpreted by the psychoanalyst as somatizations of repressed libidinal urges. He might say that they are hysterical manifestations of infantile sexual feelings; that, in effect, they are substitutive auto-erotic outlets or expressions of genital and pre-genital impulses that long ago had been blocked off and have been displaced from the genital or intestinal area upwards or from the mouth downwards, as the case may be; and that viscera, extremities and muscle groups have become thus libidinized; that all these phenomena above-described are among other things only masturbatory, anal and oral phenomena arising as the patient's automatic inhibitory apparatus becomes challenged by hyperventilation and becomes actually impaired.

I see no reason to quibble about these possible interpretations. The virtue of this particular non-verbal approach is that, as a rule, no such interpretation is required to facilitate the patient's progress in therapy. On occasion I have found a particularly sensitive or sophisticated patient offering such an interpretation purely spontaneously.

Generally speaking, though, this type of interpretation is needless because, with the discharge of tension in these particular ways, the repressed impulses become dissipated entirely. As the somatic and visceral group of tensions become dissolved or fragmented by the active vegeto-therapeutic attack, the impulses themselves are expressed, worked through and relinquished. Any interpretation thus becomes totally unnecessary—save only in a rare and isolated instance where, perhaps, the patient may deliberately invite discussion of the significance of this particular method of dissolving tensions. More often than not, insights develop spontaneously with the patient.

Reich's notion that *rigidity is frozen emotion* is thus perceived to be not merely a clever turn of a phrase. It corresponds to a biological actuality. It may also throw a good deal of light, for example, on the *flexibilitas cerea* of catatonia. The frequency of these tetanic responses during the sessions are the index to the severity of emotional repression and the fixation of vegetative energies in chronic muscular tensions. In other words, tetanies occur frequently in certain types of highly compulsive patients. Session after session is experienced in which these rigidities become the most outstanding and repetitive phenomenon. These are the particularly rigid personalities who compulsively live without apparently any kind of emotional expression. Instead of feelings, they have symptoms only—hypochondrias. Given some limited ability to express their inner-most feelings, these patients gradually exhibit less and less of the tetanic responses to hyperventilation.

Braatøy appears to have been familiar with similar couch phenomena. I am not aware that they have been noted and reported by other analysts. Braatøy notes that

> "Instead of emotional thunder, one may observe 'lightning', or what the patients themselves describe as something resembling electric shock. One sees sudden isolated clonic seizures comprising part of the body or the whole body. Sometimes such a fit is so violent that the patient gets frustrated and cautious in relation to the treatment... *The clonic fit is the expression of a dilemma."* (3) (italics mine)

What Braatøy calls the dilemma is the result of the classically described conflict between the restricting armor and the dynamic drives of the organism. Anxiety is the inevitable outcome of conflict. But the affect-lame patient is often scotomized to the existence of anxiety; previously his compulsive behavior provided an exit or substitute for the anxiety. Under the specific circumstances of therapy, the myoclonism becomes the hysterical somatization or, better yet, physiological outlet for the anxiety generated by the conflict.

When the clonisms and tetanies first set in around the pelvis or the shoulder girdle, slowly at first to be sure, the anxiety becomes so pronounced that breathing is disturbed. It becomes jerky and irregular and the exhalations are far from adequate. It is as if the patient senses trouble afoot. He concentrates involuntarily on the muscular automatisms, apparently with the intent of controlling them, of suppressing this kind of activity. This is the moment when the incipiently schizophrenic patient begins to withdraw frantically. Attention should be redirected to the respiratory process, the patient being asked and *aided* to exhale thoroughly. Merely to ask the patient to verbalize his sensations and his feelings may release enough tension to permit the resumption of trembling and the shaking off of considerable tension. Once the patient realizes by experience that he comes to no harm through these muscular activities, and again by experience of his subsequent freedom from muscular tension, he is no longer bothered, giving to the entire process his undivided attention and energy.

The mortality rate in therapy reaches a higher peak at this juncture. A small percentage may quit therapy when these relatively strange phenomena occur. Termination of therapy may also be threatened when the therapist employs the tap on the stomach to break up a cycle of tension or to end an episode of withdrawal. When either of these stages is reached, it is appropriate to cease active work of the vegeto-therapeutic type. It is far better to employ counseling and analysis on a verbal level. In this way the transference can be maintained and the patient kept in therapy long enough to relieve the massive anxiety released by hyperventilation. Once the patient can be brought to some understanding of the dynamic process he is experiencing, then and then only can he be returned to more active work. Vegeto-therapy must be fitted into a broad psychotherapeutic frame of reference to increase its efficacy and to reduce the percentage of these who fearfully leave therapy for some other approach.

A final word about these motor phenomena: they are very powerful. It could be presumed that my description of them remains solely within the literary area of figures of speech. Such, however, is far from the truth. So very real are they that most vegeto-therapists are eternally on guard during sessions with patients who suffer from coronary obstruction and other cardiopathies, bronchial asthma, gastric ulcers[1] and the like. It does not require much imaginative effort to speculate upon what would occur if a patient with latent coronary disease were suddenly to go into spasm. The whole thorax and abdominal area may become rigid and stiff, respiration may become difficult and cyanosis may be observed with the appearance of a cold clammy perspiration. The radial pulse feels rapid and bounding—which would not bode well for a hypertensive patient, for example.

In the event of a strong spasm occurring with a gastric patient, the ulcer could perforate, causing hemorrhage into the belly cavity with the possibility of peritonitis setting in later. With forced respiration, the spastic bronchial tree in the asthmatic patient may become even more spastic, rendering breathing practically impossible. For such patients I keep a nebulizer handy. There are numbers of predicaments possible in therapy—and all spell danger.

Therefore, with such patients, every attempt is made to prevent severe tetany in the first place. But if it does occur, steps must be taken to break into the tonic spasm at the first opportunity so that it does not persist for more than a few seconds. Methods usually followed are actively to shock the patient's vegetative chain of plexuses in order to release the spasm. A light tap to the epigastrium will often prove so extensive a neural shock that the patient, with pained surprise and fear, will scream loudly, double up like a ball and perhaps break down and cry. In the event that this occurs, there is little further to fear from the spasm. Should this eventuality be tardy in arising, the therapist may urge the patient to gag to release the tension. If the patient is too slow, or his hands too spastic, the therapist may push his own fingers into the patient's mouth, back of the uvula, and attempt to induce regurgitation. While this measure might strain the potential cardiac patient, it is far less of a strain than the rigidity of thoracic spasm and usually eliminates the latter.

In this connection it should be evident that self-therapy is completely impossible. Anyone rash enough to experiment in any prolonged, compulsive way with hyperventilation and the motor atti-

---

[1] At the time this was written, gastric (peptic) ulcers were believed to be caused by stress and spicy foods. This is now known to be incorrect. [Ed.]

tudes is obviously going to encounter serious trouble. There is not only the remote possibility of the emergence of repressed affects. This alone would be enough to panic the foolhardy novice. There is always the chance that schizoid withdrawals may occur and with these the unattended experimenter would hardly be in a situation to cope. The tonic spasms eventuating in tetany should be enough to dissuade anyone from non-supervised experiment. These methods should be left severely alone and never used save in the presence of a trained and experienced therapist. However, there need be little fear that many will so experiment alone. Patience and perseverance, while making a "bishop of his reverence," are rarely found in most patients. And these are the character traits supremely required for auto-therapy.

## BIBLIOGRAPHY

1. Best, C.E. and Taylor, N.B. *The Physiological Basis of Medical Practise.* Baltimore, Williams & Wilkins, 1950. p. 414.

2. Being, Robert and Haymaker, Webb. *Textbook of Nervous Diseases.* St. Louis, Mosby Co., 1939. p. 661.

3. Braatøy, Trygve. *Fundamentals of Psychoanalytic Technique.* New York, John Wiley, 1954. p. 185

4. Cobb, Stanley. *Emotions and Clinical Medicine.* New York, Norton Co., 1950. p. 78–79.

5. Fenn, W.O. *et al.* "Physiological Observations on Hyperventilation," *Jnl. Applied Phys.* I; 11, May 1949, p. 773.

6. Gibbs, Frederick A. "Value of Electroencephalography," *Modern Medicine,* July 15, 1954. p. 75.

7. Lewis, Bernard I. "The Hyperventilation Syndrome," *Annals of Internal Medicine.* 38: 918–927, 1953.

8. Montagu, M.F. Ashley. *Anthropology and Human Nature.* Boston, Porter Sargent, 1957. p. 211–212.

9. Stekel, Wilhelm. *Conditions of Nervous Anxiety and Their Treatment.* London, Kegan Paul, 1933, p. 357.

# Chapter VII

## Abreaction

"Recollection of memories without affect is without effect."
— Sigmund Freud

Some important historical factors might help to understand the nature of the problem now under consideration. Freud's early successes, after he had discarded hypnotism and employed free association, were in the specific realm of the hysterias. It is now recognized that abreaction is relatively easy to procure in the hysterias. And "cure" is dependent upon abreaction of traumatic emotional experiences. As time proceeded, Freud and the other analysts encountered problem cases outside of the hysterias. These were the so-called obsessive-compulsive cases, for example, who are notoriously affect-lame and therefore highly resistant to abreaction.

With the methods then currently employed, it was no simple matter to procure adequate abreactions. In the stage of the "transference neurosis"—which Franz Alexander termed the fourth phase of Freud's developmental process—it was discovered that the transference was the most powerful instrument yet found for overcoming the patient's resistance to facing disturbing emotional experiences. The handling of transference manifestations and the patient's resistance gradually became the center of the therapeutic process.

A few therapists such as Ferenczi, Rank, Stekel and Groddeck experimented with active methods, the aim being to evoke anxiety and other emotional reactions in heavily armored cases. These experiments were not too successful. Most of the recorded analyses of these cases, despite the creaking transference machinery, evolved on purely verbal and conceptual levels. Some symptomatic improvement was certainly achieved. But so far as ultimate personality restructuring is concerned, it seems that very little was accomplished.

According to Franz Alexander, almost two decades elapsed before psychoanalysis emancipated itself from the earlier technical formulations to be transformed into a procedure aimed at strengthening the ego sufficiently to cope with its affective problems. It was comparable more to an educational process than to the original therapeutic scheme envisaged by Freud. Sessions with the analyst came to be considered as catalytic agents, speeding up and making possible new relationships and experiences. (1) The phrase "corrective emotional experience" arose then and had a wide currency.

While there need be little quarrel with this viewpoint, from the vantage point provided by the passage of time and by familiarity with other methods, it is clear that these historical stages of psychoanalysis developed entirely as a matter of strict necessity. They developed out of the frustrating impasse experience by psychoanalysts when the admittedly important abreaction phenomena failed to occur with most compulsive patients. Their character-muscular armor was discovered to be so thoroughly organized as to render them impervious to any breakthrough of their own repressed feelings—outside of the secondary neurotic patterns already established. As I review the situation now, only Reich has satisfactorily solved this particular technical problem by his vegeto-therapy. It is a highly effective approach, eliminating the impasse previously experience by the analysts.

\*\*\*

Before attempting an elucidation of a few of the dynamic processes leading to abreaction, it might be well to detail a case at some length, since it amply demonstrates phases of this discussion.

Bob, one of the muscular types previously mentioned, is about 32 years of age. He is a powerfully built, heavy-shouldered man, with strong chest muscles developed through long workouts with weights and barbells. At first sight his history was but mildly significant. Some features stood out with stark meaning only after many therapeutic sessions. His parents separated shortly after his birth and his life was uneventful until eighteen months of age when he was kidnapped by his father who then left the Midwest and established residence in Florida. While father worked, Bob was looked after by some hired help. Meanwhile, from Kansas City his mother searched high and low for him, police and private social agencies cooperating. It was only two years later that he was found and returned to his mother.

The great depression arrived and the mother obtained some minor employment though the WPA. These were hard times for people of no financial resources. Periodically mother would get a job doing domestic work. There were times when the Salvation Army and other welfare agencies gave them baskets of food, clothes and other forms of assistance. Once in a while Bob would be asked to call at the center for a basket. He began to suffer humiliation and shame lest his friends and neighbors learn that they had fallen on such hard times.

He had gradually become a chronic bed-wetter. This behavior problem led to consultation after consultation with doctors but without alleviation. His mother nagged and reprimanded him, advertising his problem to the whole neighborhood by hanging his wet bedsheets and pajamas on the line for all to see. He suffered from enuresis until he was 16 years old when sporadic experiments with masturbation "cured" him. But the shame and possible ridicule related to bed-wetting was now replaced by the greater guilt of sex. He became quiet, shy and reclusive. Physically he was underweight and puny. Both of these factors kept him apart from his school fellows so that profound depressions set in. In late adolescence he became so ashamed of his asthenic condition and so fearful of humiliation from others because of it that he was persuaded to embark on a program of physical culture. He enrolled in a gymnasium and after a period of intense and active work developed a magnificent physique.

He knew nothing about girls; his inferiority and guilt feelings had kept him altogether apart from them. His only companion was his mother. Books and an occasional movie with her were his only recreation. In his early lonely twenties he recalls getting off a street car one evening just behind a girl whom he eyed longingly—less with notions of sex, apparently, than with some desire for companionship. He followed her to a nearby movie house, sat near her, but could not utter one word or make one gesture that might elicit any friendliness from her.

That night a curious excitement seized him. He could not sleep. His heart pounded so furiously against his ribs that he became alarmed. His mother telephoned for a local physician. A sedative was prescribed which gave him temporary surcease. Physical examination over several days followed, with suspicions being cast on the integrity of his heart. Just at this time he was also called for physical examination by his draft board. He was rejected as unfit for military service, some cardiac pathology being suspected. From this moment forward, even though no concrete diagnostic term had yet been employed, he became subject to spells of inner excitation which rocked the heart into furious activity. These would subside partially, but every now and again, subject to job and other environmental stimulation, they would flair up again.

Meantime, a fellow designer at the shop where he was employed introduced him to a girl, and as might be expected, he fell in love forthwith and with in a few months they were married. It was shortly after his marriage and his wife's pregnancy that he was referred to me for therapy. He spoke flatteringly, as though eternally watching his words, fearful lest something might emerge for which he could be reprimanded. Even after thirty-odd sessions there was always the long drawn out "ah-ah" between phrases and sentences. His heart condition worried him as he narrated the frustrations of those many long, bitter and lean years. But never was there any real venting of emotion.

Interspersed with the verbal sessions were frequent non-verbal active sessions. It was then that inspection revealed his massive muscular frame, sharply pointing to his early shame and inferiority over a puny physique. His whole body was tense. There was hardly a segment even partially free of chronic neuromuscular tension. His head was tilted leftwards on the cervical spine and his right sternocleidomastoid was spastic, thick and hypertrophied. It was a wonder that he had not developed a torticollis.

Five minutes of hyperventilation in the first active session induced a few chuckles which soon enlarged into a hysterical laughter. It persisted throughout the whole hour. The next few sessions were similarly characterized until the laughter was played out. Then, as he began to relax somewhat, vegetative excitations began to arise in his face, puckering the lips—curiously like a baby sucking a bottle.

This was the way therapy continued for a long while. He achieved some slight relief of emotional tension and became no longer subject to the excitatory spells within. Symptomatically he improved somewhat though actually there was no marked softening of the chest or belly wall. Finally I instructed him to gag every morning upon arising, having previously instructed him how to do so—exhaling constantly, never holding the breath and always with sound. After about ten days of this procedure, he telephoned me between sessions, complaining of some spontaneous nausea during the working hours of the day, some diarrhea and occasional, but brief, bouts of dizziness. He suspected infection, some intestinal influenza being current about this time. However, his physician had discounted this in the absence of fever so I had him come for a session within twenty-four hours.

As he hyperventilated, the diaphragm was found to be spastic and respiration was far from free. After about ten minutes, we started to work in earnest on the diaphragm, forcing it loose to his loud shouts. Within a few more minutes he began to sob gently. In a short time thereafter he was crying deeply so that the belly was convulsed.

Now at this time it would have been easy to have speculated over the contents of his fantasy preoccupations. I actually essayed the guess that the weeping related to his bitterness when his mother humiliated him about the bedwetting, or to his adolescent loneliness, or to his masturbation shame in the gymnasium where he saw so many other young men with such splendid physiques. Guilts about oedipal fantasies about his mother could also have been involved. But no! When he was finally able to mutter a few broken words between the gusts of sobs, he confessed to crying over his utter desolation and loneliness when he had been kidnapped and found himself away from his mother, cared for by people about whom he knew nothing and who patently cared nothing for him. It is in such ways that insight spontaneously arises. It concerns factors that might not readily occur to the therapist who, with a psychoanalytical background, would suspect a thousand things, but hardly this.

I found this an exciting and stimulating experience. From it I learned to be less prone to arbitrary interpretations, and to rely implicitly on the patient's own biological soundness once the armor had been penetrated. I now have a tremendous respect for tears and the value of crying during the therapeutic session, regardless of what the means employed to engineer them may be. It is also interesting that the patient bore no bitterness nor hostility to the therapist for the very real pain he had suffered in the process of being made to cry. There was only gratitude in that he was finally able to cry, and an all-encompassing wonder that this kidnapping about which he only been told by his mother and about which he could talk to me had engendered such an emotional upheaval that the imprints of it had endured to this day.

Insight occurs in just such ways. With adequate abreaction, memories arise spontaneously, requiring no prompting. When they do arise, they are the important ones which have been well hidden behind massive defensive barriers on both the psychic and muscular levels.

\*\*\*

**Gagging.** The device for releasing these repressed feelings are multiform. Overbreathing to produce the temporary hyperventilation syndrome has precedence over all the others; the other devices are wholly dependent upon this for their efficacy. Some of the more heroic measures must also be employed. The softening of the abdomen, including the more or less firm tap on the epigastrium, is certainly evocative of considerable affect. For the patient who cannot or will not permit himself the luxury of tears, regardless of the elaborate rationalization he employs, gagging becomes one of the most effectual means. Curiously enough, after the tears have subsided, the patient feels only love and warmth and gratitude toward the therapist instead of the anticipated anger and hate for the hurt experienced by the "punch in the solar plexus," together with the realization that only so could the patient have been brought to the overt manifestation of his feelings.

In the case quoted above, gagging was deliberately induced. In other cases the patient may cough and splutter without external provocation and appear on the verge of nausea. This is particularly true when he is asked to breathe with the tongue protruding. The nausea may be due in part to aerophagia. The more likely explanation is the diaphragmatic relaxation resulting from overbreathing. Occasionally a patient appears whose throat, chest and belly do not undergo relaxation by means of overbreathing nor probing into the belly muscles. Under these circumstances, the initiation of the gag reflex usually precipitates some outpouring of vigorous affects followed by the relaxation of the throat and diaphragm. Frequently the relaxation comes first and the discharge of affects later.

In the majority of cases, gagging has to be taught as a deliberate technique in the office where the therapist can watch and correct. Hyperventilation spontaneously provokes a feeling of nausea in a few patients. When a patient is first asked to gag, he tends to hold his breath while poking the index finger into the back of the mouth. This should be avoided. He should be taught to exhale at all times—and then exhale still more. He should be encouraged to help the gag reflex by deliberately simulating a scream while poking his finger down the throat. This can be done with the patient sitting upright, holding the emesis basin between his knees. Female patients with long, sharp nails may use a tongue depressor, but the fingers are to be preferred. I need hardly mention that a supply of paper towels or facial tissues should be available always, for tears—if not actual crying—are almost invariably an accompaniment of gagging.

The therapist should watch the muscular movements involved in the process of gagging. They can be best observed while the patient is reclining with knees raised and feet placed apart, not too far from the buttocks. When he gags in this position to induce a powerful gag reflex that might eventuate in emptying the contents of the stomach, the shoulders are thrust downward and forward, the chest tends to flatten out, the belly is pushed out and the pelvis automatically rises. In many ways, the physiological reactions of gagging, crying, laughing, coughing and the orgastic reflex are extraordinarily similar. All these processes change the style of breathing extraordinarily, and induce natural breathing. There are quite prosaic neurological rationales for this effect. In the first place Gillilan notes that "this (medullary) respiratory center coordinates the rhythmic contraction of the intercostal muscles, the diaphragm, and the laryngotracteal muscles." (3) Much later he adds that "vomiting is under normal conditions a reflex serving to rid the stomach of its contents effectively and quickly and to prevent these contents from passing into the lower intestinal tract. There is a vomiting center in the medulla oblongata very close to the respiratory centers located in the medial reticular nucleus... Changes in respiration are concomitant with vomiting, so that the two centers are closely allied." (4)

To watch these physiological reactions yields highly valuable information to the therapist. But it should never be forgotten that nothing can replace personal experience with vegeto-therapy with a competent and well-trained therapist. This is invaluable and is the *sine qua non* of using the therapy.

Before attempting to teach the patient the technique of gagging, it is better procedure to wait for some evidence of nausea and spontaneous retching. Altogether apart from the involuntary gagging that arises as the armored blocks are being dissolved, there are three other specific methods for inducing the gag reflex.

First, the patient should breathe as usual but with the tongue pointing outwards vigorously. This is fairly effective with some patients. Incidentally, it also releases the tight block in the back of the throat and neck. Patients who complain of suboccipital headaches and a stiff neck may find rapid relief through this measure.

Second, screaming loudly and shrilly, with a high falsetto, may provoke coughing and gagging in the patient with the rigid throat and neck. It can and should be alternated with shouting in as deep a voice as possible, while pushing the belly out with force.

Third, fold a small turkish towel and ask the patient to bite vigorously on a thick corner wedge. Let him clamp down hard on the wedge as though to bite through it. While biting, he must thrust the abdomen forcibly forward, pushing it out with every exhalation, while growling ferociously deep in the throat with every push. Usually only a few bite and growls suffice to induce a series of gags.

With some heavily armored and tense patients, I have occasionally recommended that every morning, as a temporary part of their matutinal toilet routine, they gag up to as many as a dozen times. They tell me—and my own observation fully corroborates their reports—that a great deal of emotional and physical tension is thus alleviated. In fact, some patients learn to use this technique in a variety of tension-producing life situations as a means of gaining relief and later, insight. The important note here is that *the need to gag occurs naturally on the couch during the treatment hour on a spontaneous level* without any coaching or prompting from the therapist. Under these circumstances the results are most outstanding.

Usually, it must be added, some resistance and hostility may be evoked at the outset by this demand for gagging. At first it seems utterly outrageous and preposterous, regardless of how nauseated the patient may feel. All of the patient's defenses rise in protest against the crudity and uncouthness of the method. It runs counter to everything most of them have lived by. However, when a brief, simplified explanation is given, or if the therapist states unequivocally that this is no time for intellectual discussion which must wait until later, the patient relaxes and complies. My procedure is to let him gag anywhere up to a dozen times, depending on the type of gag initiated.

In itself, the *style* of gagging is an admirable index to the magnitude of the inhibitory apparatus. This is highly revealing—surprisingly so. Some gag with finesse, with delicacy, without noise. Some can hardly regurgitate at all. These are, to be sure, the most difficult patients of all to handle. Their character armor is almost impenetrable and the musculature is armored and rigid to the point of petrification. They require encouragement to regurgitate with noise and *with the outgoing breath*—without concealment of their discomfort and disgust and with some fullness. Later they may come to recall much pain and embarrassment in childhood about vomiting. Others will cough and spit but still remain unproductive. Still others sneer and find the whole procedure a source of considerable amusement. Yet another group will retch with hideous completeness. Eventually a mere touch of the finger to the back of the throat results in regurgitation—with all the ease, simplicity and naturalness of a healthy, unarmored child. One sign of success is feeling the gag all the way down the gastro-intestinal tract, initiating a slight contraction in the anus. It helps to remove contractions and blocks in the throat.

It might be worthwhile here to call attention to the embryological relationship between the diaphragm and throat. Any textbook of embryology will trace the origin of the striated muscle of the diaphragm to the pair of premuscle-masses lying opposite to the fourth cervical segment of the embryo when only a few weeks old. This is the level at which the phrenic nerve enters the septum transversum. The muscle-masses migrate caudad with the septum transversum and develop in the dorsal portion of the diaphragm. Throughout life, then, it appears the close connection between the diaphragm and the throat is maintained. Chronic muscular hypertension in the one is also communicated to, or is accompanied by, tension in the other. Perhaps this is why vagal stimulation of the stomach in vomiting not only relaxes the diaphragm, but also releases the muscular block in the throat.

There is another reaction which seems extraordinary. With only an exception here and there, most people seem to experience a kind of horror or dread at the mere prospect of vomiting. No matter how "sick to the stomach" hyperventilation may make them, the obvious recourse to gagging strikes terror in them. Even the alcoholic who has often regurgitated after drinking too much liquor seems offended and disturbed by having to regurgitate in the office. The prig and the prude find themselves equally outraged. It is as if they dimly sense the emotional implicits of what is proposed.

As a pedagogic measure I have sometimes inserted my finger into my own throat to initiate the gag reflex. Once the average patient finds that I have no personal abhorrence of the gag and that nothing drastic has happened to me, he approaches the venture with less loathing and horror. The ambivalence remains, however. As their own biological structure struggles against their false moral determination to hold back, their memory may become suddenly illuminated with sharp flashes of significant reminiscences from childhood. They then recall how often they may have vomited and how easy it was to do so then, and how disturbing were the conflictual situations which precipitated their vomiting. Vivid scenes of parental squabbling pierce the darkness of their amnesia, giving clarification to the motives both for forgetting the event and for damming back the nausea.

Recollections of parental disgust at their childhood vomiting experiences also spontaneously erupt into the bright light of consciousness as they strive to follow instructions. There memories, whatever they are, are worth "working through" at considerable length. Invariably they lead to intense abreactive and integrative experiences. Tremendous emotional release is felt with astonishing flashes of understanding into current life problems with little effort on the part of the therapist.

The case of Jennie illustrates this well. For a while her gagging was wholly inadequate. It merely eventuated in useless coughing and copious spitting. She would use up almost a whole box of facial tissues after each futile attempt to gag, examining each tissue meticulously as though fully expecting to see it covered with blood. Following a truck accident many years earlier, her father had died of intra-cranial hemorrhage. Her explanation was that he had choked on his own blood.

One day, after she had been requested to sit on the edge of the couch and to try to gag, she retched a little, then turned tearfully to me asking, "Doesn't this disgust you?" She could barely believe me when, naturally, my reply was in the negative and when I reminded her, moreover, that I had asked her to do so. Memories rapidly emerged of her mother's disgust and anger with her when, as a little girl, she had regurgitated at the table during a parental scrabble in which several of the other siblings had enthusiastically participated. There was a good deal of scolding and reprimand on this score—all fully repressed until this moment.

Hitherto repressed fantasies may also erupt during the gagging attempts. For example, Jennie recalled that during a childhood bout of measles she was given an emetic. Her mother explained nothing, and certainly hers was not the gentle approach. Jennie's fantasy at the time was that mother had murderous designs upon her. The emetic was simply a potion to force Jennie to "up-chuck" her "innards" as she conceived the contents of her belly. And she was in no mood to lose her "innards" nor to be murdered by her mother.

A similar reaction occurred when she needed to scream and shout. This she fought bitterly for a long time. No matter how I dug into her epigastrium or pinched the neck muscles or moved the supra-orbital muscles up and down, she seemed determined to suffer in silence—even though on more than one occasion tears welled up in my own eyes on an empathetic basis. During one session all of this effort elicited from her a nervous query, "Don't you think I'm going crazy when I scream like this?" My only answer was to shout as loudly and as vigorously as I could several times and then to look at her quizzically. This kind of precipitation permits some very fine psychotherapy on a conceptual level. It is invariably productive of some superb pieces of insight. The value of such insight can easily be judged by the continued progress of the patient in dealing with anxieties and fears as they arise.

\*\*\*

Reich's contribution may not have appeared too valuable at first sight. A little reflection on the freeing of the throat and belly blocks and the diaphragmatic spasms that occur through gagging may perhaps yield more understanding and appreciation. During hyperventilation patients become acutely conscious of the diaphragm, no longer as a name for something in the anatomy texts which they are supposed to possess, but as a definite reality. A tense diaphragm may be symbolically considered as the somatic vice-regent of the inhibiting superego. The locus of repression, the unconscious realm where repressed emotions and ideas are supposed to be stored, may in this sense be considered the lower belly, in the vast sub-diaphragmatic spaces, dark and unknown.

In one of his essays George Groddeck has some remarks which should not be overlooked by the enterprising therapist. The wise author of *The Book of the It* and *Exploring the Unconscious* was clearly a man of tremendous insight and understanding, and some of his observations are shrewd and penetrating. Discussing schizophrenia, he remarked that the word itself indicates that between chest and belly there is erected a muscular barrier which regulates their relationship. He suggests, then, that the locus of the dissociation in schizophrenia is not really the brain but the diaphragm, that it is not dissociation in the processes of thought which is involved, but dissociation of the goals of head and chest from the aims of the abdomen. Secondly, he maintains, that such a schism takes place daily and hourly in every man, that it is intrinsically a normal process which, like all such processes, may lead however to diseased conditions when the psychosomatic defenses are used excessively.

The intra-psychic conflicts are clearly indicated in sickness. In order to hinder the invasion of the breast and the head by offensive impulses from the nether regions, the boundary walls of the diaphragm are first employed and then the walls and organs in the dome. The patient struggles to block off the forbidden impulses by a temporary, or even by a chronic, tension of the muscles of the diaphragm and the space above the navel, as well as by blowing out the abdomen with air-pockets, and in this way tries to prevent them from getting command of the voice of the chest or the wisdom of the head. Constraint and anxiety are invariably felt as sensations in the region of the diaphragm and chest (thus, precordial anxiety). That is where "wind" or gas often gathers. (5)

I would like to comment parenthetically that this allusion to "wind" is no mere symbolic statement. In vegeto-therapy one is sometimes confronted by clinical situations where enormous quantities of gas are generated. I recall one patient who respired heavily for some ten minutes, as per instruction, gradually to release a diaphragmatic block. From that moment forward and persisting almost to the end of the session, he belched and belched with loud gurgling eructations. Vast quantities of gas were expelled in this way. The diaphragm underwent a tremendous relaxing process until the entire abdomen was reported "alive" and tingling vigorously.

This technique succeeds, therefore, in reversing the common organismic mechanism of repression. If repression, by this symbolism, consists in damming back effects into the unconsciousness of visceral function, where the diaphragm is made to exercise an ever-vigilant watch, and if we can reverse the normal order of function, then we will by that token liberate affect. This unacceptable affect has been locked up in a stiff kind of belly armoring. This armoring can often be penetrated by initiating the gag reflex, especially when the nausea develops spontaneously, as it often does.

A description of how the gag reflex and some of the related methods can be used may be found in the following case history.

Loretta, 25 years of age, is a thin passive-feminine person with anorexia nervosa. Her case bears some decided resemblance to those reported and described by Cobb. (2) When she was brought to me after much fruitless treatment, it transpired that her husband had seriously thought she was insane. He had threatened to commit her to a mental hospital. There had been a couple of consultations with a psychiatrist. Rorschach tests had revealed no psychosis but a severely crippling neurotic state. It was her husband's threat to commit her that made her flee to her parental home with her little son.

The first three or four sessions were devoted to the usual information gathering. She was born in a large eastern city. When she was about one year of age, her parents moved to Kansas where they worked a farm for 12 years. She had a sister 7 years her junior of whom she was very jealous. During therapy, dreams revealed death wishes about this sister and her mother. There was a brother 12 years younger of whom she was very fond. She had the usual childhood diseases. Her mother informed me that Loretta was always nervous as a child and though she had had a good appetite, she was always somewhat puny and thin. On the farm she rode everything—horses, ponies and cattle. Nocturnal enuresis continued until she was 13 years old. Later dreams related the enuresis to suppressed sexual feelings about her father.

There was a young uncle to whom she became very attached. A cowboy in the traditional style of the West, he was slow, easy-going, mild-mannered and wore his tight Levis in a very attractive way. To this day she loves cowboy music and could dance forever to its strains.

Her school history was uneventful. Her ability was merely average and she made no attempt to work hard to improve the quality of her school work. Oral reports in the classroom terrified her so that she would shrink from attempting them or even attending school on those days when such reports might be expected. Around 13 years of age she began to date and did some heavy necking and petting, but there were no full-fledged sexual experiences until later in high school. It was then that one of her major symptoms developed. She learned to dance. From then onwards this is all she ever wanted to do. In her own words she "would rather dance than eat." The more she danced, the more meager became her appetite. Every time she could slip away from her parents' vigilance, she danced—almost danced into a nervous breakdown.

Meantime, the parents moved from the farm to a large Southwestern city. More or less simultaneously, they became religious fanatics in one of the fundamentalist sects, as a result of which they began to lecture her and moralize interminably about her sinfulness, This merely increased her determination to rebel against mother's authoritarianism and religious pressure.

Upon graduation from high school, she worked for a year as a salesgirl. The dancing craze continued and with it a fascination for sailors, especially if the uniform fit tightly and snugly. It was only later, during therapy, that she realized the connection between the sailor's uniform and the tight-fitting Levis of her uncle for whom there were strong incestuous feelings.

She met a young sailor on shore leave. Within three weeks of impetuous wooing they had sexual intercourse and then precipitously eloped to Las Vegas. Her parents did not approve of the marriage, but once it had been consummated they hoped it might prove a steadying influence and put an end to her dancing jags. A child was born in the midst of many marital problems and interpersonal disharmony. Within three years she lost both her appetite and her husband, had slipped down to some 90 pounds in weight, was weak and sick and had come home ignominiously to mother. For approximately six months her food intake consisted entirely of liquids sipped slowly and with profound repugnance since she was nauseated nearly all the time. She spent most of her days in bed.

Inspection revealed severe muscular blocks in the pelvis, upper abdomen, and neck; her face presented a drawn, anxious look. The chest appeared to be fairly flexible. Hyperventilation would rapidly induce considerable chest motility and some dizziness, from which she would withdraw into an almost catatonic state. As part of her therapy she was asked to gag every morning upon arising. She objected strongly on the grounds that it was particularly then that she felt nauseated and could not tolerate the mere thought of breakfast. I still insisted on this routine and explained that she should not wait for the nausea to develop. Rapidly the muscular inhibitions to the throat loosened up, her appetite improved immeasurably and slowly she began to gain a few much-needed pounds. Though she was still fearful of expressing anger against mother, within two months after starting therapy she was able to accept a clerical job to support both herself and her child. By this means she hoped to have an apartment of her own away from her parents and so regain her own independence. Six months later she voluntarily returned to resume therapy.

\*\*\*

**Gestures.** I will admit that some patients do confess to feeling foolish and self-conscious in the assumption of many of these motor attitudes and dramatic gestures. One patient grinned at me as I demonstrated them, saying he thought the whole thing was rather silly. Soon he started to laugh heartily. Forty minutes later he was still laughing. Generally speaking, however, self-consciousness of this type implies pride and some conceit which, in turn, masks apprehension of what others may think. Such people have to be oriented to the fact that, regardless of what they feel or do, the attitude of the therapist is permissive.

The James-Lange theory[1] is of value as a theoretical means of describing what actually occurs. Though some authorities consider that it has been largely discarded in favor of the Cannon-Bard theory[2] or the newer Papez theory[3], yet under special situations of the type we are considering, it appears to be a more adequate explanation of the phenomena than any other. The James-Lange theory has it that in response to an adequate stimulus, somatic reactions first occur and then induce the emotional response within the organism. In other words, we run from danger and then experience fear. We hear bad news, cry and then feel sad, etc. In the clinical procedures described earlier, the patient dramatizes the appropriate somatic gestures and

---

[1] Proposed independently by psychologist William James and physiologist Carl Lange, that emotions occur as a result of physiological reactions to events. [Ed.]
[2] Which states that emotions and bodily changes do *not* have a causal relationship; they occur simultaneously. [Ed.]
[3] Which proposed that the circuit connecting the hypothalamus to the limbic lobe was the basis for emotional experiences. [Ed.]

experiences the emotions that he has culturally come to associate with such gestures. Motor attitudes and emotional responses have become conditioned together since early childhood. Each patient will dramatically portray an emotion on the basis of his own conditioning and childhood training. However, the reverse is also true. Emotional responses can readily be evoked by employing the motor attitudes and somatic gestures that have become intimately bound up with them from the earliest days of life.

Corroboration for this can be obtained from many spheres. Theatrical techniques as evidenced by Stanislavsky's views are a particular case in point. Again, it is curious to note that in many religions and primitive magical rites the priest is required to make certain "sacred" gestures. These are designed to evoke moods both within himself and in the spectators. Pratt, writing on the religious consciousness, has something further to add which illumines this viewpoint. He states that the outer aids of ritualistic prayer—using the bent knee, the closed eye, the clasped hands—have a decidedly helpful effect in suggesting the religious frame of mind. This is partly due to the fact that most of the prayerful adjuncts tend to focus attention, and many have been chosen quite naturally with nothing arbitrary or fortuitous about them, having developed directly from human nature and its instinctive expression. If, Pratt continues, as is the case with millions of people, the experience of kneeling, closing the eyes, and clasping the hands has from the earliest days of one's life been associated with the emotions of reverence and religious awe, it is but natural that they should continue not only to suggest, but actually to evoke these emotions when so employed. (7)

As the hyperventilated patient gradually becomes experienced in adopting the facial gestures and motor attitudes of some emotion, vehement and overwhelming affects begin to emerge quite unexpectedly—at least to the patient. He *does* become hostile. He *does* become erotic. He *does* feel tender and tearful. Infantile, grotesque and primitive words are also used to express otherwise inexpressible feelings.

I deliberately encourage the patient to abandon himself to his feelings with as much enthusiasm as possible. All intellectual restraints or neurotic controls for the time being are thoroughly relinquished as a result of hyperventilation. There are so many restraints and inhibitions imposed on us in modern life that the neurotic patient barely knows how to function without them. And this is especially true in childhood. Naturally, the only outcome is that we feel cramped. Hostility is bound to arise under the circumstances of continued frustration. It occurs not as a result of any so-called instinctual drive, but only as a by-product of prolonged frustration. Kraines stated the matter several years ago rather succinctly in these words:

> "We must learn not to cry, not to snatch, not to demand. We must sit still, speak softly, say things we don't mean, refrain from saying those we do. We must eat food we don't like—even if we do like it we must eat it in a socially prescribed way. We must wear irritating clothes, pretend interests we do not have, conceal our boredom, mask our joy, restrain our anger, sorrow or fear." (6)

It is no wonder, then, that after some little prompting the patient feels so grateful for the opportunity to legitimately express these massive quantities of affect that have been dammed back over so many years.

At times the patient is encouraged to strike the couch with both fists simultaneously while shouting. No premeditation, no planning, no thinking should be permitted. The emotional discharges that often occur are altogether remarkable. In years of practicing psychotherapy, I have never witnessed such awe-inspiring cathartic responses. The waves of rage, fear or other emotions that overwhelm the psychic defense-systems of the patient are monstrous and bizarre. *I am above all impressed by the tenderness and loving warmth patients learn to feel and to express—things they have never known before. A fundamental change in personality structure ensues.*

Most of these dramatic gestures are well worth studying objectively, as well as experiencing and feeling subjectively. Nothing takes the place of personal experience in learning. Language is a difficulty here. Were I to say that in one way or another all are provocative of the orgasm reflex, nothing new would have been added to the earlier discussions or to the initial quotation from the work of Reich. It is only as one watches the physiological and emotional effects of these gestures and somatic attitudes that their ultimate significance may be perceived. For example, gagging produces a set of muscular movements similar to that induced by the orgasm reflex. The pelvis and shoulders are both pulled up, the head is thrown backwards and the belly spasmodically sinks in. Raising one's arms during exhalation and letting the head drop backwards constitutes a subtle kind of muscular activity, relaxation and re-education which are akin to the ultimate therapeutic goal. Any motor attitude which induces an involuntary shiver or quiver is again preparatory, for quite often the orgasm reflex may begin as a well-defined chill. Slowly or quickly, as the case may be, it spreads and becomes more generalized, culminating in the quivering convulsion of orgastic release and emotional discharge.

Even more remarkable is the spontaneous recovery of previous recollections leading to the growth of insight. It is reminiscent of current psycho-analytic formulations that the recovery of memories is not the cause, but the result of therapeutic progress. The loosening of rigid personality controls which constitute the defense mechanisms, the greater inner freedom brought about by affective discharge, give the repressed and forgotten material a chance to reappear. The conventional thought and memory schemata no longer have such exclusive predominance in the mental life of the patient. Once the affect has broken through the muscular-character-armor, there is invariably an uprush, spontaneously, of memories of previously forgotten experiences. These are of the utmost significance from the analytical point of view. Experiences of early childhood days well up unbidden, as it were, experiences that reveal themselves as the powerful conditioning experiences for the lifetime. One does not have to probe nor push the patient to force the recovery of childhood experiences. As soon as these violent affects are liberated in any quantity by breaking through the character-muscular-armor, while the patient feels accepted by the therapist, the memories well up by themselves, almost explosively.

With this hypothesis it would appear, then, that the pounding of the couch, the facial and physical gestures of affective states, serve as far more effective therapeutic stimuli than merely attempting to verbalize the emotions. When these powerful emotions were first repressed in early childhood, no intellectual equipment or memory schemata existed to express these hates and anxieties and similar affects in words. Nor, by the same token, could they be impressed on the nervous system in verbal engrammes which later might be consciously and deliberately recovered. Essentially, they are non-verbal experiences. Given an outlet in some dramatic muscular action, a dynamic sympathetico-adrenal discharge of tension occurs, which appears to render possible some degree of increasing verbalization of feeling and recovery of memory on an adult level.

A great many of the technical gestures have the effect of exaggerating the already existent muscular tensions. The motive for this may not be clear at first sight though a little reflection will soon yield up the mechanisms involved. It is really in accord with Reich's instruction that part of the work of vegeto-therapy consists of intensifying the involuntary inhibitory mechanisms.

Keeping this instruction in mind, I have often found that severely hypertonic areas could be handled with some facility. When a patient tended to pull his shoulders high, I would urge him to pull them even higher—almost to his ears—and to maintain the pull once hyperventilation had been induced. While continuing with the breathing, a cramp or some ache or discomfort might set in within a very short while. Then some vigorous movements of the arms, along the lines already indicated, would usually succeed in releasing the concealed affects and permit the tense area to relax.

The pelvis is another area where this same principle may be employed. As I watched patients breathe in the "work position" on the couch, it became patent that some could not release a partial lordosis in the small of the back. In these cases, I found I could almost slip my hand between the couch and the arch in the back. Under these circumstances I would instruct them to increase the arch in the back by pushing the buttocks backwards and raising the chest. The effect of this intensification would render the long spinal muscles around the lordosis painful and hypertonic. Then I would ask patients to reverse the position by raising the pelvis somewhat, which flattened out the lordosis on the surface of the couch. They were to maintain this attitude for some minutes while continuing a specific type of respiration. When the muscular attitude began to result in ache, I would ask them to go back to the former position. These two positions were alternated several times until the tension was dissolved and the formerly arched back could be lowered easily against the couch. And when it did, affects and sexual feelings began to make their appearance.

Many other hypertonic areas can be attacked in this manner, without the active intervention of the therapist, once the patient has settled down into the routine of therapy. That is, the therapist will not have to pound, squeeze or pinch muscles into relaxation to release affects. The patient's own efforts can be intelligently utilized once some progress has been made and once the patient comes to appreciate the scope and goal of therapy. The furrows on the forehead, the perpetual smile on the face, the chronically raised chest, the contracted toes—all of these can be handled in rather the same manner. It gives the patient a great deal of self-assurance when he discovers that by following some simple directions he can further his own psychological progress. Cooperation becomes intensified under these circumstances and far more headway can be made. It is good for the patient's battered ego to learn that he can do so much himself to dissolve his own neurotic defense systems.

It may safely be said that the average patient has but little awareness of the actual reality of the muscular armor. It is true that every now and again he gets a casual glimpse of the uncomfortable fact that he is tense and unable to relax. But he apparently does not realize that he has been living for a long while in a state of chronic tension of which he was totally unaware. As a rule the armor functions in total unconsciousness. Usually the patient does not realize in the least that his abdomen is hard and spastic, that the entire back may be almost wholly rigid and stiff no matter how often he may be able to touch his toes, that the chest is eternally raised in the inspiratory attitude and cannot let go, that the powerful muscles to the side and back of the neck are in chronic spasm, or that the muscles of facial expression register but little, so mask-like have they become. Under these circumstances, considerable effort needs to be expended not to relax them at first, as might be assumed, but to bring them within the conscious purview of the patient's perceptions. The exercises and gestures, aided above all by the partial inhibition of the cerebral cortex through the agency of hyperventilation, permit the patient to become aware with astonishing immediacy of these chronic tensions, leading to the relaxing and releasing affects so ardently desired.

Actually these two phases of the therapeutic work proceed not consecutively but simultaneously. It is not that the therapist insists first that the tensions will be intensified and second that they shall be dissolved. Both stages proceed hand in glove, and are contingent one upon the other. The tonic spasms and clonisms that develop in specific somatic areas are unique, of course, for each patient, They develop in just those areas where the muscular hypertonicity has been greatest. If he has any awareness at all—and if he has but little, it must be provided by the therapist—the specific tonic spasms indicate that there must be considerable significance in why the chest and not the neck, the arms and not the legs, the forehead and not the chin, etc., are spastic and tonic. The dissolution of the chronic spasm occurs as the tetany gradually subsides during the rest periods of the sessions or during abreaction. Then the patient may become conscious of the previous tension by its absence, by the high degree of release from the muscular spasms and by the sense of increased energy and freedom. An extraordinary somesthetic sensitivity appears to develop and is usually a source of considerable astonishment to the patient.

*** 

George was about 29 when he came for therapy. Shy, inadequate and introverted, he was a short, muscular, athletic person with powerful shoulders and upper arms. His presenting problem was the inability to converse easily with people. He appeared more or less well-adjusted sexually until he expressed the fear that therapy might modify his sexual prowess. He wanted to "screw every girl in town" as his Uncle Joe had.

Poorly educated, he was able to conceptualize his problem and verbalize his life history only with difficulty. Even after long training, free association never came easily to him. There would be long pauses, lengthening into minutes. Coaching, prodding, interpreting, discussion of transference did little or nothing to facilitate this process. Even when he was made aware of the impression of fear and caution that he communicated to me, little change was realized.

Incestuous attachment to a somewhat older sister was indicated in early dreams. After the first surprise that his little secret was revealed, he came to discuss it with, for him, a degree of facility. Coupled with this was his violent rage against a widowed father, about whom he had vivid and aggressive fantasies, murder being the predominant theme. At 17 years of age, after being apprehended in a minor theft—being saved from entanglement with the law only through the good graces of his scout master—he ran away from home because he feared that he might kill his father. This fragment of history was elicited only by great effort.

Much later he narrated that his mother had died at his birth. His father, a traveling salesman, turned the boy over to an uncle and aunt for nurture. The relationship with them became so close that he called them Mom and Pop. They became parental substitutes. When he was about six his Mom became mentally ill and had to be committed. In the meantime, he recalled incidents which revealed Pop as a philanderer which Mom discovered and about which she precipitated violent scenes. In one of these a revolver was flourished and in another Mom, from an upstairs bedroom window, fired several shots at Pop out on the street. George was a witness to these violent scenes and goaded her on.

With Mom having been taken to the mental hospital, Pop felt he could not care adequately for George who was turned over to another uncle and aunt willing to act as guardians for him and his two older sisters. It was during the four years he lived here that he ran into considerable difficulty. Discipline was applied with a cruel, heavy hand. The uncle was an alcoholic. During his drunken brawls, he severely punished George for minor infractions of discipline. In this home, George developed his incestuous attachment for one of his sisters, initiated by sexual play and investigation. On several occasions he was caught red-handed by his uncle and brutally beaten.

Meantime, his real father had obtained other employment and, having settled down in a rented house, sent for his three children to come and live with him. The oldest girl, about 15 at the time, kept house for all four of them. George felt very little companionship with his father. Antagonisms and conflicts developed, heavy punishment was meted out, and a rich sadistic fantasy life ensued.

Physically, George was a mass of tensions. *As Reich has pointed out, polymorphous muscular tensions represent and, in point of fact, are physical counterparts of conditioned inhibitions.* Hypertonus was not limited to any one segment, but was extensive. The neck was thick and rigid, face dead-pan and expressionless, chest and abdomen muscle-bound, with the pelvis and legs rigid, unbending and fixated. After about a score of vegeto-therapeutic sessions, quivering and trembling would routinely set in after hyperventilation was instituted. He began to have severe anxiety attacks and vivid nightmares from which he would awaken screaming, bathed in cold sweat. Discussion of these elicited many details of his early fears, but little was opened up about his life before six. Curiously enough, his erective sexual potency began to slip. His relationship with a girl he was living with began to go badly and soon broke up. He found himself unwilling to involve himself in other liaisons, preferring to live a solitary, lonely life. If he were enticed into a date, he experienced real fear and could not wait until he had escorted the girl home.

A good positive transference set in, with a variety of homosexual fantasies about me. Apparently he did not mind discussing these. It transpired after a while that he was using these to hide fear and hostility of me. Vegeto-therapy was resumed and the work of softening up his muscular armor continued—slowly and laboriously, but persistently. During one session, as he was lying prone and viciously slamming his pelvis into the couch with a loud bellow, the movement became more and more automatic until vigorous clonisms over which he had no control ensued. They persisted for several minutes, gradually becoming feebler until they totally subsided, leaving him breathless, weak and fearful. It was then that he was encouraged to describe first the sensations he experienced during the clonisms and then to permit whatever free verbalization of ideas occurred to him.

Gradually he learned to talk about his insane aunt, whom he had called Mom and to whom he was deeply attached. Soon he recalled what happened during those fateful years between four and six years of age when Mom had entered her schizophrenic decline. It appears that she introduced him to most of the common sexual perversions so that in those two years he led an abnormally extensive sexual life.

She performed fellatio on him, would play manually with his genitals and would give him enemas while masturbating him. She also taught him how to perform cunnilingus and forced him to do it by the hour. Occasionally he would plead, "Is this enough? Can I go out and play now?" But she would demand more and more. Her orgasms were violent, during which her thighs would press painfully on his little head. Always she demanded more. The smell of unwashed genitals still remained in his nostrils, nauseating him. I encouraged him to gag—with difficulty at first, but he soon learned to gag and to scream while gagging. Then he recalled that she would threaten him with actual castration, of biting his penis off, were he to fail to continue cunnilingus.

On another occasion she threatened him with death if he so much as told anybody else what he did with her. This apparently left a profound impression: an insane woman's intensity was not to be trifled with. He came to understand that this was one reason why he could not talk about his experiences nor free associate readily. There was survival value in silence. He came to appreciate the implications of his relationship with me. He had transferred his love, fear and hate to me and of these he could not speak until the gestures and motor attitudes had dissolved some of these inhibitions.

\*\*\*

The patient begins by play-acting. But in a short time, he becomes obsessed by the affects he had been attempting to attitudinize. The gates of hell become opened up, as it were, and demoniacal affects of which the patient was not previously aware are vividly released. Some of the better emotional features that observers have recorded with regard to psychodrama may be compared, in a very blurred way, to these striking clinical demonstrations. There is a "working through" of the most vital personality problems, not on an abstract verbalistic level, but on a realistic experiential basis, with immediacy of emotional experience.

It must be remembered that this idea is not altogether new in theory. Many psychiatrists other than Reich have indicated the relationships among gestures, bodily posturing and the evocation of childhood memories—between motor attitudes and somatic sensations and ideational processes. In a fascinating article on memory, Schachtel has some important ideas to express in this connection. They help to elaborate the meaning implicit in all these somatic procedures.

> "Since the lost experience is inaccessible to voluntary recall and incompatible with the conventional memory schemata, the question arises as to what the conditions are under which such forgotten experiences may be recalled... The accidental recurrence of a bodily posture or of a sensory perception which he (Proust) had experienced in the past, on some occasions brings with it the entire vision of the past, or the person he was then and of the way he saw things then." (9)

In other words, Schachtel suggests that the sensory perception or motor attitude may serve as a reintegrative stimulus that evokes out of the personality the whole experience of which that sensory perception is but a small part.

To resume the quotation, Schachtel continues:

> "*It is a sensation...* not a thought, as in willed recall, *which revives the past...* All these sensations are far from conceptual thought, language, or conventional memory schemata. They renew a state of the psychosomatic entity, in some respect, that this entity had experienced before, felt before. It is as though they had touched directly the unconscious memory trace, the record left behind by a total situation out of the past, whereas voluntary recall tries to approach and construct this part indirectly, coached and deflected by all those ideas, wishes and needs which tell the present person how the past could, should, or might have been."

I rather fancy that Reich would be in complete accord with this formulation of Schachtel.

The memory traces are not solely engrammes impressed somewhere within the nervous system. The bodily posture, specific groups of muscular tensions, vegetative idiosyncracies, visceral dysfunctions and psychic attitudes—all of these together comprise the indelible memory remains of different life experiences.

> "...By revival of a former sensation the attitude of the former self that first had this sensation is remobilized And thus recall is made possible of the objects and feelings closely connected with the former sensa-

tion—objects and feelings which the present self would otherwise not perceive or experience in the same manner since it thinks, feels, behaves differently and since, therefore, the conscious memory schemata are not prepared for the ready reproduction of material stemming from a historical past in which the person was different, moved by needs, interests and fears different from those that move him now, especially from those of which he is aware at present. But all experience leaves a record behind, as it were, a memory trace, inaccessible as a rule to the consciously, purposefully searching mind, revealed sometimes by the repetition of a sensation that had occurred at the time when the record was first made." (italics mine)

These gestures under ordinary circumstances will not of themselves be too effective. Some years ago, as I began to feel the inadequacy of orthodox therapeutic measures and began to experiment with more direct abreactive approaches, I wrote an article (8) describing some of these experiments. They consisted among other things of gestures of various kinds utilized in a kind of psychodramatic play-acting. Their efficiency at first surprised me and this was what motivated the above-mentioned article. As time went on, however, I began to be aware of various defects in the scheme where certain types of emotionally blocked patients were concerned. No matter how intensely they tried to dramatize certain gestures, very few genuine affects were liberated. They could pound the couch, beat the large rubber clown with a plastic hose, gesticulate vigorously, tear telephone directories to shreds, yet through these dramatic performances it was evident that they were "holding back." It was not until after the opportunity arose to undergo vegeto-therapy myself that I began to appreciate the psychotherapeutic significance of hyperventilation. Only after therapy was I able to grasp the meaning of this armored restraint. Hyperventilation of the cortex temporarily undermines the long established ability of the personality to restrain and inhibit. When oxygen-intoxication is a well-defined physiological state producing the evidences of marked personality disassociation, then these psychodramatic gestures may become effective. Then the normal inhibitory mechanisms of the cortex become overridden, permitting a free exit for pent-up emotional states. In the state of intoxication, a trivial stimulus or suggestion may trigger off considerable emotional responses which, in a sober person, would be altogether impossible.

## BIBLIOGRAPHY

1. Alexander, Franz and French, Thomas M. *Psychoanalytic Therapy.* New York, Ronald Press, 1946, p. 22.
2. Cobb, Stanley. *Emotions and Clinical Medicine.* New York, Norton Co., 1950, p. 140 *et seq.*
3. Gillilan, L.A. *Clinical Aspects of the Autonomic Nervous System,* Boston, Little Brown & Co., 1954, p. 79.
4. *Ibid,* p. 203.
5. Groddeck, Georg. *Exploring the Unconscious,* New York, Funk & Wagnall, 1959, p. 58–59.
6. Kraines, S.H. *Therapy of the Neuroses and Psychoses.* Philadelphia, Lea & Febiger, 1943, p. 46.
7. Pratt, James B. *The Religious Consciousness.* New York, MacMillan Co., 1949, p. 314–315.
8. Regardie, Francis I. "Active Psychotherapy," *Complex.* New York, Winter issue, 1951.
9. Schachtel, Ernest. "On Memory," *A Study of Interpersonal Relations* (ed. by Patrick Mullahy). New York, Hermitage Press, 1941, p. 38–39.

# Chapter VIII

## Transference

> "The patient substitutes the analyst for the most important person in his life and makes the analyst the sustainer of the central idea around which all the parapathic symptoms are encamped."
> — Wilhelm Stekel

In all relationships between two human beings, regardless of the particular level upon which they intend to operate, there is some emotional communication. Full awareness of this type of communication may or may not be realized by one or the other. In the therapeutic situation, it is customary to assume that the awareness lies with the therapist by virtue of his previous training and the insight which it should have developed. It is similarly assumed that it is an intrinsic part of his professional role to aid the patient to arrive at some understanding of the concealed implications that are presented by the relationship. Non-verbal psychotherapy offers many possibilities for the emergence of the most profound transference ties—both positive and negative. Most of these possibilities revolve around the idea that hyperventilation reduces normal critical judgment, evaluation and inhibition. Because of this, the patient's response to the therapist is more avowedly effective than might otherwise be the case. This affective reaction—the transference situation—is handled by means of the previously described technical devices of vegeto-therapy.

In psychoanalysis, the patient is urged to refrain from discussing his problems and the therapy with all individuals except the analyst. The primary motive for this counsel is that libido will not be unnecessarily spilled and wasted outside of the consulting room. Whatever comments the patient proposes to make about the treatment should be directed to the analyst. If not there is a considerable waste of energy, anxiety and transference affects which could be more wisely utilized during the analytical hour. Moreover, discussion and description of what proceeds during the session is certain to be misinterpreted by the layman who would draw quite different conclusions as to the various processes of therapy than would the patient. The interdiction therefore aims to spare the patient any upset that might result if biopathic friends and family made critical comments about situations that they do not altogether understand.

The transference situation particularly is open to much misrepresentation even by patients while in the process of receiving therapy. It has been known that friends and family often make the snide interpretation that the consulting room must resemble a boudoir more than anything else. Silence about this process is insisted upon until the patient has a clearer notion of his experience.

If the possibility of misrepresentation and misinterpretation is true in the area of psychoanalysis, it is even more true of vegeto-therapy. Many orgonomists have the legitimate fear that they will be smeared even as Reich was, and that the therapeutic system they employ will be condemned as lascivious on the one hand or sado-masochistic on the other. The fear is predicated on the basis of their knowledge of the reality of the emotional plague.

If the therapist taps a patient's belly or slaps his face or hurts the masseter during a critical abreactive episode, he may fear that if the patient talks indiscriminately about his sessions with those who have not undergone therapy, the latter will exclaim about the gross brutality of the method. This will either confuse the patient or force him into a defense of the therapist and the technique, which is needless. Or if the therapist holds the patient's face between his hands, gazing directly at tear-filled eyes, or holds him to himself while the patient cries, the cry may go up that the therapist is a gross sentimentalist who permits involvement in the patient's problems and emotional reactions, and that "acting out" may be encouraged, throwing all civilized restraints to the winds.

Behind all of this is, as I have said, legitimate fear based on the actual fact that they have already witnessed the abuse and ridicule too often heaped on psychoanalysts. That the latter have sexual affairs with their patients is an old canard which has not diminished with the passage of time. Generally speaking this is false and a malicious slur against honorable men practicing a difficult therapy. Some orgonomists who have had more than their just share of bitter abuse and vilification have some apprehension lest their techniques conjure up plague images of licentious and unbridled sexual passions being pandered to in the privacy of the consulting room.

It is true that a patient here and there may make a direct sexual overture to the therapist, but these advances can usually be well managed and used by the therapist in the service of the therapeutic regimen without acceding to the patient's request. Once in a while a patient does come to therapy with the eager or apprehensive anticipation that the transference carries with it the implication of sexual intercourse with the therapist. Such patients have to be disillusioned promptly of their fantasy and re-educated into the realities of therapy and the actual meaning of transference. Overt sexual acts have no part in vegeto-therapy. At certain times during the dissolution of specific muscular tensions, sexual feelings and excitations may emerge and are as much to be welcomed as tears, anger or fear or any other affective response.

But just as the therapist does not permit the patient to strike or kick him during abreactive sessions, so also he does not permit the patient to use him as an object for sexual gratification or satisfaction. It is this emergence of healthy sexual feelings which will drive the patient to seek orgastic fulfillment elsewhere in the event that there is no adequate satisfaction in the marriage relationship. This is one reason why some marriages fall apart during therapy. They had been maintained solely on the basis of guilt, compulsion, religious faith or legal obligation. Therapy would not have been needed in the first place had adequate orgastic satisfaction been possible. The sexual drive, awakened out of its neurotic armorings, is the prime instinctual factor that impels the patient to seek life fulfillment—but not at the hands of the therapist.

Any accusation, then, that the therapist is a libertine or a sadist is utterly absurd. His sole purpose is to strip the patient of his inhibitions, of his muscular-character-armoring that has stifled growth, satisfaction and fulfillment.

Meanwhile, plague reactions have to be avoided. They are a distinct menace. For this reason, no doubt, Reich has been sparing and cautious in his descriptions of techniques and office procedures. It would be difficult to obtain a mastery of the method from reading Reich's works. Judging from the few autobiographical fragments he has published, the caution is justified. Though I have thrown caution to the winds in outlining the major technical procedures, it is my hope that the benefits will far outweigh any possible misrepresentation of what the therapy and the therapist propose to accomplish.

There seems to be no question but that formal orientation in the psychoanalytic manipulation of the transference is indispensable to the therapist, even though he may use different methods to cope with it. The success or otherwise of vegeto-therapy depends on the recognition of the transference and its management. It is true that in many instances the transference can be manipulated readily by attacking the muscular armor. Latent hostility and resistance can often be readily discharged once the hyperventilated patient is aided in releasing or dissolving specific muscular tensions. In other instances no such facile device is adequate to enable the patient to understand feelingly the situation in which he finds himself involved.

All too often, as the armor is softened, there develop attitudes toward the therapist which an adequate anamnesis demonstrates are the literal reproductions of earlier attitudes to parents or parental surrogates. Under these circumstances, there is no alternative but to deal with these attitudes on a verbal level in very much the same orthodox manner as they are dealt with elsewhere. They must be exposed, thoroughly ventilated and, if necessary, explained to the patient; otherwise a formidable block develops to the detriment of a successful outcome to therapy.

For example, a 29-year-old male, Ernie, an obsessive-compulsive character with a long history of juvenile delinquency, was lying on the couch breathing softly and easily according to my instructions. Though Ernie had had a number of previous sessions, on this particular occasion he seemed singularly uncooperative. He did everything that was expected of him, yet I had the impression that this was merely external compliance covering some inner resistance. After working on his very angry-looking sterno-cleidomastoid muscles and the muscular digitations on the lateral aspect of the thorax, he grabbed both my wrists and viciously glowered at me as though he would like to attack me. Then he began to scream and cry. It was his complaint that I was forcing change on him with threats of termination of therapy—though this topic had never previously been broached.

After the tears had subsided—a period of some 20 minutes had elapsed—he was asked to verbalize his impressions of the accusation against me. Throughout this time, as I held his head, I asked him to look at me so that I could clearly see his eyes and so that he could observe possible changes of emotional expression in my face as we talked. Once the abreaction had exhausted itself he talked bitterly of his father's brutality and neglect. Father's constant harangue was "Look here, young man, you've got to change your ways—or get out!" Often his father would beat him with a razor-strop, following which Ernie would have fantasies of murder. He would talk to himself in the privacy of the barn or woodshed and say, "Change? Never, you old son of a bitch! You can beat me or kill me. But change? Never, never!" He was bitter, too, that mother had been present during some of these thrashings but, impotent and powerless like himself, had not interceded on his behalf. His fantasies, therefore, were cruel and violent, with savage murder as the predominant theme. All of this fantasy and affect, under therapy, he had transferred to me as the therapist. And though many physical and psychological improvements had been obtained, we both had noted an underlying resistance to any lasting biological release. This he suddenly understood with a clear flash of insight, as this transference reaction came to be thoroughly verbalized and conceptualized.

Later Ernie developed another piece of valuable insight which also brought with it several recollections that had previously been blocked off. In accordance with my instructions he had been vigorously kicking the pillow which I had held at the foot of the couch. Shortly afterwards, he turned face downwards on the couch while I loosened up the hypertonic and painful rhomboid muscles. As he lay relaxing afterwards, he became aware not only of the familiar tingling sensations in the legs and back, but a rather unfamiliar feeling of weakness and sickness. The area between the shoulder blades felt uneasy and empty, to use his language. As the minutes elapsed, a look of bewilderment arose on his face. When I urged him to verbalize his feelings, he recalled it as something with which he was already familiar. He had experienced it during the period when he was an avowed juvenile delinquent. He had been sexually promiscuous with both boys and girls, had stolen tires and other equipment from automobiles parked on the streets, and had raided the alleys for scrap metal and other junk which he could sell. This weak, sick sensation he recalled experiencing when he was about to be scolded by his father with "I don't know what we're going to do with you. You're incorrigible. We'll have to send you to a reformatory." The apprehensive feelings also arose when there was the possibility that the police were going to catch up with him, as they had on several occasions. He finally managed to repress these feelings in the muscular tensions of the back, belly and legs.

I like Groddeck's formulation that, in therapy, the important consideration is not so much the evocation of unconscious material or heightening recollection of earlier traumatic events, but *the elimination of inner resistances,* the character-muscular armor. If this be so, and in general this viewpoint has nowadays gained wide acceptance, then by means of the elucidation of the transference situation with vegeto-therapeutic aid many severe characterological resistances may be broken down.

Groddeck also offered some significant contributions to the transference relationship fostered by physical contact. So far as his therapy was concerned, he used manipulation as one of his major operational tools so effectively that he approximated some of the therapeutic goals envisaged by Reich. A certain harmony of feeling on the biological level between doctor and patient is the fundamental basis of medical treatment. This is the fundamental thesis he elaborates so far as transference is concerned. The term "biological" indicates that this important factor in treatment has really little to do with the intellectuality and skill of the physician, but arises from the interrelationship of two human beings and their mutual emotional responses. One does not need a great deal of experience to know that the influence of this factor in healing is almost entirely dependent upon physical contact. By its very nature, thought Groddeck, the use of massage compels a closer physical contact between doctor and patient than does any other form of treatment, not excepting even surgery. And just as the first massage consistently and invariably affects the patient both pleasantly and unpleasantly, so does every succeeding one. Thus he states almost dogmatically that massage, in whatever way it is carried out, must have some affective influence upon the unaccustomed organism and that it is an important, though incalculable weapon for psychotherapy. What we call transference and resistance appear during the course of the massage to aid or to hinder. (4)

In non-verbal therapy, transference attitudes are elicited more readily because of the more intimate body relation of patient with therapist. The close physical contact, the state of semi-nudity, the exposure of latent affects by the direct attack on the muscular armor—all of these facilitate a very profound form of transference. And it is for this very reason that the therapist utilizing these biological approaches should be more than prepared to deal with them.

Whitaker and Malone wrote,

> "The authors believe that physical contact is a technical aid in the therapeutic process. It is liable to the problems noted above and it is as certainly true of positive affect and warmth as it is of aggression that unless the therapist has appropriate feeling in himself, it can be dangerous. The authors have found that holding the patient during a crying episode, or offering to rock the patient during a period of deep regression into infantile living brings to the therapeutic relationship certain proprioceptive and sensory modalities which make a significant contribution to the therapeutic process itself. The therapist may also find help by utilizing the nursing bottle with nipple. Here the therapist assumes on a behavior level the active maternal role in the patient's regression to a crucial infantile experience." (12)

Physical contacts unequivocally facilitate a positive transference. This relationship must at all times, then, be perceived by the therapist if the warm positive feelings are not to be transformed into malignant hatred. As a result of the positive transference that such attitudes engender, the patient learns to feel and tolerate a wide series of emotions and affects that transform his personality. The affect-lameness naturally disappears and so does the contactlessness of which such patients have long complained.

It furthers the possibility of a deeper transference relationship. As the patient becomes more and more able to function from the center of his own biological core, from a feeling level he develops a profound set of feelings for the therapist. This set of feelings is, of course, compound. It consists, as we might suppose, of infantile dependency feelings, needs and yearnings which have remained unsatisfied since the earliest years of his life. These have been released by virtue of the therapeutic process itself and so are rendered labile enough to be transferred to the person of the analyst. In this way, much of the "unfinished business of childhood" can be brought up to date. However, this is only one part of the process. The rest consists of a newly developed capacity to function soundly and realistically on the present-day level. *The patient feels*—and in the realization that he is being "reborn" and re-structured through the good offices of the therapist, a great deal of warmth, gratitude and love develops on this basis. Much depends on how much love the therapist is able himself to feel and communicate to the patient. This is the *sine qua non* of the entire therapeutic process, despite all the attendant paraphernalia of vegeto-therapy.

Ernie is a good case in point. He had been a particularly difficult patient to handle over a long period of time. There was always the possibility that one careless or misjudged move on my part might precipitate an act of extreme violence from him which would vitiate a good prognosis. Therapy, therefore, had to proceed slowly, laboriously and painfully. Several months after the incident previously described, some work had to be done on the spinal muscles in the area of the lower dorsal and upper lumber vertebrae. The muscles were stiff and rigid; tight cords could be palpated. Into this area I dug my knuckles to bring about a physiological relaxation and to elicit the usual affective responses. He screamed, yelled, shouted and thrashed around on the couch, pounding with his fists in a futile unproductive way. Soon all of this stopped, while he helplessly rolled over on his side facing the wall and buried his head in his hands. He was curled up like a ball, more or less in the fetal position, crying like a baby. Easily, I rolled him over to face me and gathered him up in my arms, rocking him and patting him gently on the head and back as though he were a hurt youngster who needed affection. Soon he looked up at me from his tear-filled, bloodshot eyes just in time to see that my own eyes had become tear-filled also. He could hardly believe that I could feel with him to that extent. And, haltingly, he stuttered, "Why, doctor, I really believe you love me." Of course I nodded my head in agreement with his statement, all the while looking into his eyes which lost their hard, glassy and lackluster look and became loving themselves. From that day forward his progress in therapy proceeded rapidly. His musculature softened up phenomenally. He originally had had a chest which resembled a block of concrete more than anything else. Many of the disturbing neurotic traits, such as repetitive fantasies about killing me, murdering my family, raping my female patients and stealing my library dissipated utterly and thoroughly. His own relationship with his wife quickly became more adult and mature, and he was able to deal more realistically and successfully with his contracting business which had suffered until then because of neglect by reason of his proneness to fantasy.

Summing up, the vegeto-therapeutic process is deliberately calculated to heighten the intensity of the transference. *It intensifies the patient's capacity to function on a feeling level.* The physical state of near-nudity, the permissive attitude of the therapist to every type of abreactive state induced in the patient, the bold assault on spastic muscles, the actual body contact, and the occasional feelings of utter helplessness and dependency—all of these appear to foster the emotional relationship between patient and therapist.

Spurgeon English (3) has laid down the proposition that love and touch are inseparable and indivisible. For most of us love and the warmer emotions cannot arise from the depths without some tactile stimulation. He also advises that the cooperation necessary for social conformity on an adult realistic level is not possible without affection and tactile stimulation. This is certainly true of children. And since it is evident that the therapeutic process temporarily reduces the adult patient to the extremity of feeling and behaving like a child, it is equally true of the average adult in or out of therapy. For what we love, we want to touch. It is his contention also that misunderstandings which arise through wide separation are cleared up on close contact. And Montagu also wrote that there exists a certain amount of evidence indicating that cutaneous stimulation in an adult who has had an inadequate amount of it in childhood may relieve the person of a disorder which is related to that inadequate cutaneous stimulation. (6) This is the essence of the vegeto-therapeutic attitude to the positive transference.

This, as we know, is not the only type of transference that may be elicited. Just what kind of transference is established between the patient and therapist needs to be corroborated by the ordinary means of communication. This is why, in my estimation, an occasional verbal session is an absolute essential. For it is then, and only then, that the therapist is able to determine the fundamental attitudes of the patient. Only in this way can he learn of the variety of memories and fantasies that flit through the patient's mind as he pursues instructions to breathe, exercise, scream, shout and cry.

It should be obvious to any psychoanalytically oriented observer that regardless of the apparent intensity and vigor with which a patient pursues some of these gestures and exercises, he is bound to indulge in a variety of fantasies. Much of the work is deliberately designed to utilize most of the energy and time of the patient to reduce the opportunity to fantasize to a bare minimum. Nonetheless, one has only to watch a patient for a short period of time to become aware of the automaticity of his performance after the first few gestures.

Such activity should not be ignored or underestimated. These fantasies are likely to be significant to the process under way. When verbalized and analyzed, though not necessarily at length, they will go far towards releasing the patient's energy and enthusiasm. So often I have perceived patients engaging, after a while, in movements in an automatic or mechanical way. Little increment follows when this is the case. The expenditure of a few minutes or even the whole of an occasional session to permit the ventilation of such fantasies improves the quality of the patient's active couch-work. Some reductive interpretation in terms of character-structure, without the accusatory element entering into the interpretation, is of inestimable value here. It is imperative that the therapist realize the significant role he plays in the patient's mental and emotional life. His own efficiency cannot help but be improved so far as that particular patient is concerned.

Yet the conventional Reichian viewpoint here also needs to be reiterated. The therapist must of necessity have undergone enough vegeto-therapy himself to have achieved the orgasm reflex and, with it, the emotional and biological release that is a corollary. He must be able to function on a profound feeling level. If this has been achieved, he will find himself possessed of a sharp and penetrating tool with which to aid his patients. The orgonomists dislike the word "intuitive," but rather than use some of the debatable terms they have fostered, I prefer to state that the therapist often senses or intuits the patient's feelings without having to interrogate him about the contents of his fantasies.

At the beginning one is inclined to be sceptical about the reliability of this intuitive faculty as an operational tool. But after a time, and with clinical experience, one learns that it is quite reliable and can be used freely in the office. Perhaps it is less intuition than development of a keen perception that gathers up and evaluates a wide variety of subtle sensory data which may be summarized or interpreted in fractions of a second on an unconscious level, so that one suddenly knows that such and such is the process developing within the patient. It may well be akin to what Theodor Reik has so eloquently called "listening with the third ear." It cannot be very distant from feeling the "expressive language of the living," which is Reich's term for the same creative event.

Be that as it may, verbalization of inner activity is still useful and should not be altogether dispensed with. Regardless of whether the therapist insists upon verbalization or feels his way into the clinical situation, it is evident that the patient seems to experience almost every single phase of his childhood in relation to his parents. His emotional repertory extends from "a to z." And it is a very broad and intense spectrum of emotional experience. There are moments during the assault on his muscular hypertonicity when he indulges in fantasies of murder and revenge and feels an almost inexhaustible bitterness and despair. Later, as he whimpers and sobs, he may come to feel completely helpless and dependent. Memories of all the many earlier moments in his life when he felt similarly alone and in need of love crowd into his mind. There are moments when he is suffused by the warmest kind of love and affection. These he may momentarily repudiate as strange proprioceptive sensations are evoked, again awakening out of the darkness of his memory, distinct recollections of being pleasurably stroked by a parent after being tucked happily into bed. A rapid departure may follow. He may become sullen and resistive, unable to tolerate the sheer sensual pleasure of these vegetative excitations and streamings. The therapist's attack on his anxiety-laden musculature may then eventuate in overt hostility, hardly different from what he once knew when being spanked as a youngster, or rejected by a parent, or bullied by an older sibling. At this point, well-defined memories and fantasies surge forward, clamoring for expression and verbalization to release the fear and hurt he once knew.

Some of Stekel's views about the transference are useful. (10) He believed, along with most other analysts, that in therapy the patient does indeed transfer to the therapist feelings and attitudes that were generated in earlier years within the family milieu. Nonetheless, he felt that if these feelings do not interfere with the smooth course of therapy, the therapist should not interfere with them. They are best left alone, to be quietly and deftly manipulated by the therapist to the ultimate advantage of the patient. Only if they are excessive in any one direction, interfering with the forward progress of therapy, should these attitudes be ventilated and elucidated.

Positive transference attitudes may be perceived by the zeal with which the patient cooperates with the therapist. For example, no matter how difficult some of these gestures appear—and actually they are all but impossible in some types of armored character structures—the patient struggles powerfully to perform them. It is evident in the early phases of treatment that the patient struggles not because he realizes the value inherent in the gesture itself, but because he wishes to please the therapist. He will go far out of his way to ensure that the therapist likes him. He turns up for the session promptly, never misses an appointment, and regardless of the intensity of his symptoms, works very hard on the couch.

This may be a transient phase, to be succeeded by being late for the appointment, forgetting the time of the appointment, or by confusing the therapist's instructions. So far as the latter is concerned, hyperventilation is at least partially responsible. But it is far from the entire explanation. When one closely questions a patient who seems to be doing everything all wrong, one detects the build-up of intense hostility. Sometimes verbalizing it facilitates adequate discharge. In still other cases more active measures, of the types already described, are called for. And then, during the pounding, punching, breathing, exercising, the patient abreacts sufficiently to be able to follow the therapy and get over the negative phase of the transference.

It is customary in conventional psychoanalysis to restrict some of the patient's activities at the outset of therapy in order to dam back libido and facilitate the discharge of anxiety on the couch. The homosexual may be asked to refrain from all homosexual activities while undergoing analysis. The compulsively promiscuous girl has to make a strong effort to restrain her promiscuity so that the underlying sexual anxiety may be brought to light more vividly. The alcoholic must avoid alcoholic excesses. The restraint intensifies the concealed conflicts. This kind of procedure is widely pursued and without a doubt is effective.

Generally speaking, however, this procedure can be avoided in vegeto-therapy. Complete reliance is placed on the therapy itself to eradicate the symptoms by changing the structure without compulsively insisting upon restraint. Self-regulation is the cornerstone of the entire system, together with the concept of self-determination. What the patient does is entirely his own business and he must assume responsibility for his life from the outset. There is no need for artificial restraints of any kind to elicit anxiety or to disclose the hidden unconscious conflicts. Sooner or later, hyperventilation and the vegeto-therapeutic armamentarium does its insidious work. For a while the patient may be entirely unaware that anything is happening to him in his daily life. But the day comes when a homosexual experience is rejected, or the promiscuous girl refuses an offer for sexual contact, or the alcoholic turns down the chance to get drunk. And under these circumstances, no one is more surprised than the patient. No one has insisted that such experiences be refused. Yet the patient did refuse—and for the moment is unable to understand his motives or behavior. It may take a little while to appreciate the fact that an entire set of values have been transformed, that biological substructure has been radically altered. This seems a far sounder course in therapy than anything else.

As in other psychotherapies, resistance phenomena are commonplace. Again, as elsewhere, they require to be recognized and understood. With the gradual softening of the muscular armor and the reduction of excessive tonus, the patient is slowly transformed into a person capable of *feeling*. This could be quite a frightening transformation for one who years ago was compelled to develop armoring in order to *avoid* feelings. The nearer the therapist brings the patient to this goal of sensing and feeling himself, the more anxiety is likely to be generated. *Therapy of any variety, when successful, is bound to provoke anxiety.* In fact, there will be occasions when the therapist must deliberately induce anxiety. But it is the end-product of this phase of therapy that the patient naturally chooses to avoid. It is on the basis of this avoidance, then, that resistance occurs. If the intensity of the anxiety and other feelings is dimly perceived beneath the protective armor as being overwhelming, the resistance to the continuance of therapy will be in like proportion.

Methods of dealing with this increasing gradient of resistance are manifold. First, the therapist may temporarily desist from active therapy. A session or two of skillfully handled verbal communication is usually adequate, particularly when the patient is aided in the realization of the constant theme running through the employment of vegeto-therapy: that the more he relaxes his muscular armoring, the more he opens himself to the re-experience of infantile affects blocked off years earlier. With the patient coming to understand that these are infantile affects, having little or nothing to do with his adult experience, he is usually willing to experiment bit by bit with coming in contact with them. As he learns that nothing particularly devastating occurs to him as he experiences his own body sensations or his infantile emotions, much of the resistance and reluctance to continuance of therapy vanishes.

Second, if a good positive transference has previously been established and has been continually reinforced by the gentleness and consideration of the therapist, the patient will experience little hesitancy or resistance. The therapist who realizes that the patient fears his body sensations will therefore make no attempt to push therapy beyond the session-by-session tolerance of the patient who will then be likely to offer less resistance.

Third, a head-on attack can often be provocative of a considerable dent in the armoring. Those muscles particularly involved in the process of resistance—and it must be constantly remembered that any psychic process is both muscularly and viscerally related—can be palpated and singled out as being especially tonic. The patient may be asked point-blank with what part of his body does he feel he is resisting. He may indicate that it is with the back of the neck, or with the fleshy digitations of the serratus magnus below the axilla, or with a tight hard belly, or with the buttocks, or the calves of the legs, or even with the curled up toes. To whatever area of tension the patient points, all the attention of the vegeto-therapist may be directed. A particular set of movements may be suggested which will work those parts to alleviate the excessive tonus and so release some of the resistance. Moreover, the therapist may himself attack the areas mentioned by squeezing, manipulating, pinching, etc., and thus encouraging the patient to *feel* the resistive attitude locked up in the tight musculature. Anger, tears or anxiety can thus be located and released.

Fourth, this approach itself may provoke resistance. A great deal is expected of the therapist in the form of skill, dexterity, accuracy of timing, pre-judging the readiness of the patient, etc. He must be ready to evaluate whether or not the patient can tolerate this direct attack on the armoring which harbors the resistance. If the patient is not ready, the attack may well prove abortive and succeed only in evoking more resistance.

Finally, when none of these approaches succeed in releasing the resistive mood, a vacation from therapy may be suggested. This may be as short as merely missing one session. Or it may extend for as long as three months—even more. But whatever period is suggested, provided a good transference has previously been established, when the patient does return for therapy, the resistance is considerably modified and therapy can proceed at full speed ahead.

There is another viewpoint which is important in this connection. The resolution of the negative transference which is expressed in the resistance is the *sine qua non* of good therapy. So long as hostility remains latent and unexpressed, the patient's neurotic problem has not been adequately dealt with. If the resistance can be challenged effectively and the patient provoked into spontaneous manifestation of the repressed anger, he releases to that extent a powerful source of energy which can be turned to everyday usefulness. This is confirmed by statements made by Reich relative to the developmental problems of the child. In addition to direct sexual inhibition resulting from attachment to the parents, there are guilt feelings due to the enormous hatred which accumulates during all the years of living in the familial situation.

Reich thought that if this hatred remained *conscious,* it could become a powerful individual revolutionary force, enabling the patient to break family ties and become the initiator of actions against the original conditions which created the hatred.

A final criticism refers the possible results of these somatic methods to the transference situation alone. It was claimed that they have little value in themselves and that the really useful operational tool was the transference itself. This is a variation of some of the views of Groddeck, enunciated earlier. I doubt if Groddeck, after due consideration, would have altogether concurred with the criticism.

I cannot deny that the transference is useful, or inevitable, or indispensable. Indeed, I have insisted that the solid transference is the *sine qua non* of any therapy. But it seems to me that this begs the question. If conservative psychoanalytic therapy, employing the transference as it does, achieves merely intellectual insight in the affect-lame patient, but is ineffectual in changing his stereotyped neurotic responses, the patient is accused of having chronic and severe resistances. It rarely happens that a critic within the field itself assumes that there is a technical deficiency in the psychotherapeutic approaches now current. Yet it is a common inference that the technical efficiency of vegeto-therapy can only be due to the transference.

Current psychological approaches are ultimately sterile in the severe neuroses. It is quite often asserted that even when conventional psychotherapy is successful, the patient evinces a curious emotional flatness. Even when the transference has bloomed into full-flower, and has been analyzed up hill and down dale until the neurotic symptom-formation has been dissipated, the affect-lameness in modified form still persists. It remains affect-lameness no matter how modified or rarefied it appears to be. The somatic methods developed by Reich and briefly delineated here appear to be more than effectual against such neurotic manifestations. Apparently they succeed where not even the analysis of the transference neurosis did. Stekel used to dismiss his patients after three to six months of analysis, regardless of whether or not the transference had been successfully analyzed and whether or not the pathological symptoms had vanished. The opposite technique also has been in vogue—of retaining the patient through hundreds of hours of psychotherapy until, it was hoped, the emotional block could be made to disappear. Time and money are both saved by employing vegeto-therapy.

Regardless of the type of therapy, the transference is always an integral part of the treatment. But only with the non-verbal methods are transference feelings evoked in such an active form as to assure a greater likelihood of successful treatment of the affect-lame person. And it succeeds with reasonable promptness. This is the empirical clinical fact upon which I insist. It swiftly eliminates the theoretical objections which are not based upon actual experience.

\*\*\*

Hyperventilation reduces the critical activity of the cortex and so permits the freer emergence of spontaneous affects and autonomic excitations. During these states of temporary suspension of normal "set," the patient is rendered far more susceptible to suggestion. For the purpose of this discussion, suggestion may be defined as the uncritical acceptance of any idea. It is accepted that a person intoxicated with alcohol may be triggered into motor activity by suggestion without subjecting his impulse to any kind of critical evaluation. Impulses to motor activity may be more readily stimulated during inebriation than at most other times.

This susceptibility to suggestion is a formidable two-edged sword during therapy. Hyperventilation is one factor, the transference relationship with the therapist is another. Both factors have to be considered together as responsible for this heightened degree of susceptibility. Yet an occasional therapist seems unaware of the laws of suggestion and the possibility of negatively affecting patients by his statements. One therapist has told some patients, before they had grown to an understanding of the facts, that as a direct result of treatment they might become impotent or frigid and that their ability to write or paint or engage in any of their usual skills might become impaired. Some were told that their "marriages would go on the rocks." This "therapeutic negativism" could be highly dangerous and might cause much apprehension in sensitive patients. I have since learned that this approach was used and recommended by Reich, and is standard operating procedure among some orgonomists. This procedure is also used in dealing with the transference situation. It is rationalized that the neurosis is being challenged in one form or another from the moment the patient enters therapy. Direct statements are made, sometimes before the patient is capable of appreciating them on a feeling level.

In a major sense it is understandable that the therapist was expressing therapeutic prognosis. Sometimes, as the compulsive patterns are broken down as a result of the concentrated attack on the muscular armor, it is true that some drives, learned skills, artistic abilities and personal relationships are apparently affected adversely. All good psychotherapy must produce similar reactions with the evocation of considerable anxiety.

In most instances, the patient can be reassured that this is only temporary. Usually these traits are restored later, minus the compulsive push so characteristic of the neurotic. Even many faulty marriages may anchor themselves on a more stable basis when one of the marriage partners has completed therapy, although in the intermediate phases it may appear as though the marriage were foredoomed to dissolution.

When therapy approaches a critical phase the couple may indeed separate and live apart from one another. Temporarily confused and filled with anger and remorse and guilt, they do not know whether the separation will be temporary or permanent. The confusion is welcomed by the therapist. It represents the breaking-down of the hard and fast neurotic standards by which the patient has hitherto lived. Moreover, out of this confused state may emerge the hidden feelings and motivations which the patient may have to live by for the rest of his life. Therapy and the separation act like catalytic agents to precipitate latent emotional capacities. For a while, though, the patient may experience many affective difficulties, being forced to fall back on his loneliness, despair and anxiety. Many a successful therapy has been concluded only because of such an eventuality. It forces the patient to yield to his own desperate and powerful emotions when previously there was, as it were, no vital need to confront the pride, shame, hate or love. Perhaps this situation is required before the patient is able to let go to his own need to cry.

Some patients appear to "coast" through the therapeutic process. There are no drastic personality changes until life steps in to accelerate or cooperate with the work of the therapist. The marital split may be one of these life interventions. The appearance of impotency, loss of artistic skill, sudden disgust with employment, or even a major illness are other interventions of life which may bring the patient face to face first with his shocking inner confusion and then with buried motives and feelings which must be experienced.

With recovery of the full capacity to feel, the confusion and anxiety disappear and the creative talents and skills return for ready use, subject to self-regulation rather than compulsion. But to prognosticate overtly and too soon to the patient in or out of the hyperventilation state, is a grave psychological error that cannot be too roundly condemned as a method.

While on this topic of criticism of current therapeutic procedures, a warning needs also to be expressed regarding dogmatic interpretations of what facial expressions, gestures and motor attitudes mean in terms of personality traits and character-structure. That they have subconscious meaning to the patient goes without saying. Deutsch (2), Werner (11) and others have established some of the principles involved here. Sheldon (9) *et al.* have attempted to relate physique in a broad way to temperament. But this is not to say that certain lines, wrinkles, furrows, ridges, facial expressions, etc. have a specific characterological implication which therapists, having completed therapy themselves, can interpret. Sometimes some highly questionable deductions are spontaneously made from chronic facial attitudes, without even inquiring of the patient whether or not he attaches any meaning to them. Naturally, there is some empirical basis for these observations and deductions. In many of Reich's writings are found several passages which provide the orgonomic interpretation for such deductions.

As indicated above, this concept has enormous significance to the orgonomists. And in a major sense they are right. A good deal of meaning may justly be given to impressions they receive from the patient's attitudes, posture, behavior and general appearance. This is standard in contemporary psychiatry; any good book on case-study emphasizes much the same thing. (5) But the orgonomists go one step further. They believe that with the peculiar insight developed by the restructured person, such signs as lines or furrows on the face, expressions of the eyes, and so forth, can be interpreted *almost* as if the old "science" of physiognomy were valid and was being revived. Some become dogmatic about the "expressive language of the living" and behave as if it were a well-corroborated science and not essentially a highly personal art. There are no dogmas here despite this belief.

There is, however, a certain inevitability in the evolutionary development of these concepts from the relative simplicity of the approach made originally by Reich in his work on the character armor. His attitude was that the important factors in an analysis were not so much *what* kind of material was repressed in the unconscious, but *how*. The approach dealt more with the *kind* of person undergoing therapy. What were his attitudes, his chronic characterological approaches to the process, and how did he react to it? What did he look like? What were his gestures, physical or otherwise?

Reich earlier found that patients did not mind discussing their physical or neurotic symptoms. These were experienced rather as one might a foreign body in the eye or a splinter of wood in the finger—as not really oneself but as something unpleasant to be gotten rid of. But when he approached one of their character traits such as timidity, aggressiveness, penuriousness or haughtiness, a good deal of resentment was shown. The patient felt insulted as if he were being attacked. Having carefully observed the characteristic attitude of the patient in a variety of situations, Reich would attempt to imitate it in such a way that the patient might perceive his own character traits. It was like holding up a mirror in front of the patient's face. At the same time, however, the adoption of the patient's character attitude evoked similar emotions in Reich, provoking a species of empathic identification. It was only a short step from the perception of these stoutly defended character traits to the identification of facial, bodily and other signs, symptoms and mannerisms as clues to the basic temperament of the patient. If these, too, were called to the attention of the patient, some resentment would also be experienced.

Wolstein wrote:

> "To challenge the patient is to evoke a mosaic of defenses. This may be useful as a time-saving device and may bring to light many of the repressed trends which might otherwise remain repressed for a much longer period. But it does not contribute much more to the successful analysis of defenses and the repressed trends underlying this. It does not provide a base for their understanding and control in the feeling knowledge of the patient and will probably fail because therapeutic results on purely functional bases are integrated in a mechanical way." (13)

Vegeto-therapists do, however, challenge the patient's neurosis routinely, and they reject Wolstein's notion that therapeutic results are integrated mechanically.

The patient bitterly resents being told he is hostile, contemptuous, fearful, lascivious or whatnot. He has come to therapy to be helped to overcome neurotic barriers preventing him from enjoying a larger, fuller life. He is in the predicament in which we find him largely because of his lack of awareness and understanding of the very principles which enable him to function as a healthy biological organism. He is also neurotic because of various pressures that have been brought to bear upon him by virtue of training, education, social position, religion, economic status and so on. As a result of these events he has been forced to develop a protective psychic armor—the character—the mechanics of which are essentially irrational and unconscious. To challenge him with unconscious material is a grave error. This constituted one of the principal theorems of Reich in the "character analysis" stage of his development. Premature analysis of unconscious material was rejected by Reich as leading to a sterile analytical situation. The patient might intellectually acquiesce to a given interpretation or statement, but the defensive façade would remain unshaken and the patient would remain affect-lame. By opening up the character resistances, the very neurotic traits by which the patient had lived and functioned, then, perhaps, the underlying emotions which he had been attempting to ward off and repress might percolate through and be discharged. Statements, accurate or otherwise, prove in the long run to be futile and unnecessarily prolong the whole therapeutic venture.

This criticism has been well stated by Rogers who wrote that:

> "There is the greatest temptation to most counselors, whether they are psychiatrists, psychologists, guidance counselors, or social workers, to inform the client as to his patterns, to interpret his actions and his personality to him. We have already seen the type of reception this is likely to receive. The more accurate the interpretation, the more likely it is to encounter defensive resistance. The counselor and his interpretation become something to be feared. To resist this temptation, to interpret too quickly, to recognize that insight is an experience which is achieved, not an experience which can be imposed, is an important step in progress for the counselor." (8)

Obviously great care needs to be exerted here. I have known of more than one questionable assumption having been committed on this basis by some well-intentioned therapists. Yet any college sophomore taking a course in general psychology will recall examining scores of pictures and photographs and being asked to name the specific emotion depicted. In the overwhelming majority of instances it was found to be fairly impossible to specify an emotion from the gesture, expression or facial stance. The capacity for emotional expression may be inborn and unlearned, yet the form and style it may take is wholly dependent upon familial, environmental and cultural factors.

In all fairness to the orgonomists, however, it must be realized that there is a world of difference between the college sophomore and the trained and experienced vegeto-therapist. This difference is crucial. It would be interesting to conduct a similar experiment with a group of therapists and compare their results with those of the above-mentioned college students.

## BIBLIOGRAPHY

1. Baker, Ellsworth F. "A Grave Therapeutic Problem," *Orgone Energy Bulletin,* Vol. V, No. 1–2, 1953.
2. Deutsch, Felix. "Analytic Posturology," *The Psychoanalytic Quarterly,* XXI, No. 2, p. 196. 1952.
3. English, O. Spurgeon. "Sex and Human Love," *About the Kinsey Report* (ed. by D.P. Geddes and E. Currie). New York, New American Library, 1948, p. 101–102.
4. Groddeck, Georg. *Exploring the Unconscious.* London, Daniels & Co., 1933, p. 46.
5. Menninger, Karl A. *A Manual for Psychiatric Case Study.* New York, Grune & Stratton, 1952.
6. Montagu, M.F. Ashley. *Anthropology and Human Nature.* Boston, Porter Sargent, 1957, p. 211–212.
7. Reich, Wilhelm. *The Cancer Biopathy.* New York, Orgone Institute Press, 1948, p. 328.
8. Rogers, Carl R. *Counseling and Psychotherapy.* Boston, Houghton Mifflin Co., 1942. p. 195–196.
9. Sheldon, W.H. *The Varieties of Temperament.* New York, Harper Bros., 1942.
10. Stekel, Wilhelm. *Techniques of Analytical Psychotherapy.* New York, Liveright, 1950.
11. Werner, Heinz and Wapner, Seymour. "Sensory-Tonic Field Theory of Perception," *Jnl. of Personality,* Vol. 18, No. 1, p. 88, 1949.
12. Whitaker, Carl A. and Malone, Thomas P. *The Roots of Psychotherapy.* New York, Blakiston Co. 1953, p. 225.
13. Wolstein, Benjamin. *Transference.* New York, Grune & Stratton, 1954, p. 95.

# Chapter IX

## Affects

"This type of emotional experience as it occurs during treatment we call 'corrective emotional experience' and we consider it the most important factor in all uncovering types of therapy."
— Franz Alexander

Emotions have been described in many ways by different authorities. There are at least two basic definitions that may be considered useful in connection with this thesis. The first is that emotion is a stirred-up state of the entire organism with cerebral, visceral and behavioral components. The second is that it is a disturbed psychological condition which can best be described as disintegrative to cortical behavior patterns—although under certain conditions it may lead to a better adjustment.

It is the basis of this thesis that hyperventilation, by reducing cortical inhibition, permits the eruption of some "stirred-up states" of the organism. Other facets of the vegeto-therapeutic work also release these affective states. It would appear, then, that once these stirred-up states are induced, a "disintegrative reaction" occurs to established cortical patterns. They temporarily disrupt the remaining inhibitory patterns, permitting the further exit of emotions. We might say that a reciprocal cycle of events is instituted. Hyperventilation gently disturbs the habitual blocking of emotions by the cortex. Once this state is achieved, emotions can be released. These in turn progressively diminish the capacity of the cortex to inhibit—in which case emotions continue to flow more or less freely. This reciprocal cycle facilitates abreaction so that session by session it becomes easier for the patient to break into the circumscribed bonds of his neurotic inhibition.

Not only do a complex series of physiological phenomena occur on the basis of overbreathing, but gradually the patient becomes acclimated to and tolerant of his own body sensations. Out of these vegetative excitations, affective reactions develop. At first they may arise with difficulty in the affect-lame person. One can watch the bitter resistance put up by some patients to the possibility of feeling anything. A constant battle is waged on the couch between patient and therapist, between the armor and the biological core. With repeated sessions which reinforce the conditioned familiarity to feeling states of different types, the battle slowly subsides and the affects become relatively easier to elicit and tolerate.

This data has been clearly described by those who have experimented with hyperventilation. Best and Taylor note:

> "It is after the first five minutes that certain temperamental differences may also emerge. Whereas many, perhaps more cautious, keep themselves well in hand...there are others, perhaps more adventurous, who develop symptoms more quickly... Of the latter group some become somnolent and a few will appear amused and if set laughing have difficulty in controlling themselves. *The condition has been described as one of mild intoxication.*" (1) (italics mine)

The earlier quotation from an essay by Mittelman is also corroborative and should be re-read in this connection.

In itself, the motor response is of the utmost significance. There is a phrase current in psychotherapeutic circles that the superego is soluble in alcohol. In other words, the inhibitory function of the cortex can be disturbed by any intoxication—hyper-oxygenation being one of them. The neurotic control lost, temporarily, then repressed or inhibited emotional states, depending upon the individual and his past history, are capable of bursting through into open manifestation. *In vino veritas* also is apt in this connection. Quite often in the intoxication induced by overbreathing, there is a startling revelation of the status of the underlying personality. A 36-year-old woman who appeared suave, sophisticated and more or less well-adjusted, gave an altogether different impression during couch-work. After merely five minutes over-breathing, she was behaving like a petulant, spoiled five-year-old little girl. Therapeutic work under the circumstance is difficult, to say the least.

It is worth re-emphasizing the significance of these findings. The neurotic patient ordinarily cannot demonstrate his feelings. If he does have any available, they are invariably distorted. They have been blocked off for so long that to all intents and purposes he has lost a significant part of his personality. He has become a mere shell. He cannot cry; there are tremendous resistances to this. He cannot get angry; he may be just nasty and sarcastic. He cannot love; he merely suffers from his own rigidity, deadness and emptiness. Under the stimulus of hyperventilation, this one significant fact emerges: he can be brought, by stages, to feel some emotional response and with some vigor. Reich has skillfully elaborated this finding into a highly workable set of techniques designed to eradiate affect-lameness.

Best and Taylor observe that "the condition suggests a loss of control of the upper over the lower neuron, a marked contrast to the state of affairs at the beginning of the experiment." (2) This is a superb neurological definition of the dissociation induced by hyperventilation.

Elsewhere, in another connection, Gellhorn notes that

> "The conclusion arrived at from these experiments, that the emotional pattern is regulated by subcortical structures, particularly the hypothalamus, is supported by various clinical observations. Misfits with absence of cerebral hemispheres due to disturbances in fetal development may show almost continuous crying... The observations of Head who found in hemiplegic patients that stimuli applied to the hemiplegic side evoked marked emotional responses (warmth was felt as exceedingly pleasant and a prick as very painful) seem to indicate that *the emotional response is increased in the human if the inhibitory cortical influence is eliminated...*
>
> "*Apparently functional or surgical elimination of the cortex leads to an overactivity of the subcortical centers.* In the presence of the hypothalamus, overactivity appears in the form of sham rage in animals, and in increased emotional reactions in the human... Effects of a functional decortication may occur in disseminated sclerosis. Wilson characterizes this disease by the presence of euphoria and increased emotional display. Emotional over-reactions are very common, leading occasionally *to spasmodic laughing or crying.*" (5) (italics mine)

All of this is a further corroboration of the validity of this thesis. Vegeto-therapy temporarily incapacitates the critical function of the cortex, releasing the subcortical centers where the basic nuclei which mediate instincts and emotions are located. Pavlov has expressed it thus: "The whole cortex is a mosaic made up of excitatory and inhibitory points affecting the activity of the organism; as these points have a reciprocal function the cerebral hemispheres manifest a mobile equilibrium." (9) Since it is always a dynamic equilibrium, the blocking of any of a series of cortical points disturbs the established equilibrium. This can only mean that therapy interferes with the neurotic equilibrium of the patient. Thus an entirely new basis for operation becomes necessitous—an equilibrium on another more liberal basis. It is on this basis that there occurs what Reich called the re-structuring of the personality. It represents a reorganization predicated on the basis, not of repression nor of compulsive morality, but of self-regulatory expression of the whole organism.

Some of the technical devices used in therapy appear to evoke affects which are in no way related to the immediate therapeutic device. For example, after a few minutes overbreathing, one may ask a patient to shout or scream without the therapist doing anything physically to elicit the scream. Yet, if the patient is persuaded to scream, often a variety of unexpected events occur. Some patients begin to tremble almost immediately, as though the effort to scream has disturbed the precarious neurotic stability of the armor. A few others, after shouting loudly, may feel anger welling up and discharge it by pounding vigorously on the couch. Another few soon begin to whimper and break down in profound sobbing.

This approach is perhaps one of the simplest and most direct of the methods to be used in eliciting affects. It might be assumed that its effectiveness lies in the fact that most people have not dared to shout or scream since they were children. The veneer of good manners, social etiquette and fear of emotional display effectively sets up a barrier against anything quite so uncouth and infantile as a shout. An individual here and there will not comply with the request to shout because he has associated this with insanity. Only insane people scream, yell and shout. And since he is not insane, he must firmly decline to scream. All sorts of arguments and rationalizations will be presented to avoid the necessity of breaking through the armor to permit the emergence of affects.

One patient explained that while on the delivery table with her first child, she screamed and cried without restraint. However the obstetrical nurse reprimanded her severely, cautioning her against disturbing nearby patients, and advising that if she continued in such unrestrained emotional expression she could go "stark raving mad." The fear of being considered crazy was therefore adequate to block any kind of abreaction, no matter how much stress and strain she experienced on the couch during treatment. A good deal of orientation was needed before she was able to discard such inhibitions.

These rationalizations can be effective in blocking therapeutic progress, so fearful has the patient become. I have known a few patients to quit therapy rather than shout. In such cases, discretion being the better part of valor, the termination of therapy can best be avoided by not pressing the patient too hard and switching over to verbal communication.

One patient with chronic rheumatoid arthritis was incapable of screaming. Superficially she seemed a placid, easygoing person of some 38 years for whom any show of hostility was altogether out of the question. She had a typical passive-feminine character structure. Yet her history was marked by parental rejection, familial strife of the basest type, economic insecurity, a poor social adjustment, many frustrated love affairs and two abortions—all before the age of 21. After the second abortion she incurred arthritis and all medical treatment was unsuccessful. After a session in which she was verbally prodded and encouraged to scream without result, a significant memory spontaneously emerged just prior to the next session.

At seven or eight years of age, she engaged in a fight with an older sister who, more robust and powerful, knocked her down and grabbed her long hair. In this way, the sister dragged her along the garden pathway. It was excruciatingly painful and she screamed continuously with pain. Just inside the house, Mother heard these screams and jumped prematurely to the conclusion that something had happened to the older sister. She ran out of the house to investigate. When she found that this was merely a childish squabble and that nothing had happened to her favorite daughter, she took a switch across the neck and back of the younger sister. Under the circumstances her more or less unconscious interpretation was logical enough: "If you scream you get beaten." Once this memory had been worked through clinically, she became capable of screaming loudly without being physically prompted, thus expressing a little of her accumulated pained feelings. Very quickly her rheumatic shoulders and arms relaxed, with much of the tension and chronic pain being alleviated. This is not to imply that she was "cured" by any manner or means. However, the otherwise inevitable progress of the disease appeared arrested and clinically she became well enough to hold a job, the first employment in seventeen years of physical invalidism.

Another most effective device is the sharp tap to the abdomen. At first sight this may sound a brutal or sadistic method of eliciting emotional responses. In point of fact, however, most patients later come to recognize its effectiveness and express gratitude that the method was used. It, too, will elicit scornful laughter, anxiety, rage, fear and tears, either alone or in conjunction with muscular activities which presage the orgasm reflex. In the neurotic patient, the belly is invariably heavily armored as though the abdominal contents are being specially guarded against intrusion. Complete exhalations go far towards softening the whole belly area, permitting the emergence of some of these feelings. But there are patients whose abdominal armoring is so rigid that adequate respiration has become almost impossible. The unexpected blow to the belly acts as a nervous shock which releases these vegetative contents. The shock and release may even result in urination on the couch or in evacuation of the bowels immediately after the session. Nearly always the expected emotional discharge and muscular quivering are the welcome outcome of the attack, thus facilitating the continued progress of therapy.

"It wasn't so much the pain that made me scream," remarked one patient. "All right, it was the pain that started me off, but that wasn't really too bad. Anyway, it disappeared fairly quickly, and in its place I could feel a rage, a terrible rage such as I've never known before—at least that I could remember. And all I could do was scream and scream and scream!"

I personally never objected too strongly to any of these physical ministrations during my own therapy; perhaps this may be interpreted as a masochistic trend on my part. I doubt it, however. Nor can I admit to any sadistic pleasure in administering this phase of therapy to my patients. In any event, I must register the conviction that it is a valuable component of the therapeutic regimen despite the fact that occasionally some patients indignantly terminate, or threaten to terminate, therapy at this juncture. Resistance also may arise if there is the possibility of its further use. Some object strongly to being "pushed around" or being "beaten up," as they term it. It might be well in such circumstances to analyze the resistance and examine the indignation that is evinced. Historical factors will always be discovered that account for it. They become intrinsic parts of the negative transference that arises.

Yet in most cases, if the timing is good, the attack of the belly wall will result in the total surrender of the organism to its own feelings. The sudden shock to the recti muscles causes contraction. This shortening of the muscles pulls the chest downwards and the pelvis up. It is preparatory to the orgasm reflex itself. The timing has to be good, however; otherwise there is no yielding or surrender, merely resistance and hostility to the therapist. For the chronically repressed patient who is severely affect-lame on the basis of blocked-off hostility, there may appear no alternative but to "beat him up" as some patients term it with characteristic exaggeration. Other psychotherapists appear also to have found that such so-called physical attacks on the patient are highly effective, resulting in fewer emotional impasses than often occur with more conventional approaches. For example, Whitaker and Malone wrote:

> "Aggression by the therapist may be used to augment anxiety. It is used frequently to fragment the defenses of the patient and to break through the pseudo-adultness of the patient to find his infantile need... Actual physical aggression has been used by the authors with deteriorated schizophrenic patients; and where, in some instances, years of therapeutic endeavor have failed to reach the psychotic patient, active and intense physical assault was effective in opening up an emotional relationship between the therapist and patient on the basis of which therapy could proceed... To be adequate to the patient's needs, it must be personally appropriate to that patient, and not displaced from another area." (10)

In other words, the therapist must have undergone intensive therapy and shed his own armor to a considerable extent before methods of this type can be employed.

An interesting response to this actual aggression on one compulsive patient—in this instance, pressing with the thumbs on the spastic masseter muscles at the angle of the jaw—was that he swiftly leaped from the couch and, after smashing a small table lamp, stood in the middle of the floor swearing vigorously and eloquently at me, screaming and crying at the same time. His anger and rage were so deep and genuine that later, when I held his head to my chest, he could hardly believe me to have been without any resentment for the stream of hateful invectives he had hurled at me. The realization that he was not rejected, despite such an intense outburst, fostered a deep emotional relationship which augured well for his therapeutic progress.

Some patients approach their sessions with what appears at first to be nonchalance—others with some degree of eagerness and pleasure. The therapist needs to be reminded that things are not always what they appear to be. I have previously mentioned a patient, Jennie, with a 3-year-old son. Between these two there was always friction—a friction which the mother realized was wholly irrational. There seemed to be little she could do to control these irrational bursts of irritability and anger towards her little boy. She had had some conventional psychotherapy before her son was born, and had approached vegeto-therapy with what appeared to be a great deal of eager anticipation. However, it soon transpired that there was an enormous amount of caution in whatever she did—breathing, raising her arms, moving her hips, softening the eyes, sticking out the tongue. Though she gave the impression of being extra-cooperative, closer inspection revealed a great fight to control possible feelings that might emerge from the therapeutic work.

She complied with literal exactness to every instruction. If she was hurt, she yelled—and so forth. On one occasion I tapped her in the epigastrium where there seemed to be a great deal of tension. She screamed and kept on screaming. I sensed this was artificial. I poked her in the belly, again and again, some nine or ten times. The artificial scream ceased. She began to flail her arms about protectively.

The scream took on another note. Fear was written all over her. Within a few seconds she was panic-stricken, yelling, "Stop it! Stop it! You're killing me! You're killing me!"

This was one of those occasions when the therapist must go along with whatever opportunity presents itself to open up the armor more thoroughly. Forced respiration was instituted, helping to lengthen her exhalations. Soon a spate of tears let loose, continuing for fifteen minutes or so. After its subsidence, I encouraged her to talk about what she had felt and experienced during the active part of the session. As she spoke a fine quiver and tremor began to develop; she was encouraged to talk despite this, to let it take its course, fearful though she might be.

A great deal of her history was known to me, information gathering having been conducted during previous sessions. But some of the amnesic and, emotionally speaking, most significant gaps now began to be filled in. She was the youngest of ten children, nine girls and one boy. The marital life of the parents was marked by periodic squabbles, petty bickering and internecine warfare. The relationships among the siblings was not too dissimilar. Discipline was applied with a firm and harsh hand. In her thirteenth year, a couple of days before Christmas, Jennie was rude to her father—she "sassed" him over some trivial situation. He approached her with open hand, before which she ran, seeking shelter in the bathroom. Angry at her hasty exit, father chased her and, pushing into the bathroom where she cowered in a corner, belted her cruelly with his heavy razor strop. Hurt, humiliated and weeping, she screamed when it appeared he had lost his temper, "Stop it! You're killing me, you're killing me!" This screaming acted as a cold douche, as it were, and restored him to his senses. As he silently strode from the bathroom, she muttered *sotto voce*, "Go to hell! I wish you were dead!" Upon hearing this, father's temper returned—and the beating with the razor strop was resumed.

A few days later, right after Christmas, an accident occurred to the ice truck which her father manned. He was knocked down on the icy street, suffering a concussion and a fractured skull with internal injuries. A few hours later, in the hospital, he was dead following cerebral hemorrhage.

The next few years brought considerable hardship to the family. The older girls were obliged to curtail their education and obtain jobs to augment the family income. Mother scraped, skimped and labored to the care of the large family. One by one the girls married and left the family home. The only boy had previously left, destination unknown. Finally, only Jennie remained. Her relationship to mother was marked by hostile outbursts and difficulties of one kind or another. Occasionally, Jennie fantasized that she would never be able to marry, her role in life being to look after mother. Occasionally, death-wishes would creep into her mind. Her mother's demise could be the only solution to her problem, but guiltily they would be dismissed. In her early frustrated twenties she met an architect with a good background and education with whom she fell in love. They announced their engagement—but within a couple of weeks her mother became ill. Months of medical treatment transpired with intermittent epileptoid fits and hallucinations before eventually a diagnosis of cerebral arteriosclerosis was established. After marriage, mother became such a problem to the newlyweds in their home that she had to be committed to a mental hospital. From then on, Jennie developed severe guilt reactions with much self-accusation—she was responsible for mother being in the mental hospital.

During another therapeutic session, when she was well-hyperventilated, I gently manipulated the sterno-cleidomastoid muscles on both sides of the thyroid. Again, a kind of hysterical alarm intervened. To relax the cervical segment, she was asked to gag. Here all sorts of resistances emerged. She would glower at me between gags, muttering, "I hate you. I could kill you!" As she developed insight from these procedures, she realized that when she felt I was killing her, she was abreacting her much earlier feelings that in his rage her father would kill her. Second, she realized that she had blamed herself for his death. If she had not wished him dead, he would not have been killed. When he died in the hospital, an older sister who sat by the deathbed reported he had choked on his own blood. Jennie would not gag in therapy, fearing she would rupture a vessel that might result in a similar kind of termination as her father's. Third, she feared mother would discover she had killed her father and that according to the terms of *lex talionis* she in turn would be killed. Fourth, all the hardships that the mother and the entire family endured as a result of her father's accidental death were to be laid at her doorstep. It was no accidental death, but murder. Fifth, the years of privation and deprivation that eventuated in mother's sickness were due to father's murder and, therefore, also were to be attributed to her. All of these factors, then, were responsible for her mother's commitment and for her overwhelmingly guilty feeling. To assuage her guilt throughout the years, unconsciously she had tried to identify herself with the mother. In so doing, she recapitulated with her own child the abominable relationship she had had with her own mother throughout her own lifetime.

Some of these she had been able to conceptualize, but it remained for the attack on the epigastrium, the pinching of spastic cervical muscles and the gagging to release the repressed feelings which had become anchored in these segments.

Little probing is required to elicit this kind of insight and psychological material. It seems to go hand in hand with the somatic and affective responses that the patient makes to the several experiments of therapy. The occasional verbal session enables him to communicate these to the therapist, facilitating not merely a further discharge of affect-laden memories, but to enable him to understand himself so much more completely. It helps the patient to understand how his personal history and interpersonal relationships within the family setting have gone to shape his present character-structure in all of its warped aspects. This understanding and insight, with the gradual dissolution of the character-muscular armor, reveal to him the methods he must employ to change his environment and his responses to that environment.

Conditioning must play a tremendous role in the therapeutic process. As therapy proceeds session by session, little hyperventilation may be required to initiate the psychological and physiological reactions. After several sessions have been experienced, the patient's cortex may have become thoroughly conditioned to the therapeutic situation. Cortical intoxication may be induced with only a few deep respirations—and its inhibiting activity curtailed rapidly. I have seen patients take barely half a dozen deep respirations in the treatment position when a profound state of relaxation ensues, in which a light touch here and a gesture there suffice to initiate tics, twitchings, choreiform motions, together with emotional responses of anger, rage, fear, depression and tears. These vegetative excitations tend to appear readily without any particular emphasis on respiration.

Some of the involuntary muscular activities that occur in connection with the eruption of some affects are worthy of discussion. Laughing, crying, coughing, gagging, yawning and the orgasm reflex have this in common to the observer: the muscular contractions in each are extraordinarily similar. Vomiting is accompanied by a convulsion of the body, a rapid folding of the epigastrium with a forward jerk of head as well as pelvis. From the energy point of view, *strong waves of excitation run from the middle of the body upwards and downwards towards mouth and anus*. These convulsions, Reich noted, accompany deep expiration and a wave of excitation from the diaphragmatic region to the head on the one hand and the genitals on the other. In vegeto-therapy any and every emotional response is welcomed both for its own sake and because it represents a major change in character structure. In most cases, the bodily movements accompanying these affects are premonitory of the orgasm reflex.

Gagging has already been discussed in detail. Coughing in itself is hardly important enough to warrant much consideration here. A few patients evince a "nervous" cough as soon as they assume the work-position. One man coughed incessantly whenever he should have shouted. Stifling of sobbing sounds may result in coughing and spluttering. It produces a severe throat block akin to the classical *globus hystericus*. Once shouting and crying have been achieved, the tight throat is relaxed and the resultant cough disappears.

Crying, yawning and laughing occur so frequently during vegeto-therapy that I feel they demand more than casual mention.

**Crying.** If you have ever watched a person weep from deep down in his belly when he has been overtaken by grief or by inexpressible loss, and perceived the spasms and convulsive abdominal contractions that literally shake the organism, immediate understanding arises concerning its importance to the whole process of vegeto-therapy.

Crying is a normal and genuine need of the organism. It is a profound emotional response to hurt, grief, fear or a loss of one kind or another. But because of discipline and authoritarian attitudes which impose punishment for such expressive types of behavior, it is a capacity that most of us lose long before adolescence rolls around. Patients will often recall during a crying episode parental reactions to their tears when they were young. "If you keep on crying, I'll really give you something to cry about." This, perhaps, is the most common of all experiences that ultimately sets up the inhibition against crying. "Only sissies cry" is another of the diabolical prompts blocking off this most natural of all affective responses. "You make us very unhappy by your crying; you should be very grateful for all we have done for you." These are only samplings of the anamnestic prompts that have resulted in repression.

Under these and similar circumstances, the need to cry is choked back. This is best accomplished by tightening the throat, as though to choke back one's feelings. A chronically contracted diaphragm is necessary to prevent the belly spasms that accompany crying. And to keep the diaphragm in this condition, a raised rigid chest is also required. All these events mirror themselves in lackluster eyes and in the face, eventually becoming chronic—and so lost to awareness. With the loss of awareness there is also a loss of function. Later one finds oneself wholly unable to cry, even when one needs to very badly. I have known many patients who recount sorrow and tragedy and despair with perfectly dry eyes. They will speak of their wish and desire to cry, knowing full well what tears would do for their grief. But no tears will come. And the pain in the chest and the tight gut and the choking lump in the throat persist so that they can neither eat nor sleep. This they know. Thus they long for tears which never flow. With this chronic tension, what wonder that alcohol has become so necessary?

Julie, a patient with severe anxiety tension reactions, continually struggled during each session against her own need to cry. Even though she was aware of the tremendous tensions she had to generate to block off the tears, there was no yielding whatsoever. "I can't go around crying all day," she would moan on the couch. I had to remind her gently that nonetheless she could "go around all day" with severe pains in her neck, shoulders, chest and abdomen—pains which attracted her constant attention and all her energies—pains which could be so readily alleviated by one good cry. Many sessions were necessary before she would permit this affect to break through her muscular and characterological inhibitions.

The inability to sob carries with it the burden of the inability to breathe fully. The chest becomes fixed in the chronic inspiratory muscular attitude. Almost impossible is a long and full exhalation. The business of childhood thus remains continued and unfinished, perpetuated into adulthood through the agency of involuntary muscular blocks. And this defeats the innate biological tendency towards completion or closure through adaptation. With a rigid musculature, adaptation is relatively meaningless.

Being forced by therapy to shout, scream and cry releases the tight block in the chest and belly. The throat spasm may be a little more difficult to release, but gagging and inspiring with "crowing" sounds may facilitate loosening of the throat. As these involuntary blocks become dissolved, the individual gradually learns to sob with his whole being when the life-situation demands it. He no longer has to suffer silently, nursing a horrid hurt inside with no means of emotional release.

When the patient begins to cry on the couch, regardless of the technical device used to break the block, it is common practice to touch his arm or to put one's hands on his face, to show sympathy in some similar way. It is very comforting to the patient, giving him a profound sense of security and empathy with the therapist. The latter assumes a significant parental role; he must show that he, too, can be loving and tender. So often at this stage I have heard patients mutter between sobs, "I feel so young" or "I feel so utterly helpless." It facilitates the emotional growth of the patient to experience the therapist's firm direction in breaking the crying block and then to be enfolded by his love. This is something to be experienced first; it is rather overwhelming. Many a negative transference that long defied solution by conventional means has been utterly dissolved in the warmth and love that arose after anger and tears had been elicited and when the patient had been held by the therapist. The transference reaction that it fosters is invaluable, evoking as it does emotional responses belonging to an earlier period of life. Above all, it helps the patient to complete the unfinished business of childhood when, perhaps, he had longed for love and understanding where neither had been forthcoming.

In the consulting room the therapist works steadfastly and consistently in the direction of enabling the patient to dissolve his muscular blocks and to wash them away in a stream of tears. Once the door has been opened, patients report long periods of crying between sessions. Sometimes tears appear to be evoked by almost any stimulus. Sometimes they will retire at night to bed and cry themselves to sleep as they once did when children. They need to be encouraged to let this phase of things exhaust itself, as it eventually will.

Under these circumstances, there are full clonic spasms and convulsive movements and quiverings of all the muscles of the diaphragm, belly, chest walls and the throat. As the sobbing subsides and the patient begins to experience the tremendous relief afforded by frank and open crying, there is a metamorphosis of emotional response. Relief through sobbing may pass perceptibly to pleasure and orgastic sensations as the body, relaxing spontaneously, passes into the involuntary natural movements of the orgasm reflex itself.

One final word in this connection. When the tears will not arise, the therapist would do well to re-examine his efforts in connection with the first (i.e., ocular) segment of the armor. He may find the eyeballs tense and immobile and the superciliary muscles cramped. Work should be resumed there to engineer a dissolution of the tension. Rather than hurt the patient myself, I have often asked a patient to dig the fingers of both his hands into the occipito-frontalis and in this way raise and lower it with great vigor. The underlying tissues may be very painful, and the patient should be instructed to make any kind of open noise that pleases him or helps him to express or tolerate the pain. The area soon feels altogether congested and, as hyperventilation proceeds, tics may arise.

There is an old hypnotic technique which may be enlisted on behalf of vegeto-therapy, although the intent is different. The therapist slowly moves his hand up and down about a foot or so from the patient's face. The patient is instructed to follow these movements with his eyeballs. The motion is up and down, from side to side and any other series of movements that may occur to the therapist to achieve mobility of the extrinsic eye muscles. Forcing the eyes to open wide and then shutting them tight a number of times will also go far towards activating this area. It still astonishes me to discover that such activation of the eye segment may release tension in the diaphragm and abdomen, permitting the free eruption of crying.

**Laughing.** Mention has already been made of the spontaneous emergence of laughing jags. Chuckling and a contagious laughter develop during various stages of therapy. While in most instances, but not necessarily all, this is defensive, representing avoidance of other far more disturbing affects. Nevertheless it is never criticized nor rejected by the therapist. On the contrary, it is welcomed and the patient is encouraged to express it fully. It may become so contagious that the therapist will be obliged to laugh himself while watching the patient. This in turn catalyzes the patient's responses so that he laughs more and more. I recall one man who began to laugh early in the session. His laughter continued throughout the rest of the hour. His diaphragm was exhausted at the close of the session. A week later when he returned for the next session, he had only to lie down on the couch when again he began to chuckle. It also lasted for the rest of the hour. This persisted for four or five sessions.

Superficially interpreted, it is at the very least some type of emotional activity. For the patient who has habitually hidden all of his feelings, it may represent a tentative effort to slough off part of his protective armoring. Moreover—and this is important—quite often the laughing may progress to such an involuntary level as to become explosive and deep. It may well up from the depths of the organism. Watching the physiological accompaniments of such behavior, one perceives almost identical muscular processes as occur with crying. The whole organism participates. The muscular movements proceed from the diaphragm and belly. Even tight chest walls are obliged to move freely until the chronic inspiratory spasm is released. The body rocks with this activity. When it persists, it facilitates deep respiration. The body becomes bathed with perspiration, dizziness is often induced followed by an overwhelming weariness. A breakdown of some neurotic controls is inevitable under these circumstances.

The laughing involuntarily induces a relaxation of most of the chronically hypertensive muscles all over the body which the patient, by his own conscious efforts, might have been unable to achieve.

After a long round of laughing, relaxation will occur with full easy exhalations, with the patient becoming more aware of the ease and pleasure involved in the flow of air in and out of his lungs. If there has been adequate therapeutic preparation, the easy convulsive reflex of the orgasm may ensue. At other times, before the reflex is able to occur, the laughter precipitously culminates in open crying.

Laughing sometimes occurs on the basis of ticklishness. Some patients are sensitive to touch and respond to tactile stimulation with broad laughter. Any attempt to touch them, no matter how gently or lightly, results in different types of protest. History-taking usually indicates that in many ways they are frightened people who have learned to repress the gross manifestations of their fear. They have developed reaction-formations that are socially acceptable, but which are personally devastating. They are the "yes" people who are eternally busy being nice to everyone. They cannot bear to hurt anyone's feelings, acquiescing and agreeing so that their own feelings may not be hurt. The more they say "yes" to others the more they consolidate their own social armor which continually says "no" to their own creative feelings. Their ticklishness in therapy could almost be construed as "leave me alone," "don't hurt me," "I'm frightened to let go."

One man, about 48 years of age, who came to therapy for the complaint of intermittent impotency, would become extraordinarily ticklish after a few minutes of hyperventilation. I would only need to touch—and lightly at that—the neck muscles or brush with my fingers the lateral aspect of the ribs and he would roar with laughter, pulling away from my fingers. He would beg me not to tickle him. When I persisted, the laughter became more strange, with peal after peal of robust laughter shaking his entire body. Gradually the underlying psychological signature emerged. Ordinarily he was fairly affect-lame, with the mask of a cultured European gentleman: high-chested, good carriage, suave, sophisticated, reserved and with a wide range of intellectual interests. His history revealed isolation and rejection in childhood, very little affective impact from his parents and little ability to express his own feelings. He had developed a great deal of contempt for most people he came into daily contact with—contempt which was hidden under haughtiness and arrogance.

He was not particularly proud or arrogant when hyperventilation swept aside his restraints and showed him to be a sensitive, frightened and lonely person. His defense against these feelings had been contempt, and it was this character trait which culminated in his impotency. It is difficult to be sexually potent with people whom one despises.

**Yawning.** The patient may be in the work position on the couch, verbalizing on whatever topic has arisen for discussion. All goes well and there are no unusual phenomena attending the session. The topic exhausts itself, at which time the therapist may recommend the return to active non-verbal therapy. The patient takes a couple of deep breaths, yawns lightly, and proceeds with the breathing. After a half dozen more exhalations, there is another yawn; a few more exhalations and yet another. Gradually the yawns deepen until, as the therapist watches, each successive yawn produces a thoroughgoing quivering of the body. There is a great deal of muscular loosening up with yawning—but it would seem as though the patient is able to achieve little satisfaction from the yawning. The activity does not achieve at first what he feels the yawn should produce, but as one watches, the yawn throws the head backwards, pulls the shoulders down and forwards, induces a quivering in the pectoral muscles and even draws up the pelvis.

In other words, as with so many of the phenomena that spontaneously arise in vegeto-therapy, there is a gradual preparation for the orgasm reflex. The yawning is not merely due to the need for additional oxygen. The patient obtains and uses all the oxygen he is capable of inhaling. Braatøy (3) has suggested that this constant incomplete yawning is evidence of light fear which induces an alert, watchful attention and thereby restricts breathing. Some vegeto-therapists suggest that this compulsive repetitive yawning gives evidence of a state of boredom. It implies that in his daily activities there is a continual ennui—of which, perhaps, the patient is not normally aware. But it is there. And behind boredom there is a barely concealed hostility and anger with the life-situation which has produced the boredom—be it employment, family or love-life. The anger can often be elicited by showing the patient how to let the terminal phase of the yawn pass into an angry gesture.

If no attempt is made to interfere with the repetitive yawning and the patient is encouraged to proceed with the exhalations, the occasional quiver induced by the yawn may become more generalized. If this does occur, then some of the tension related to the "on guard" state is shaken off and a profound yawn with much sound develops which does finally satisfy and give relief. Many of the tight chest and neck muscles may then be seen to relax; the breathing becomes easier and more effortless. Crying may then ensue. I am also led to believe that yawning at first is an hysterical substitute for tears. But later it becomes the herald of profound relaxation.

If the tension persists, then active measures may be taken to break into the vicious cycle. Any of the measures already described to discharge hostility and anger may suffice. Jabbing the pelvis upwards from the couch to the accompaniment of a loud shout very often is adequate. Or the more gentle approach of having the patient raise his arms towards the ceiling with every exhalation, in a gesture of supplication and yearning, also is useful. At other times, the patient may be asked to turn over and the therapist palpates the back. The muscles between the shoulder blades may be found rigid and unyielding. Working on them with the thumbs will provoke anger and unalloyed spitefulness—perhaps followed by tears and the emergence of the sought-after tender feelings. But in any event, yawning will have stopped and relaxation will have occurred.

**Rage.** Of all the emotions which plague modern man, anger or aggressiveness is the one he has least learned to cope with. From early childhood when he first hears that "nice boys (or girls) don't throw temper tantrums," to his acquisition of social and cultural conventions of polite behavior, etiquette and good manners, most of the time his hostile feelings have to be kept in abeyance. Once in a while, under considerable stress, there may be a volcanic eruption of anger, following which there is shame and remorse with pious determinations to prevent its recurrence. The outcome of these rages and guilt responses is neuro-muscular tension. The current widespread incidence of colitis, hypertension and coronary seizures is eloquent testimony of this repression and tension.

Many psychotherapists attempt to come to terms with this hostility by various devices. A common recommendation is regular athletic activity with the use of imagination. While hitting a golf ball, for example, one is enjoined to fantasize that one is striking the senior vice-president, the foreman or the wife. The wife is counseled to behave similarly while she is engaged in the performance of her household chores, to beat the bed while making it or to strike the floor with the broom while sweeping it, and so forth. In some institutions, there is a complex program to release the aggressive feelings of psychotic patients. It has been my experience, however, with patients who have undergone lengthy psychoanalysis that very rarely are the most subtle muscular tensions released. One has but to observe such a person breathe on the couch to realize the extent of his muscle-bound condition. The inhibitions remain.

So far as rage and anger are concerned, one does not have to scratch at the surface for too long to release these affects in the average neurotic patient. In a few instances, simple hyperventilation alone appears to stir up the organism to such a peak that discharge occurs almost immediately. Such patients need little verbal prompting or other aid from the therapist. In the event that anger does arise but appears to be somewhat restrained, the patient is instructed to beat the couch vigorously with both hands, either open or closed into a fist. The whole arm should be encouraged to participate in this movement so that muscles of the shoulder girdle and the superior chest can be employed and relaxed. Shouting, growling, cursing should accompany such movements. The patient may get fairly well carried away by these gestures and experience real gusts of genuine aggression. (Sound-proofing of the office becomes a necessity.) I have seen patients arise from the conventional work position, kneel on the couch and thump hard at the mattress for all they are worth. They contend that more force can be put into the punch from this position and more hostility discharged. After such angry eruptions, tears may appear—in which case a feeling of release and relaxation follows, with well-defined streamings and bio-electric sensations.

Other patients who have constructed rigid reaction-formations against anger and thus suffer inwardly, need considerable prompting and goading by all the vegeto-therapeutic devices available. Under such stimulation, the aggression released is prolonged and impressive. The release also provides clear glimpses into the meaning of the neurosis for which they came to therapy. It sometimes occurs that very little abreaction of rage is engineered until, after a long period of therapy, the patient has finally succeeded in crying. This appears to unlock the inner restraints. The crying may continue for several minutes at a time, repeated throughout many sessions. Eventually the crying may take on a vicious, aggressive quality characterized by shrill screams and choking sounds. The patient may punch, kick and want something to tear or twist—all the earmarks of an infant's temper tantrum. I have sometimes given the patient a thick turkish towel to twist, tear or pull upon—and this series of gestures provides much satisfaction. At other times, I have given the patient an old telephone directory, instructing him to tear it vigorously into tiny shreds. A great deal of effort and concentrated fury is devoted to this. After thousands of paper fragments have been carelessly tossed hither and thither, the office has sometimes given the appearance of having been ravaged by a cyclone. Later I ask the patient to collect the fragments into the waste paper basket, using all the profanities and obscenities that he can command.

At the outset there may be a profound reluctance to the manifestation of such feelings. The underlying fantasies connected with such rage may have been connected with murder and sadism, which of necessity had to be subjected to inhibition and repression. Such patients present a picture of almost frightening neuro-muscular tension. Their rigidity is generalized and of severe proportions.

During these responses and abreactions, it might be well for the therapist to push his chair a little distance from the couch—a good foot or two. The oxygen-intoxicated patient who is annoyed can kick very hard, without much discrimination—which, after all, is what one is attempting to achieve. Many a patient has muttered imprecations from closely clenched jaws. The threat is that he "would like to take a swing with clenched fists" or "deliver a good kick" at me or "a punch on the nose." Fortunately, it has never been my experience to actually be assaulted by a patient under these circumstances. However, there have been occasions when a patient has attempted to kick or strike out at me. At times, both my hands have been grasped angrily by a patient glowering hatred, but merely looking quietly at the patient's eyes assuages the possibility of attack. Some considerable agility and nimbleness is certainly required to deal with these happenings. Generally speaking, I do not think that the therapist has much to fear from the average patient—provided his diagnoses have been more or less correct. The average neurotic or maladjusted patient may threaten, but rarely will he permit himself to assault the therapist. Danger might conceivably be expected from a psychotic, from the chronic alcoholic or from the psychopathic personality.

Nevertheless, one colleague has told me that on a few occasions he has actually been punched by a patient. Hyperventilation does loosen the psychic controls, and when sensitive muscles like the trapezius or the sterno-cleidomastoid are firmly pinched, one should be prepared for almost anything. The method of dealing with this type of situation is, as I have intimated above, to look directly at the patient's eyes or, if need be, slap his face thus providing enough of a shock to bring him to his senses. One gazes at the patient's eyes until the latter show a softened appearance, when as a rule a show of tears and weeping terminates the possibility of further violent abreactions at the therapist's expense.

Progress has to be slow and methodical. Each successive session should be devoted to softening one armored segment after another. With the dissolution of each segment, or part of a segment, a little resistance will have been dissolved and a little affect discharged at the same time.

Dreams may occasionally be brought to the therapist by the patient. Their manifest content points to a fear of losing control with the possibility of a tragic accident occurring. This material may be briefly interpreted so that the patient's awareness of his fear of aggressive feelings may be heightened. With the abreaction of hostility by all the methods described, the dreams gradually change in noticeable ways. The fear of losing control is the predominant factor that gradually disappears.

But time and patience are required of the therapist. He needs to evaluate the patient's inhibitions and to determine if the softening-up process should be rapid or prolonged over many sessions before encouraging the abreaction of anger. Even the overtly hostile patient may not be willing to release anger on the couch, no matter how unpleasant his family claims he may be to live with. A variety of rationalizations may be offered. These should be methodically challenged, one after another, to strip him of superficial defenses. If successful, the patient will evince anger spontaneously, without arbitrary prompting by the therapist. But he may still require to be aided and guided so that as much as possible is discharged with a minimal residue. If the patient can be brought to tears after an upsurge of anger, the session is far more likely to be terminated with positive feelings of warmth and friendly contact with the therapist.

**Fear.** Enough has already been said of hyperventilation both by way of quotation and description to indicate that it induces quivering, trembling and twitching of muscles and of limbs. As the skin cools and the extremities tremble and shiver, the patient, without appreciating the physiology of these somatic responses, begins to experience fear. One need only to experience personally a little of this trembling and quivering to appreciate how easy it is to become afraid under these circumstances. It makes little difference as to whether one is intellectually oriented or not. Familiarity with physiological principles does not appear to diminish the intensity of the apprehension experienced as one feels so many unaccustomed physiological events occurring independently of one's control. Fear emerges—this is the simple basic fact. Some patients will blanch, others grit their teeth to control the fear; others unequivocally call out for help. Much later on, towards the end of therapy, just prior to the actual advent of the orgastic reflex, a similar fear sometimes appears. Just prior to the doubling up of the organism in the full easy convulsion of the reflex, some patients scream with unalloyed terror.

Under the stimulus of this emotion a vast adreno-sympathetic discharge is elicited which overwhelms all critical understanding. In small quantities, the suprarenal hormone is said to be synergistic to acetylcholine. In greater quantities it inhibits the latter. Thus, during the trembling which occurs as a result of hyperventilation and vasoconstriction, most parasympathetic responses, dependent upon acetylcholine for their transmission through the synapses, are inhibited. From this moment forward practically all responses are sympathetic and sub-cortical. They represent a true emergency response to fear in which reason and parasympathetic adjustment are out of the question. This status continues for a considerable length of time until the responses have died down during the period of relaxation. Gradually, then, with the reduction of adrenalin discharge, the inhibition of acetylcholine ceases, permitting parasympathetic impulses to express themselves.

The prolonged and concentrated attention to the work while the therapist attempts to break down abdominal and inter-thoracic tensions so as to permit more extensive breathing has an exciting effect on the cerebral cortex. Morgan has already explained this. But the cortex will tolerate excitation only up to a certain point. From that moment forward fatigue sets in. As Pavlov has indicated, "the exhaustion in a cortical cell consistently leads to the appearance in it of an inhibitory process." (9)

In other words, the cortex, which ordinarily by virtue of early training acts as an inhibitor of the subcortical structures, now undergoes inhibition itself. This releases the prolonged control over the old visceral brain, whose effect upon the rest of the organism is now manifested in a more marked and vigorous way.

One of these diencephalic structures is the hypothalamus which is known to play a significant role in the regulation of body temperature. Cobb states it is the center for the integration and externalization of the motor impulses that cause emotional expression. It is, moreover, "the head ganglion of the autonomic nervous system which mediates so many of man's emotional manifestations: blushing, sweating, erection of hairs, palpitation of the heart, raised blood pressure, urination and defecation, to mention the most obvious." (4)

At much greater length and with more detail, Grinker asserts:

> "Not only does the hypothalamus integrate all visceral and autonomic activity, but it functions as a balancing mechanism between the parasympathetic and orthosympathetic divisions. The parasympathetic system...furnishes the brake upon activities, conserves resources and reserves, and builds up tensions. The orthosympathetic system lies exterior to the visceral organs and enhances the functions of the sensorimotor apparatus, increasing its functional output. It is concerned with catabolic activity in massively discharging internal tensions. The fine cooperation of these two divisions results in the balancing of effects and the maintenance of an integrated regulated internal milieu, within certain limits of stress." (6)

Then Grinker goes on to state what is most significant to this theme, that:

> "Although hypothalamic activity integrates all autonomic functions, it includes but few somatic responses. Panting, shivering, running movements, and clawing are the extent of somatic responses from direct excitation of the hypothalamus."

I must interpolate that these somatic responses are common phenomena in the vegeto-therapeutic process. During the relaxing phase of the treatment, after a prolonged bout of hyperventilation, as the muscular tensions are being dissolved, the patient will often complain of chilliness and gooseflesh. Very soon shivering, diffused itching, panting and clonisms develop on a purely spontaneous level.

> "We can compare the relaxation of the hypothalamus to cortical autonomic centers as the extrapyramidal motor system to cortical motor areas. *Removal of the latter results in overactivity of the previously inhibited extrapyramidal system. Removal of the cortical autonomic centers results in overactivity of hypothalamic functions."* (7) (italics mine)

Many compulsive and obsessive patients claim ordinarily not to be subject to fear or panic. However, these are the patients who become especially disturbed or frightened during therapy when trembling and twitching occur sporadically in isolated muscle groups. Fear seizes them with an awful immediacy as they become aware of the possibility that their controls and lifelong defenses may be submerged in the welter of a rising tide of vegetative excitations. These are the phenomena that give them some degree of recognition of their previous affect-lameness.

Cortically they are not conscious of anger, fear, the need to cry, or any other affects. They are hard, cold and controlled, living their life out by reason, so-called, and by neurotic symptoms of many kinds. But soon they come to realize that in this series of physiological events the body is actually crying, or showing anger or experiencing fear. On the basis of this dichotomy—the language of the body versus the conditioned lameness of the cortex—they come to appreciate the meaning of their neurosis more clearly, This appreciation dawns on them with ever stronger meaning during each succeeding session, until integration and restructuring of the personality become real possibilities.

But until then they suffer, for fear and anxiety are not readily tolerated. An inner struggle is perceived as they become seized by the clutch of fear in the gut and as they trace back the historical origins of these feelings, sometimes to serious and grotesque familial traumata. The battle to tolerate this loneliness and inner misery—and to accept it—has to be fought again and again. There will be many times when the patient will come to doubt his ultimate ability to triumph and to discharge this affect. Only the warmth, love and sympathy of the therapist can aid the patient to gird up his loins and repeatedly face the terror that lurks within. There is no substitute for a solid transference to bring the patient through such emotional trials and tribulations.

## BIBLIOGRAPHY

1. Best, C.H. and Taylor, N.B. *The Physiological Basis of Medical Practice.* Baltimore, Williams & Wilkins, 1950, p. 414.
2. *ibid.*
3. Braatøy, Trygve. *Fundamentals of Psychoanalytic Technique.* New York, John Wiley, 1954, p. 167.
4. Cobb, Stanley. *Emotions and Clinical Medicine.* New York, Norton Co., 1950, p. 49.
5. Gellhorn, Ernst. *Autonomic Regulations.* New York, Interscience Publishers, 1943, p. 189.
6. Grinker, Roy. "Hypothalamic Functions in Psychosomatic Interrelations." *Studies in Psychosomatic Medicine* (ed. by French and Alexander). New York, Ronald Press, 1948, p. 54 *et seq.*
7. *ibid.* p. 62.
8. Pavlov, I.P. *Conditioned Reflexes and Psychiatry.* New York, International Publishers, 1941, p. 57.
9. *ibid.* p. 64
10. Whitaker, Carl A and Malone, Thomas P. *The Roots of Psychotherapy.* New York, Blakiston Co., 1953, p. 224.

# Chapter X

## Goal

"Everything natural and great is simple... Complexity is a life expression peculiar to the armored... The simple, straightforward, immediate, periodically leads in irresistible fashion to orgastic plasma convulsions."
— Wilhelm Reich

**Vegetative excitations.** The average patient's intolerance of his own body feelings has often startled and amazed me. When vegetative excitations well up from within, there is a well-defined sensation of something happening. Of this there is no doubt whatsoever. This *something* may be chills and tremblings, a wave of warmth with perspiration, a tetany followed by profound relaxation, the emergence of feelings and affects, or some almost indescribable proprioceptive sensations which are reported in terms of motion or movement of something within such as "tingling," or "buzzing," or "pulsating," or "prickling." Whatever the excitation or sensation is, it is remarkably distinct and cannot be explained away or negated. For most patients it is an entirely new kind of experience to which they respond, as to most new experiences, with some little alarm.

I am thinking specifically of Mary, who, after breathing faithfully in the prescribed manner for some minutes, gradually succeeded in achieving some relaxation of shoulders and belly. This should have encouraged her since one of her major complaints had been severe muscular tension, especially during sexual intercourse, preventing her from achieving an orgasm. Instead, however, she began to gasp, sob and wriggle with all the earmarks of considerable discomfort. Since all of this wriggling prevented the continuation of active vegeto-therapy, she was asked to talk about the sensations that were troubling her. She described tingling and prickling sensations in the legs, ascending from her feet to her thighs and hips, sensations which also "buzzed" along the spinal gutter. There was some previous familiarity with such vegetative excitations. Quite often she had been awakened out of a sexual dream by this buzzing and tingling, and the anxiety would keep her awake for hours. Long futile periods of sexual intercourse that did not culminate in an orgasm tended to induce similar physical sensations. Occasional verbal discussion enabled her to appreciate the simple fact that these were her own body energies attempting to break loose from chronic tension.

When she could be persuaded to delay her fear responses just long enough to watch and feel these sensations more or less objectively, she gradually came to realize that they had at one time accompanied feelings that her religious and family training had labeled as "bad." The fear of her own bodily sensations was equivalent to the fear of her own emotions. Sensations and emotions co-exist, like two sides of a single coin. Re-education was the most important procedure at this point, learning how to accept and tolerate her own body with its responses.

Every psychiatrist and psychotherapist has at some time or another encountered patients such as Mary who routinely describe intense physical sensations as an integral part of their anxiety attacks or emotional upsets. At first I thought that they augured well for a favorable prognosis in vegeto-therapy, for having already experienced these autonomic excitations they would rapidly become acclimated to the deliberately induced form of such sensations and be willing to proceed enthusiastically further. It now becomes apparent that the patients who experience such a profusion of tinglings and paresthesias are actually affect-lame. They have lost all contact with their emotions. It transpires that only when the threat arises of experiencing a genuine gust of feeling of any kind that anxiety develops. In the place of feelings they now have body sensations. It is as though, in dealing with a two-sided coin, the patient cannot cope with the obverse side of the coin, and the reverse is so frightening that it literally "scares the devil out of me," to quote one patient.

This fact has to be recognized during therapy. Such patients not only need to be encouraged to relax to their organ sensations, but have to be taught that such vegetative excitations can be deliberately induced by little more than overbreathing. Again and again with such patients, I have asked them to take a chance on hyperventilating long enough to induce the full flow of tinglings and paresthesias and then they can stop and relax. As they realize that such indeed is the case, some of the terror is relinquished and they are willing to proceed just a little further. Then they need to understand that such vegetative excitations are integral parts of the total psychic experience that we call emotion. At the beginning of treatment, the patient may report a great variety of such body-sensations. The earliest reported areas are in the hands and feet. Some experience tinglings in the face and elsewhere, dependent upon where the original muscular blocks were located.

As therapy progresses, it is noteworthy that most patients report very few such tinglings, etc. By then he has learned to flip the coin as it were, and to experience his emotions and feelings in their true form with immediacy and not through their somatic equivalents. They are related, it is true, but the vegeto-therapist constantly seeks to eliminate the primary condition of affect-lameness. And while at the onset of therapy he may be content to teach the patient to accept his own body sensations, later he will surely attempt to orient the patient to their emotional equivalents—whatever they may be. For example, one schizoid girl would experience a good deal of quivering in the buttocks which set off clonisms in the thighs and pelvis. Much later, as she approached the end of therapy, she came to realize the connection between trembling and the extreme loneliness she experienced as a child.

Another patient, a 29-year-old male with severe obsessions, loosened up well save in the legs and feet. These would tingle profusely, but under no circumstances would they quiver or tremble. As therapy wore on, he recalled a period in his boyhood when his mother would bathe him daily. After the bath, she would rub him down with a coarse turkish towel and sprinkle talcum on his genitals. Since he was a big boy, he was capable of having erections. But since he feared what mother would think or do—he recalled from bedwetting experiences that mother respected no confidences—he struggled against genital stimulation by tensing his legs, feet and toes. This he had practiced for so many years that the lower extremities were a mass of severe involuntary tensions.

When the patient's response to the quivering and other body sensations is positive and less fearful, they come to describe these feelings as "soft," "most delightful," and *inside* the bones rather than superficially on the skin or in the surface muscles. For the first time in their lives a wholeness is perceived—such as, "For the first time I feel I'm becoming connected all over." Or, as another patient volunteered when he was asked what these feelings were doing to him, "It's made me alive!" I think this is saying a very great deal for any kind of therapy.

Psychotic patients are also familiar with these electrical body sensations. Some paranoid schizophrenics are capable of describing them fairly accurately, despite the delusional nature of their interpretation. There is a relationship between what the psychotic feels spontaneously and what the neurotic patient feels while undergoing vegeto-therapy. This does not imply that the latter are being converted to psychotics, as once was actually suggested to me. Rather, the therapeutic process may throw a great deal of light on what is really occurring to the person who develops psychosis. In other words, there must be a disordered cerebral metabolism in the psychotic, as a result of which many sensory barriers and thresholds are lowered. This lowered threshold permits the awareness of various somatic and visceral processes, of which normally the average person is totally unconscious. It is only when this awareness arises in an otherwise unprepared person that delusional interpretations may develop, centering, of course, around the emotional conflicts of a lifetime.

Familiarity with this kind of phenomenon must have led Reich many years ago to interpret vegetative excitations in terms of orgone energy. So often patients describe their sensations *as if* an electrical energy were coursing through the nervous system. Long after the above had been written, I came across a footnote in the book by Braatøy, mentioned earlier. He confirms my inference here and wrote: "My guess is that the observations of such phenomena contributed to Wilhelm Reich's start on his 'electrical' speculations. It is a pity that in his further work he did not take time to correlate his observations with elementary electro-technic and neuro-physiology." (1) It is also a pity that Braatøy did not elaborate his thesis. Originally, Reich was content to explain these reported sensations with the libido theory. Later, he resorted to the more familiar concepts of bio-physical or neural energy. With the passage of time, he felt more and more convinced that, despite his patients' clumsy expressiveness, they were right in believing there was an electrical energy which poured into them during the therapeutic session.

Incidentally, there seems to be an extraordinary parallelism between Reich's orgone concept and what Jung calls *mana*, borrowing an anthropological term[1]. Jung has much to say about this energy phenomenon. While to be sure there are enormous theoretical and philosophical differences between Reich and Jung, on this energy concept they appear to be united. Jung's patients experience *mana* via their dreams; Reich's patients while they are working on the couch.

> "Whence this new idea that thrusts itself upon consciousness with such elemental force? And whence did it derive the power that could so seize upon consciousness that it completely eclipsed the multitudinous impressions of a first voyage (of Robert Mayer) to the tropics?... The idea of energy and its conservation must be a primordial image that was dormant in the collective unconscious... The most primitive religions in the most widely separated parts of the earth are founded upon this image. These are the so-called animistic religions whose sole and determining thought is that there exists a universal magical power about which everything revolves...something which the American investigator Lovejoy has appropriately termed 'primitive energetics.' This concept is equivalent to the idea of soul, spirit, God, health, bodily

---

[1] One has only to read the last chapter of *Cosmic Superimposition* and one is forced to compare Reich's cautious "functional rationalism" as he calls it, with the writings of Jung which have been labelled "mysticism." There are many resemblances indeed which should not pass without notice. Perhaps the major, if not the only advantage of Reich, is a simple manipulative technique, which, like Hatha Yoga, brings mysticism within the purview of objective study and clinical experience. The sensations and feelings that are experienced by the patient on the couch are not very far removed from some of the classically recorded mystical experiences, save that religious terminology is not used.

strength, fertility, magic, influence, power, prestige, medicine, as well as certain states of feeling which are characterized by the release of affects... This power-concept is also the earliest form of a concept of God among primitives and is an image which has undergone countless variations in the course of history... According to the old view, the soul itself is this power..." (6)

*Mana* may well be Reich's orgone energy, which in turn *may* be a real, measurable energy detectable by instruments not yet at our disposal. Some people are inclined to believe that a great deal of research now under way concerning the "electro-dynamic field" theory may eventually corroborate many of what they consider to be Reich's startling and unproven "hunches." These friendly critics merely deplore the fact that Reich felt compelled to invent a new terminology and did not take time out to see how his findings and operational concepts could be fitted into modern scientific nomenclature. For the time being I am inclined to simplify the whole idea to a bio-physical energy, the product of combustion, coursing within the organism. It is physico-chemical in nature and function.

McDougall wrote:

"The energy which all agree is regarded as converted from the potential chemical form to some active form within each neuron upon its stimulation, must not be regarded as confined to the neuron within which it has been liberated, but as capable of flowing on, passing into and through other neurons, so that each neuron serves not only as an irritable conductor of excitation imparted to it, but also as a channel through which the energy liberated within it and also the energy liberated within others with which it is in functional connection may flow from place to place within the nervous system." (7)

According to this formulation, although the nervous system is a mechanism for the transmission of impulses, it is also something more. It is a reservoir of energy. The afferent impulses coming in through the sense organs serve to tap this reservoir. They cause the stored-up energy to be transformed from the potential to the kinetic form. It is this energy thus transformed which is to be conceived as flowing out over the various efferent pathways to give rise to the action of muscles and glands. It is also this energy which, liberated from the inhibition of the cortex, is experienced as coursing through the organism during the relaxing phase of the therapeutic session.

The simple tingling of the earliest phases might also be explained easily in terms of relaxation of the vascular system, with increased internal respiration and combustion. It would seem that as a result of hyperventilation and the wider excursions of the diaphragm, the visceral capillary beds dilate and became engorged with blood. The continued diaphragmatic action stimulates the abdominal and thoracic viscera, massaging the capillary bed, forcing the chronically constricted capillaries to relax. One might liken this process to that which occurs when one shakes one's hand vigorously for a few moments. Invariably one becomes aware of a warm glow with profuse tingling. The active shaking results in the centrifugal forcing of a quantity of blood towards the terminal and peripheral capillaries. Under this impact, they are obliged to dilate. Thus they come to accommodate a greater quantity of blood, producing warmth and glowing. Sensory nerve fibers become stimulated, in response to which vasomotor impulses dilate the capillaries and venules, promoting better drainage of blood from the area involved. This complex set of activities must of necessity be connected with the well-defined set of body sensations which arise viscerally. This, perhaps, more readily than any other explanatory device, would account for the sense of well-being and improved physical health which is the result of a term of therapy.

When the patient arises from the couch at the close of a session, he may complain of dizziness, weakness or fatigue. It seems to me that this is a direct result of hyperventilation which has accelerated glucose metabolism. A mild hypoglycemia is the outcome of both prolonged hyperventilation and the adrenal discharge that accompanies emotional catharsis. It has been my practice for some time to keep a jar of hard candy in the office. Sucking a piece or two immediately after the termination of a session apparently supplies enough glucose to end the feeling of weakness and dizziness so that the patient can go on his way without excessive bodily discomfort.

As time proceeds, the light tingling becomes metamorphosed into well-defined prickling, almost like "pins and needles." Then it becomes heavier, a throbbing—a pulsation, even like the *sound* of the whirring or buzzing of an electric motor. In fact, many patients have described their sensations as if they were connected to a battery delivering direct current. Others, more sophisticated and informed, speak of a galvanic current with a gentle sine wave superimposed. It is these latter energy phenomena that are most difficult to explain.

The vitality of the child is well known. It appears as if there is a more or less inexhaustible fund of energy from which he draws. A little boy of three or four, for example, barely keeps still. He moves about—walking, running, climbing—practically all day until eventually at night he collapses in his bed, to sleep deeply and soundly, oblivious to all external noises. What happens to this vitality?

It is reasonable to assume that as the months and years go by he is subjected to more and more discipline, more and more restrictions, more and more criticism on an emotional level. Many of his crude, undisciplined behavior patterns are hardly acceptable to the adults around him. Under threat of punishment he is forced to restrain his feelings. As I have indicated earlier, inhibition and repression are not solely psychological processes. They are invariably accompanied by and sustained by neuromuscular tensions. By means of chronic muscular tension a state of relative emotional control is achieved—a neurotic restraint of which ultimately he loses awareness entirely. It becomes completely involuntary.

However, to sustain any kind of tension requires the expenditure of energy. If the emotions to be repressed are manifold and powerful, then a considerable quantity of energy is needed to repress them via the channel of muscular tension. The maintenance of a perpetual guard over unacceptable and undesired feelings requires involuntary mechanisms of inhibition in the form of tensions which, over a period of many years, deplete the personality of kinetic energy. What wonder, then, that the repressed neurotic patient invariably feels tired and exhausted! What wonder, too, that even with superficial psychotherapy to release some of the latent conflicts and emotional tensions a great deal of this fatigue and exhaustion is relieved!

The dizziness, vasoconstriction, trembling, tetany, paresthesias and energy-sensations are manifold evidences of the hyperventilation of the brain. Under the stimulus of so much oxygen, metabolism in the brain is extraordinarily heightened. Before fatigue overtakes some cortical cells as a result of overbreathing, the heightened oxidation of glucose in the brain must have generated vast quantities of energy. Probably it remains in a potential form when cortical inhibition sets in. During the last phase of the session when the patient, while relaxing, attempts to become more aware of proprioceptive perceptions, there is an awareness of a circulation of this kinetic energy through the neural pathways. The various sensory thresholds appear to have become lowered because of excitation and inhibition succeeding each other rapidly in the cortex. As a result of these altered neural thresholds, a greater quantity of energy can circulate in the vegetative chain, while simultaneously the patient's somesthetic awareness of its circulation is heightened. It might well be that this energy circulates a great deal if not all the time, but because of the normally high neural thresholds, there is usually little awareness of it. A great part of the therapy is devoted to heightening the patient's awareness of himself and diminishing proprioceptive thresholds.

A considerable alteration of these barriers or thresholds must follow as a result of hyperventilation and the oxidation which it fosters. It is part of the Reichian hypothesis that this energy, in process of circulation, aids in the dissolution of some of the visceral tensions that the therapeutic process cannot reach directly, and that this energy in itself has a decided therapeutic effect on the viscera that it is able to reach and so to charge.

"Dead" areas have to be rendered glowing and alive by their infiltration with energy before the orgasm reflex can occur. "Dead" areas are those where, despite hyperventilation, abreaction and manipulation, there is no sensation of tingling, streaming or pulsation. Where no such sensations arise, it is assumed that muscular blocks of one kind or another prevent the free circulation of neuromuscular energy. The task of the therapist is to loosen up these areas individually so the patient may become aware of the stream of vitality and power that surge through him. There is little mistaking "live" areas for "dead" areas, or vice versa. A rigid area rendered tetanic through hyperventilation may be perceived after relaxation has set in to be pulsating with energy as definitely and as clearly as if the moist pad of a sinusoidal generator were placed on that area.

There is yet another viewpoint to be considered here in relation to these energy phenomena. It was enunciated by Groddeck that, in the course of time, life brings about certain functional disturbances and anatomical changes of little importance to the healthy man, but which eventually come to retard the recovery of the sick man. He claimed that nearly all of these can and should be put right at the cost of some trouble and care by means of massage. The fact remains, avers Groddeck, that certain lower parts of the adult body always contain an excess of fluid; they always contain edemic tissue. This edema of particular body regions goes unnoticed because it develops imperceptibly over a period of years. A great part of our unconscious mental energy is consumed merely in protecting oneself from pain emanating from these water-logged places. From the moment that it no longer becomes necessary to devote unconscious attention and psychic energy to the avoidance of pain, the power thus set free can be utilized for other purposes, for the task of recovery. (5)

***

**Orgasm Reflex.** The problem of when conventional psychotherapy should be terminated has always remained unanswered, ultimately because there are no exact criteria that determine the end of therapy. (5) Some therapists superficially feel that therapy should terminate with the elimination of whatever symptoms the patient presented initially. Others feel that it should end when the doctor-patient relationship has been wholly explored and reestablished firmly on a realistic basis without infantile fantasies and dependency feelings. Still others feel that this termination should occur when the patient's dealings with the world—his family, his job, his co-workers and his community—have become entirely factual and realistic and without elements of fantasy and compulsion. In other words, they stress social adjustment. (10) These are all dependent upon evaluation by both the doctor and the patient in joint agreement. But nearly all agree that this evaluation is quite arbitrary and without any basis in any measurable objective terms. (2)

Perhaps most of this discussion can be summarized in a quotation from Clara Thompson:

"Originally cure meant the relief from symptoms... Today, in addition to relief from neurotic suffering a person is considered cured when he is capable of relating to other people with a minimum of parataxic distortions in his behavior, and when he is free to develop his powers as far as his education and life circumstances permit...

"It is obvious that absolute cure does not exist. We live in a sick society with which he must make some compromise, and probably no one exists who is so healthy that he can make all the compromises necessary for survival without occasionally resorting to mechanisms of escape, or at least temporary denials of reality... The decision to stop treatment should be by mutual agreement with the realization that life may yet stir up more difficulties which can then be coped with as they arise." (9)

Certainly we can agree that there is no generally accepted standard of "cure." In fact, the word "cure" has to be enclosed in quotation marks and followed, perhaps, by a question mark. *By contrast the orgasm reflex is in fact the one goal of vegeto-therapy.* It comprises a distinct goal to be achieved, and is the standard by which "cures" can be compared. It is more realistic, well-defined and factual than most of the other arbitrary standards of most forms of psychotherapy. With its achievement, vegeto-therapy is to all intents and purposes completed. By this standard the patient has been able to get rid of muscular inhibitions which interfere with full biological and emotional expression. He is capable of tension discharge in a natural, healthy manner by means of the orgasm reflex. It is a positive standard not arbitrarily imposed on the individual from without, but is strictly determined by the biological factors within the organismic makeup of the individual.

All the therapist should do is assist the patient to clear away those neurotic obstacles interfering with the achievement of this basic standard. When achieved, however, it is to be understood that then, and only then, is the patient really capable of continued emotional growth. Should any life-situation arise to provoke anxiety and tension, he has at hand the tools by means of which to discharge the tension and deal with the problem on a realistic level. He will "feel" his way through it. So often patients will come for a session all keyed up, tense and anxious and totally unable to cope with even the most trivial problems. By the time the session has been completed, and a total organismic state of relaxation achieved by the discharge of neuromuscular tension, most patients will offer the statement that the problem appears more soluble than before. This is even more true after the orgasm reflex has occurred. It represents the attainment of emotional and biological maturity. Reich calls this stage of growth that of the "genital character," and its hallmark is the ability to function, not without tension, but to discharge it effectively at regular intervals.

The orgasm reflex has been clearly, fully and frequently described by Reich. It is best appreciated first by personal experience, and then by further observation with patients. It occurs on the couch only as the direct sequel of intensive therapy and the acquisition of the ability to breath naturally. Of necessity the muscular armor will have had to be softened sufficiently for the individual to be able to bend and yield to himself. Affect-lameness will have been a pathological state left behind, and the organism will have become capable of sincerely experiencing tears, yielding to pleasure, anger or sexual excitations without fear. Many of the patient's life-problems will undoubtedly have been previously exacerbated by the therapy, plunging him into the depths of acute feelings such as sadness, despair and loneliness. Only from this basis can the reflex occur.

The orgasm reflex consists of a series of wave-like contractions beginning in the gluteals, and extending to the abdominal muscles which tend to flatten out the chest, while the shoulders and pelvis move upward, inward and forward. There is the sensation of the belly "caving-in." This may be initiated merely by free breathing, or as the result of easy myoclonic movements—crying, yawning, gagging; any sincere experience of emotion may start it off. Whatever the precursors are, it may begin with a sudden chill darting through one's body, or a feeling of extreme warmth. The skin becomes pink and warm, moist with a fine perspiration. The eyes are expressive with lively, active pupils.

As it develops, it is as though the shoulder and pelvic girdles were gently rolling toward each other in a soft, rippling series of waves. Some patients come to feel as if there were some kind of energy propelling them into doubling up. I, myself, have often felt as though there were bars pushing themselves up through the heels, while at the same time there was a yielding of the whole abdomen. It is as though the body, once the muscular tensions had softened adequately, were being pushed by an energy into the orgasm reflex. There may or may not be genital excitations, depending upon the patient.

Experiences of this kind, repeated throughout the years, must have impelled Reich to postulate orgone energy as an explanatory device to cover these and other phenomena which the orthodox psychologist can scarcely conceive of. In spite of this neurophysiological thesis, I cannot feel entirely that his explanations should be discarded until they have been thoroughly examined and investigated.

The reflex culminates in the eradication of total tension as though this vigorous and convulsive quivering of the body shook loose involuntary rigidities which could not be softened by volition or vegeto-therapy. Once in a while a patient will describe the reflex as a normal sequel of his sexual activity. As a result of this the patient describes feeling freer emotionally, is capable of accepting tender and soft feelings quite naturally, automatically discards compulsive characteristics, and derives infinitely more satisfaction from coitus than had been the case before. Many of the difficulties experienced previously in the sex life appear to be discarded as the result of this reflex.

It must again be affirmed that no conscious volition enters into the production of this reflex. No suggestions are given directly or indirectly to the patient by indoctrination or otherwise. It just *happens.* And as a rule it happens when the patient least expects it. Sometimes towards the close of a dynamic session, when the patient has succeeded in breathing freely with the whole thorax and abdomen, has discharged hostility, made gestures and grimaces successfully, sincerely experienced a simple direct emotion of any kind followed by soft and warm feelings of tenderness and has been instructed to stretch out and relax, then this phenomenon may occur.

It may begin as already indicated with a marked chill, or with a diffused warm glow spreading all over the body. It may change into a tingling sensation which gradually undergoes a metamorphosis into what can be called the galvanic charge. This seems at first to *grip* clonically the long muscles of the back, buttocks, the inner thighs and the shoulders. Very soon, much to the consternation of the patient initially, there may be a few bicycling movements, or perhaps the shoulders may gently jerk forward. The pectoral muscles twitch. Other twitches may appear here and there throughout the whole body. The pelvis begins to rock up and down, easily, pleasurably and without any effort. If the patient is instructed not to resist this rocking motion, but to watch it carefully while breathing easily, pulsating sensations seem to concentrate below the softened diaphragm and in the recti muscles, and then the wave-like motions softly occur. This is the orgasm reflex. With repetition and with encouragement it has a profoundly maturing effect on the entire person. The personality develops the capacity to function as the adult "genital character" described by Reich.

The therapist has to be on guard for two pitfalls—they are dug for the unwary. Both relate to simulation of the movements of the orgasm reflex. One is voluntary, the other involuntary.

The first occurs as a result of the patient struggling desperately to impress or to please the therapist. The latter may have inadvertently slipped some clues as to what he expects. To avoid suggestion, the less said to the anxious patient the better. In a transference situation, where he will do practically anything to gain the therapist's approval—or where therapy itself is creating such anxiety that he wishes it were over and done with—he will make bodily movements which he may think bear some resemblance to those of the orgasm reflex. The major difference is that they are characterized by considerable belly and back tensions. They also appear to be performed with muscular strain instead of occurring naturally and effortlessly. Furthermore they are wholly unproductive of any vital character restructuring. The patient's endopsychic problems remain unaltered.

The second possibility arises out of the real progress of the patient in therapy itself. Couch-work may produce strong pelvic streamings or pulsations. Should these occur too early during the therapeutic regimen, the falling anxiety may be evoked. This is nothing but the fear of his own body sensations—orgastic anxiety. In this event he may fall back on muscular tensions as a means of armoring himself against both the pleasurable streamings and their counter-cathexis of anxiety. This emotional conflict may be such as to demand repression; muscular tension is the psychosomatic bulwark of repression. At this stage of therapy, however, the repression with its accompaniment of muscular tension is dynamic. It is accompanied by vigorous bodily movements which to all intents and purposes block the orgastic reflex, yet simultaneously give the appearance of being the total body movement of surrender. It, too, is characterized by stiff abdominal and dorsal tensions, leaving the patient fatigued, even exhausted at the close of a session. Nightmares may occur from time to time, as well as a resurgence of former psychosomatic dysfunctions, until the conflict has been resolved through everyday living or therapy.

Reich stated that *the factor which changes the human structure from "sick" to "healthy" is the emotional bio-energetic coordination of the organism.* The orgasm reflex is merely the most prominent indication that coordination has actually happened. Respiration, breaking of muscular blocks, resolution of rigid character armor are nothing but tools of reintegration of the organism. They are, however, often mistaken for a therapeutic end in itself. To mistake mere tools for the end itself is the result of bad thinking due to lack of co-ordinated knowledge of the organism, a narrow judgment which does not fit the breadth and the depth of human emotional diseases. It is not a matter of "muscles" or of "breathing," but of understanding in which ways cosmic orgone energy came to form plasmatic moving substance, and in which ways cosmic orgonomic functions are present in all activities of the human animal.

This is Reich's viewpoint. And while some may or may not feel disposed to accept his orgone theory, at least the essential positive attitude is one to which attention should be given. It represents a dynamic outlook created by a vital, seeking and creative personality.

It might seem appropriate here to discuss briefly what Reich has termed orgastic potency, since there is a well-defined connection between the two concepts. Many people seem to believe that by orgastic potency Reich referred to the characteristics of a person who, like a "stud," was in a state of perpetual sexual readiness. It recalls an English poet who some decades ago expressed this stud-like attitude in these words: "Take thy fill of love when, where, and with whom thou wilt…" Despite the fact that very clearly Reich has dissociated himself emphatically from such a Bohemian or promiscuous viewpoint and has clearly defined his terms, many people who should know better persist in this gross misinterpretation.

For Reich, the orgasm is primarily a biological form of *energy discharge.* Some form of this exists in the simple cell and other elementary forms of life. In man it has become a highly complex phenomenon. But energy discharge is characteristic in all instances. *Tension is gotten rid of and replaced by relaxation.* In our sex-negative culture, conditioning has been so extensive as to set up enormous endopsychic obstacles to biological discharge in this basic orgastic form. The result is that the average heavily armored neurotic—no matter how frequently he may copulate—rarely achieves a total discharge of psychosomatic tension by this means. Kinsey's reports enumerate the number of orgasms experienced by those interviewed. But this number of orgasms does not necessarily imply that sexual satisfaction was obtained. Reich long ago contended that quantity is relatively unimportant; it is the *quality* of the coitus that counts. By quality is meant the extent to which tension and anxiety are dissipated. It is this factor that is all too often ignored. Where there is inadequate discharge of tension, profound feelings of satisfaction and inner peace may be absent. If love, tenderness, warmth and the orgasm reflex have not arisen from coitus, some dissatisfaction will be experienced. Promiscuity develops as a secondary drive, emanating from the fundamental biological wish in every living organism for fulfilment and gratification. The neurotic, with his sex-negative indoctrination, eternally hopes that his next sex partner will enable him to achieve full orgasm, full satisfaction, full discharge of tension. And when this fails to occur, he is compelled to go forward in his quest for a more satisfactory love partner, or become impotent or frigid as a gesture of protest.

Many years ago Reich stated that orgastic potency is *the capacity for surrender to the flow of biological energy without any inhibition, the capacity for complete discharge of all sexual tensions through involuntary pleasurable contractions of the body.*

The more chronic muscular tension the patient has discarded, the more his sexual activity is characterized by the genital convulsion at orgasm. In line with most of Reich's findings, emphasizing the psychosomatic unity of the organism, pleasure and tension-discharge express themselves appropriately in the muscular and visceral activity of the organism. Donald F. Geddes said that

> "love is much more than an affair of the heart. It is also an affair of the lungs, the blood pressure, the actual flow of blood—that is, the parts of the body to which it is directed in larger or smaller quantities; the whole nervous system, and the endocrines—the glands which pour out, upon occasion, into the blood stream, chemicals capable of many effects." (4)

The orgasm is an activity of the whole organism—psychic as well as physical. And while the emotional facets of the orgasm have been adequately dealt with elsewhere, it remained for Reich to insist that it must be accompanied by vigorous visceral and muscular activity. If not, then anxiety has become predominant as a result of familial, environmental and religious pressure, creating too powerful an armor for the biological energies to break through. The muscular convulsion occurring with the orgasm is in every way similar to the bodily convulsion that occurs on the treatment couch as a result of the vegeto-therapeutic work.

It is essentially an involuntary vegetative mechanism. It *does* indeed represent the surrender of the individual to his own biological makeup. It cannot be induced by an act of will—nor by any compulsive determination. It *is* involuntary. However, the laws of learning apply here, as they do to other skills that have to be acquired. All the methods and techniques described earlier are devices with a specific motive. By these devices, the patient gradually *learns* how to let go, to give in to himself, to surrender to "the flow of biological energy without any inhibition." No trick suffices here. No artifice will accomplish this. It cannot be faked. But stage by stage, facets of the armor can be destroyed piecemeal so that eventually, in a powerful orgasm of surrender, the pleasure-convulsion takes over and the patient "bends" to himself. It is a fearsome thing, watching the patient resist this necessity and inevitably give in. Every bit of his moral training and early conditioning runs counter to natural surrender. "Hanging on to the bitter end" as a life-attitude has become invested with all the hostility, frustration, despair and bitterness of a lifetime.

And it represents, too, a major convulsion of the personality to discard these accumulated emotional burdens of the lifetime.

That these concepts must be interpreted in the setting in which they were originally placed, and are capable of severe distortion if care is not used, is proven in a recent book by William Silverburg. In this work, the author takes Reich severely to task for the assertion that mental health is synonymous with orgastic potency. Silverburg concedes that "in the male, mental health does not exist without orgastic potency, though the existence of the latter does not necessarily guarantee mental health." (8) Despite the great care that Reich took in defining his terms, it is quite clear that Silverburg actually has in mind a physiological potency—what Reich called "erective potency." There is a great difference between orgastic and erective potency. Reich certainly realized the difference, even if some other psychiatrists have not. In fact, when the German psychoanalysts of the 1920s were still contending that the ability to perform coitus successfully was the fundamental criterion of a successful analysis, it was Reich who first insisted that these two notions were different.

So far as erective potency is concerned, the male experiences an erection and is capable of introjecting it in the vagina—or, in the case of a male homosexual, has enough of an erection for the purpose of fellatio or rectal intercourse. The penis can be moved with more or less rhythm, and the ejaculation occurs with an orgasm of more or less pleasurable intensity. There may or may not be a discharge of accumulated emotional and physical tension. There may or may not be a strong compulsion towards immediate repetition of the act—a clear indication that discharge of energy has been far from adequate. No matter how often the erectively potent male achieves an erection or performs coitus or experiences some sexual satisfaction, he may still remain as cold, hard, cruel and compulsive as he was before. It was said of Herman Goering that he loved women and children, but this in no way altered his arrogance, blustering egotism and viciousness.

In his *Function of the Orgasm* Reich has methodically and at great length delineated what orgastic potency is. He has defined his terms to imply that it is not erective potency—it is a great deal more. It presupposes the massive discharge of neuromuscular tension.

Moreover, it must induce the subjective awareness of total body pleasure (not genital only) and of the complete organismic surrender to the quivering convulsion of the orgasm reflex itself. These three experiences are the *bona fide* criteria of orgastic potency. Merely to have an erection with which to perform the sexual act may be a great step forward for the anxious or compulsive patient who has previously suffered from sexual impotency. But it is not orgastic potency. Silverburg, like many another modern critic, has not read Reich's work closely enough, perhaps has not yet experienced the orgasm reflex himself, and therefore has misunderstood him. And in so doing he has disseminated a criticism which is not based on the facts.

## BIBLIOGRAPHY

1. Braatøy, Trygve. *Fundamentals of Psychoanalytic Technique.* New York, John Wiley, 1954. p. 185.
2. Buhler, Charlotte. "The Process-Organization of Psycho-Therapy." *The Psychiatric Quarterly.* Utica, New York, April, 1954. p 11.
3. Freud, Sigmund. "Analysis Terminable and Interminable," *Collected Papers,* Vol. V. London, Hogarth Press, 1940. p. 316.
4. Geddes, Donald Foster. *An Analysis of the Kinsey Reports.* New York, Mentor Books, 1954. p. 25.
5. Groddeck, Georg. Exp*loring the Unconscious.* London, Daniels & Co. 1938. p. 50–52.
6. Jung, Carl G. *Two Essays on Analytical Psychology.* New York, Pantheon Books, 1953. p. 67.
7. McDougall, William. "The Sources and Direction of Psychophysical Energy." *Am. Jnl. of Insanity.* Vol. 69.
8. Silverburg, William V. *Childhood Experiences and Personal Destiny.* New York, Springer Publishing Co. 1952. p. 251.
9. Thompson, Clara. *Psychoanalysis: Evolution and Development.* New York, Hermitage Press, 1950. p. 241–242.
10. Wolff, Werner. "Fact and Value in Psychotherapy." *Am. Jnl. of Psychotherapy.* New York, VIII:3, p. 466.

## Chapter XI

### Self-Regulation

"(The goal of psychotherapy) is that of transformation; it seeks to transform the negative protest and rebellion of the patient into positive expression of the rebellious urge… It is anti-adjustment, anti-conformity, anti-passivity."
— Robert Lindner

**Restructuring.** Long before the orgasm reflex finally occurs, a great deal is happening to the patient. The characterological changes occurring with the use of these somatic approaches are both impressive and startling. Many of the psychological symptoms just seem to slowly melt away and disappear. Sometimes the patient is hardly aware of their disappearance until a relative or friend calls his attention to such a fact. Or until, in the course of a discussion with the therapist, he suddenly becomes aware of freedom from a previously disturbing symptom. Timidity, shyness, obsessive trends, compulsive patterns, anxiety, phobic episodes of a startling nature and many other symptoms gradually subside.

Sometimes, however, there is a marked exacerbation of physical symptoms which first arose in earlier periods of life. At other times, to indicate the subtle effect of the therapy on a biological level, by destroying the character armor there may emerge occasional rounds of great physical exhaustion, severe anxiety, depression, despair, disillusionment and marked mental confusion. It is during these rather lengthy periods of reorganization that the transference relationship stands the patient in good stead. There are times when the patient becomes penetratingly aware of moods and feelings originating in childhood, feelings against which he then had to armor himself. Loneliness seems almost beyond all others to be the feeling that wells up from the past. One becomes aware, listening to such patients, of the awful and long periods of loneliness that the child must experience. Loneliness in which there is no love, in which there is nothing to do but suffer—or to develop compulsive traits of hyperactivity to block that awareness.

Gradually, however, these things disappear, to be replaced by healthier, positive and more constructive personality trends. It tends to confirm Reich's theorem that the character and muscular armors are really two poles of the same neurotic defensive system. And that a therapeutic attack on any one pole has a profound effect on the other.

This aspect of the therapy needs to be elaborated. Most apologists for any kind of psychotherapy, whether of the verbal or non-verbal type, rarely paint an adequate picture of the very real and emotional distress suffered by the patient as his lifelong defenses collapse. He is then confronted by anxiety. One first has to experience this eruption of anxiety to appreciate its enormity. Whether the therapy consists of free association, digging into forgotten memories of the past, discussion of childhood attitudes, or attacking the muscular tensions—all of these technical approaches constitute attacks on chronic defense mechanisms. And such attacks give rise to fear. This is not tolerated too well by the patient since, of necessity, there once had to be painful meaning to the erection of these stout bastions of the psyche. And once these bastions are no more, the psyche is vulnerable, painfully and bitterly vulnerable to all the pain of the past. Under such circumstances, one can only cry. There seems to be a barely concealed but inexhaustible reservoir of tears. They flow and flow and there seems to be no end. But gradually the tears wash away the pain and the hurt and the fear. And in the very act of crying, there is growth and progress.

In the meantime, the anxiety is considerable. Sometimes it is not experienced directly as anxiety *per se,* but rather in symptomatic form. The most common form, perhaps, is dyspepsia and this is remarkable for some people who have never known the meaning of indigestion. One woman developed a stiff rigid stomach with intermittent nausea as a result of which she could retain no solid food for weeks. She lost several pounds of body weight. Her physician could find no organic pathology despite careful and painstaking examination. This persisted until she was able to break down in tears, when the entire syndrome vanished. Another patient, a 46-year-old compulsive, began to suffer from insomnia. It took more than fifty sessions before it began to subside. The dissolution of the muscular throat block with the ability to cry was responsible for gaining freedom from this disturbing symptom.

One doctor who came into therapy in his early fifties very rapidly found his muscular armoring attacked. Armor was no more an intellectual postulate or necessity, but a matter of dreadful experience. He described it at the opening of one session in these words: "I feel as if I were some prehistoric animal that had been frozen solid in ice for 100,000 years. Now the thaw has set in, the ice slowly begins to melt, and I am beginning to come to life. But it is terribly painful, this thaw, and I don't know if I dare let it continue."

Still another patient would wake up out of deep sleep with no feeling of anxiety at all. He would turn over, attempting to return to sleep, when he would become aware of what he thought was the bed shaking. As he turned his befogged attention to this phenomenon, he realized it was not the bed but himself. As he concentrated still more attentively, it dawned upon him that he was not perceptibly shaking, but that he had tachycardia. He palpated his own pulse rate which he found to be in the neighborhood of about 150. He had insight enough to realize that this was an anxiety symptom and had developed enough self-awareness to turn over on his back to relax and to continue to become more conscious of the cardiac thumping.

It is in such ways that the anxiety precipitates itself as a rule. "Fear may be experienced in the pit of the stomach, the back of the neck, the buttocks or even in the big toe," wrote Margaret Mead, "depending on how you were reared, what parts of your body you were taught to identify with the emotion of fear." (2) Very rarely does it seem to occur in purely psychical form with the affect-lame patient; only later, in the course of therapy, does he develop the capacity to feel anxiety as anxiety. But its emergence in any form is regarded as indicative of the gradual dissolution of the muscular armor. Once this emergence begins, other repressed affects cannot be far behind.

These anxiety manifestations are likely to recur over a long time. Some medical orgonomists usually intercede on the patient's behalf when these disturbing symptoms show signs of becoming overwhelming and prescribe mild sedation of one form or another. Perhaps in this connection tranquilizers may have some usefulness. Sedation allays the intensity of the anxiety and the overwhelming quality of the total psychosomatic response while vegeto-therapy is continued, until the disturbing affects have been wholly discharged.

Reich offers an explanation vastly different from that given by the therapist trained along more formal lines. He suggests that as the restrictive armor is attacked, the personality is laid open once more to vegetative excitations or body sensations. Though the armor is softened up, the patient habitually attempts to use the old neurotic ways of dealing with these reawakened excitations. Considerable conflict is the result. It is this conflict which produces the "falling anxiety" as Reich has termed it. It is the fear or anxiety which invariably arises at a certain stage in therapy. The nearer the patient draws to "yielding" and "surrendering" to his own biological sensations, the more anxiety emerges. It is a fearsome thing to watch a patient almost on the verge of the orgasm reflex—yet fighting furiously to restrain himself. It is reminiscent of some of the sensations experienced in sexual intercourse. Patients will describe again and again the mounting pleasure of coitus. Then, as they approach that wonderful moment of explosive release, there seems to be an awful pause. It is only momentary; I doubt if it could be timed in terms of a fraction of a second. But it is there. It is as though perched on the edge of a tremendous precipice one was to be plunged in the next instant into screaming eternity. There is a moment of awful hesitancy—and then one plunges. And all anxiety and fear vanishes and the whole organism is convulsed in the overwhelmingly pleasurable discharge of orgasm. That instant of awful hesitancy is experienced again and again. But on the couch in the course of vegeto-therapy it is not an instant. It is prolonged indefinitely. The patient's fear of giving in to his own vegetative excitations from which he has been alienated so long seems a terrible experience. It is laden with extreme anxiety which he resists for as long as he possibly can. It is the therapist's help, encouraging, prodding, stimulating—the solid basis of the transference situation—that eventually enables the patient to make the plunge. Then he discovers there was nothing to fear; it was only awful fantasy and anticipation.

Expatiating on this, Reich wrote that the appearance of falling anxiety is a sure index that plasmatic excitations and orgastic sensations are beginning to function in the total organism. Some of the signs of falling anxiety are dizziness, "sinking feelings," falling dreams, feelings of oppression in the gastric region, nausea. These and others characterize the breakdown of the armor, which is accompanied by orgastic sensations, involuntary muscular spasms, hot flushes, tremors, itching sensations, etc. These biological symptoms are represented as a generalized anxiousness and insecurity. Roughly speaking then, the therapy has to pass through the following stages of loosening of the armor: orgonotic sensations, breakdown of the armor, clonisms, falling anxiety, increased plasmatic excitation, orgastic sensations in the genitals.

One may be inclined to give only a figurative meaning to the phrase the "falling anxiety." That would be a mistake. It is an actual clinical experience—and at times a terrifying one. The sensations that patients experience during sleep, when they dream of falling off a cliff or are hurled from a high tree, are almost identical with those felt by patients while wide awake, working on the couch. Some relate it to the sensations of falling experienced as a modern high-speed elevator comes to a rapid stop. One patient, a movie fan, compared it to the roller coaster scene in Cinerama, when almost the entire audience gasped. I, myself, recall clutching frantically the sides of the couch as the falling anxiety gripped me during one phase of my own therapy. I had shouted several times with as much vigor as I could muster. Apparently it forced the diaphragm to relax, for with its wider excursions I began to feel as though my abdomen were caving in. There was a flushed feeling, with dizziness, as I felt myself careening downwards through the couch, falling wildly in space. It marks a distinct piece of therapeutic progress.

Reich further explains it by saying that since in fright, excitations and body fluids are withdrawn to the center of the organism and since, further, in the case of actual falling, this process takes place as a total organismic response, the idea of depth and of falling must be the same as the sensation of central excitation in the organism.

Not only, as indicated earlier, do forgotten symptoms of old physical maladies reappear—costiveness, headaches, rashes, myalgias and neuralgias, coryzas, enureses, etc.—but a gamut of repressed emotions well up almost from nowhere and appear to all but overwhelm the personality. Childhood needs, fears, doubts, hostilities, dependencies, envies, jealousies, etc., arise once more with all the strength they once had. More often than not, however, these are not immediately perceived as having belonged to an earlier period of time, but they become attached to present-day events, circumstances, people, etc. It is this dynamic displacement which renders the patient so disturbed. His responses to life-situations today seem so inexplicable and so absurd. And what makes the whole situation much worse—there seems to be at little he can do about them.

Some verbal therapy in the form of discussion of anamnestic details is strongly indicated here. Time should be spent at this stage of therapy communicating on a verbal level. It tends to produce penetrating insight into the disturbing problems and events of childhood, which while previously remembered had been apparently stripped of their affects and thus sterilized into safety. Insight develops more or less spontaneously to give considerable insight into what happened to these repressed affects and biological energies. The economy of the personality does not permit their total disappearance. They had merely become transformed into a narrowing of the mental horizons, a stricture of the ego, into pathological phases of character development, into heightened muscular tensions and into the "predisposition" for one kind of illness or another. Bodily posture, specific groups of muscular tensions, vegetative idiosyncracies, visceral dysfunctions, all of these *in toto* comprise the indelible memory remains of different life experiences. And this is, in effect, what Reich regards as the "language of the living."

Therapy reverses this process, stripping the armor wide open. Anxiety, of course, is the immediate result of such an attack. No attempt should be made to minimize the significance of the vast eruptions of anxiety. For this reason, therapy imposes a temporary but considerable strain on the personality. The patient becomes sorely tempted to quit the process producing this strange evocation of evanescent and transient but highly disturbing symptoms. If nothing else, the anxiety and resentment become displaced onto the therapist and his ministrations. The minor bruises and discomforts experienced during the assault on the tense musculature become highly over-determined and their significance greatly distorted. More than anything else, the transference and its discussion on an analytical level are required to help the patient appreciate the value and meaning of his experiences and, above all, to give him the reassurance and security he so badly needs.

**Auto-regulation.** One of the important ideas for which Reich unequivocally stands is autonomic regulation of function—whether in the sexual, intellectual or any other biological area. He claims that if the infant were not basically interfered with biologically by having neurotic parental standards forcibly imposed upon it, it would be able to be wholly self-determining throughout its lifetime. Most people, when first introduced to this idea, stand aghast at it—as if any individual "would go completely to hell" if permitted to express himself freely on an animal or biological level. I have heard parents say that if they let junior select his own foods, for example, they would consist solely of chocolate bars, hamburgers and pop. At first, this sounds *almost* as if it could be so—until one becomes familiar with some basic experiments.

The most important of these experiments which wholly corroborates the concepts of self-regulation and thus vindicates the Reichian viewpoint is cafeteria feeding. A group of several children was selected, ranging from six months to two or three years of age. At feeding time, they were confronted by trays containing small portions of as many as twenty to thirty different foodstuffs. In the case of very young infants, when any one food was pointed to, the attendant spooned it out and helped the child eat. If it rejected the food by spitting it out, no attempt was made to force or cajole it into eating. Selection, apparently, was made on the basis of visual and olfactory interests. At the close of the experiment, after some months, it was determined that the selection of the foods, so far as concerned basic food elements such as minerals, vitamins, proteins, etc., would not be other than would have been prescribed by a nutritional expert. In other words, the infant *selected*—it was not cajoled. There was no imposition of authoritarian dictates—no matter how sound or reliable. The infant was left to his own devices—and prospered.

This fact has long been known about animals and their biological needs, yet it has always been questioned with regard to humans. But this question only indicates how thoroughly environmental pressures of a neurotic culture invalidate the natural capacity for self-regulation of any and all biological functions. What has been discovered with regard to food, Reich insists is true in all other areas. If biological urges are permitted to operate without interference from compulsive moralities, they regulate themselves in a totally realistic manner. Freud was afraid that id impulses would operate to the detriment of the organism in a modern society. However, Reich believed that Freud failed to differentiate between primary and secondary drives, and that the basic inborn biological drives and needs have the innate capacity to regulate and adjust to the environment in a realistic manner. Morality is not required. It is the result of repression which forces secondary and pathological or substitute drives into expression. These latter, once developed, certainly require regulation, discipline and perhaps compulsive suppression. The biological core of all living things has functioned for eons solely in terms of expression, necessity and adjustment—survival is its keynote. Morality, compulsive imposition of norms and social inhibition create pathological people whose resultant sado-masochistic needs, if unchecked, may drive mankind into total extinction.

This point of view is characteristic of all of Reich's writings, from the earliest to the latest. It is most succinctly expressed when he says that *the inability to experience natural sexual gratification regularly leads to development of secondary impulses, in particular, sadistic impulses.* Most schools of psychotherapy admit a similar possibility. They differ mostly about methods of dealing with this sadism.

Reich's approach is simple. If biological impulses when armored and dammed back result in sadistic expression, then the main line of attack is against the armoring. This is the personality area requiring the heaviest artillery. If the defenses are shattered, however, some critics believe that the person will not be able to withstand the full impact of his sadistic impulses. This seems a highly specious argument. First of all, the fragmenting of the defenses is not instantaneous but slow and gradual. And secondly, the energizing factor in the defenses is nothing else but the hostility itself. Therefore, as the defenses crumble piecemeal, so also is the hostility being discharged and dissipated. When eventually the armor has largely crumbled, by the same token so will the mass of sadistic impulses have been discharged. Then the individual comes face to face with his own biological urges, with his own pleasure needs, his own demands for "natural orgastic gratification." And in these, without the armored distortions, there is no danger.

Though admittedly idealistic, Reich's "genital character" is still more in accord with general scientific thinking. To that extent it can be usefully employed. It can serve as a reasonable goal towards which the individual patient can be directed so long as it is understood that there is no compulsive forcing, no insistence that the patient conform to the characteristics of this theoretical schema.

Reich describes the essential characteristics of the genital character under several headings.

The genital character's thinking takes its orientation from objective facts and processes. It differentiates between the essential and non-essential—or less essential. It attempts to detect and eliminate irrational, emotional disturbances. Its nature is functional, neither mechanistic nor mystical. Judgment is the result of reality testing. Rational thinking is accessible to factual arguments and functions poorly without factual counter-arguments.

Motive, goal and action are in harmony in the genital character. Motives and goals have a rational social goal. Motives and goals, on the basis of their primary biological nature, strive for improvement of the living conditions for the self and others. It is what could be called social achievement.

In the genital character, the sexual life is essentially determined by the basic natural laws of biological energy. Pleasure in the happiness of others is a matter of course, as is indifference towards perversions and repugnance towards pornography. The genital character is easily recognized by the good contact he has with healthy infants. To his structure, it is obvious that interests of children and adolescents are largely sexual ones, and that the demands resulting from these biological facts should be fulfilled. This attitude is spontaneous, no matter whether there is corresponding knowledge. Today, it is precisely such fathers and mothers—unless they live in a favorable environment which supports them—who are exposed to the social danger of being regarded as criminals. They deserve the exact opposite, the maximum social protection. From the centers they form in society will one day come rationally acting educators and physicians. The basis of their lives and their actions is the happiness in love which they experience. Yet today, parents who would let children live in terms of healthy natural laws would be in danger of being dragged into court by someone infected with the emotional plague and of losing their children.

The genital character follows the development of a work process in an active manner, by letting it take its own course. The interest is essentially directed towards the work process itself. The end result comes about without any special effort since it is engaged in spontaneously. The product of the work process is an essential characteristic of biological joy *in work.* This leads to a sharp criticism of all present methods of early upbringing in which the activity of the child is determined by a pre-made work product. Anticipation of the product and the rigid determination of the work process chokes off the child's own imagination—that is, his *productivity.* Pleasure in work goes hand in hand with the ability to develop enthusiasm. Compulsive morality is exclusive of genuine enthusiasm. A child who must build a pre-planned house with *given* blocks in a *given* manner cannot use his imagination and therefore cannot develop any enthusiasm. It is not difficult to understand that this basic trait of authoritarian education owes its existence to the pleasure anxiety of adults. It always strangles the child's joy in work. *The genital character guides the work achievement of others by his example and not by dictating the product and work methods.* This presupposes vegetative motility and the ability to let oneself go. All of these ideas are subsumed under the single heading of genitality.

**Insight.** As therapy proceeds the patient may develop some extraordinary insights without any intervention by the therapist. This occurs not on the basis of intellectualization—which is all too often merely defensive and evasive—but upon the basis of re-experiencing emotional situations in rather the same manner in which they had once occurred.

One 47-year-old male presented the immediate problems of impotence and alcoholism. His mother had been a religious bigot, a frustrated wife and a harsh disciplinarian. It was her intention that her son should learn to play the piano and play it well. She kept him practicing for hours at a time, scorning his desire to play ball with his friends or to engage in other compensatory recreations. These were the ways to sin and she would have none of them. He came to hate her with an indescribable hatred. He would plot awful revenges on her—but all of these fantasies were of no avail. Finally, he hatched one plot which was demoniacal. He would take a single musical exercise and play it exactly one thousand times. In this way, he would force her medicine down her own throat. She rebelled and the neighbors complained, but he gloated. He persisted in this method systematically. Ultimately he did become a very fine pianist. In fact, his critics had often said that his technical virtuosity was superb—and his soul empty. On the couch one day, after an ample demonstration of his hostility through pounding and screaming, he realized for the first time that his musical skill was nothing but a secret outlet for his hostility.

Another piece of insight arose in a 36-year-old woman who, prior to marriage five years earlier, had been a school teacher, albeit an unhappy one. She was highly nervous, compulsive and prone to excessive alcoholic ingestion, ostensibly to keep her husband company when he drank. Her hands and fingers were constantly plucking with athetoid motions, the sequel of St. Vitus' dance at the age of eight years. This had been preceded by a severe mastoiditis which had invalided her for months. All through her life she had felt isolated, inferior and rejected.

During one vegeto-therapeutic session, tears spontaneously arose following a few minutes of some muscular automatisms of the shoulders, arms and hands. When the spell of weeping had subsided, she began to speak about a recollection that had just welled up. While confined to her bed as a youngster with Sydenham's chorea, she once overheard her younger sister talking outside her bedroom window. The sister was inviting some of her little friends to peep through the window and watch her sister "jiggle." The entire notion of being on show like a freak at a circus side-show was utterly traumatic, coming as it did after a long period of sickness and debilitation. But this recollection helped the patient to understand with a great deal of clarity how her feeling of isolatedness and inferiority had developed.

The patient usually requires no prodding from the therapist. Once the armor has loosened sufficiently to permit the exit of repressed affects, understanding also dawns spontaneously. These insights may be re-synthesized into the conscious ego and integrated with the other contents of the adult psyche for present-day utilization and understanding.

On several occasions, so vivid can these spontaneous memory recoveries be that I have seen patients become practically hallucinated, temporarily, as they recalled powerful affective experiences of an earlier year. The vision of a father beating a boy or a mother discovering and scolding the child engaged in masturbatory practices, become vivid, real experiences. Significantly, while beating a pillow which he had fantasied was his father, one patient became hallucinated by the picture of his father beating him. His verbalization was not, "I can recall father beating me," but, "He *is* beating me!" and, "He's *still* here!" and the pounding took the form of violent expression of the aggressive fantasies that were engendered at the time of the beating. Another patient, after making the gesture of hostility, leaped up from the couch, his face distorted with wild rage, screaming, "I'm going to *kill* him. I *will* kill the son of a bitch!" His father had been dead for many years.

Still another patient, a charming lady with a passive-feminine character structure, had a pathological history. As a girl, three of her brothers would entice her upstairs to their bedroom where, in the closet, they would seduce her into engaging in fellatio with them. On one occasion at least, she was discovered by her mother who adopted the attitude that this nasty behavior was the sort of thing that might be expected from boys but most certainly not from nice girls. She was severely punished and ostracized for several days. During this period, she felt considerable hostility for her mother. This hostility had been previously recalled quite clearly during analysis, but at no time could she be induced to discharge effectively the emotions she once had felt. During one session, after the initiation of somatic procedures, she not only tore a telephone directory with slow, deliberate and insidious destructiveness, but swore vigorously at me, to whom she had previously transferred mother attitudes. Her language was comprised of obscene words she had picked up in her girlhood from her brothers during her sexual experiences in the upstairs bedroom. Tearing the directory pages, she glowered at me malignantly while thrashing her feet on the couch and muttering unprintable words through closely gritted teeth, with monotonous repetitiveness. For the first time, after some forty sessions of previous conservative psychotherapy, she became capable of re-experiencing affect—and tolerating it, too.

I am quite aware that these abreactive phenomena occasionally do occur in the normal process of orthodox analysis. All that I insist upon is that in the case of the resistant or affect-lame patient, the defenses have been erected so stoutly as to prevent the possibility of abreaction. The compelling and significant purpose of these somatic techniques is to break through the controlling barricades and to permit the free eruption of the hitherto repressed emotions. Their function thus serves to shorten the term of conventional psychotherapy in the severely inhibited patient.

Non-verbal psychotherapy rapidly destroys the neurotic equilibrium. Once even a few body feelings sneak through into open manifestation, the old rigid homeostasis has been destroyed. The person can never be quite the same again. New equilibriums have to be created on a more realistic basis, demanding the toleration of bodily feelings and actively participating in the discharge of normal biological urges. Profound changes in personality thus come about solely on the basis of the breakthrough of the vegetative impulses, feelings and emotions. And this breakthrough is made possible by first rendering the cortical inhibition less absolute, less inflexible and less dominant.

Though vegeto-therapy is highly effectual, it still is not to be considered an omnipotent magical formula. Effort is still required of the patient. Perhaps this is one of its major claims of superiority over the more conventional verbal approaches. One bequeaths a set of tools to the patient which he can use as required. As therapy goes on, the patient becomes more sensitive and perceptive of the process he is undergoing. Cooperation becomes more than possible. In fact, between sessions many patients will deliberately use these operational tools as means of coping with emotional problems and anxiety-producing situations as they arise.

Often a patient will report that while driving a car on the freeway, he will shout as loudly as possible to relax a tightening diaphragm and discharge mounting tension. Or, while walking on the street, he will make a "crowing" sound in his throat during inhalation to relieve a laryngeal spasm. Others will tell of lying down on a bed at home in the conventional therapeutic position and throwing the hips up with much force while shouting. Still others will fall back on encouraging deep respiration until it becomes easy and natural. Under these circumstances, emotional discharge becomes a ready possibility of which they avail themselves often.

Yet it is no magical pill, no magical potion. It requires sincere effort on the part of the patient, effort to shed himself of infantile controls inculcated by his parents or their surrogates. It demands an honest and adult recognition of the tremendous creative potentials inhering within the biological organism. It also demands a frank facing of the pathological elements residual in the whole concept of the armoring. The patient requires to understand that therapy means restructuring—not merely the elimination of a disturbing symptom. Vegeto-therapy must be understood as implying that the very character structure from which all neurotic symptoms arise must be completely changed, resulting in what might be called the birth of a new individual.

Gerhard Adler says,

> "It happens only too often that a patient expects at the beginning of an analysis that the psychotherapist will, by some magical means, simply rid him of his symptoms without ever touching the rest of the structure of his life, with which he is quite satisfied. The analyst is only too often supposed to be a kind of 'medicine man,' who will make the symptoms disappear from outside. The truth is that nobody can be cured until he

is prepared to accept the need for a more or less complete reorientation of his life. To put it in a nutshell: *the healed person is not the original person minus a symptom, but a newly orientated person* in whom, through the new orientation, the necessity for the symptom, and therefore the symptom itself, has disappeared." (1) (italics mine)

After considerable therapy, Ernie, previously mentioned, presented a dream in which he had enormously large testicles. In the dream he commented, "Well, my therapy is certainly doing something." The dream was significant in that it managed to draw together a number of tangled motivations that, up to that moment, he had not been able to integrate. For example, one of the several motives for entering therapy was the seldom verbalized belief that he was a genius. In therapy he would be "discovered." He had no idea in what technical area his genius lay, but that was of small moment. Later, he also voiced the fear that his genitals were ridiculously small. In fact, he recalled that many of his playmates would mock him when noticing his genitals at the creek where they swam and call him "little dick." This always bothered him.

Of the several siblings in his family, the one immediately succeeding him was mentally defective. He recalled how he would beat this poor little imbecile to force some kind of learning on him. It seemed important to him to force Donald to learn *something,* anything, he didn't care what. If Donald managed to learn something, the odium attaching to his deficiency would be lessened. Ernie experienced much shame in having to be accompanied here and there by Donald who would soil himself often, resulting in ridicule from the neighborhood children. He recalled noticing that Donald's genitals were rather undeveloped. The fear gradually took form that there was a blood-taint in the family, a taint of mental deficiency that would sooner or later produce its telltale marks on him.

He spent many hours questioning his mother about her background to discover if there were other mentally retarded members in her family. His mother had, in fact, a younger brother who had been retarded; he was killed in an automobile accident. His mother foolishly expressed some attitudes which implanted many doubts in his mind. She wondered if God were not punishing her for her sins, unnamed, by giving her a mentally retarded son. She wondered if it would have been better had she remained unmarried. None of this reassured Ernie in the least.

When he masturbated, which was often, one motive was to increase the size of his penis. This would prove that he was not like Donald. It was not until many years had elapsed that he realized that all through grade and high school he would not compete scholastically or athletically with other children for fear that his own stupidity would be exposed. Occasionally during an altercation with his father, the latter would rail at him, "What the hell is the matter with you? You must be completely stupid!" Though this would fire his fantasies about getting even with his father, nonetheless these remarks merely confirmed his secret fears that he was just like Donald.

Though he repressed his inferiority feelings as much as he could, they stayed with him constantly. After his discharge from the armed services—where often he was intoxicated and went AWOL and for which he was almost court-martialed—the belief did emerge that he had some concealed genius. He became an ardent follower of Count Alfred Korzybski, to whose writings he was introduced while a student at a trade school, and became an active member of one of the general semantics chapters. While he did acquire some facility in handling semantic concepts, his inferiority and inadequacy remained. It was this that eventually drove him to seek psychotherapy.

Even then he shied away from any detailed discussion of Donald for fear that I would determine that he, too, was mentally retarded and dismiss him. But he soon came to realize the compensatory mechanisms involved in the fantasy of being a great genius. It had clearly served to disguise his anxiety about the possibility of being a mental defective and about having small genitals. It was also related basically to the Oedipus situation and his fear that with his tiny penis he could never succeed in satisfactorily performing coitus with his mother. Castration fantasies were also connected with this complex set of situations, especially since on the farm where he was raised he had often watched his father castrate piglets. With all of this he was sure he could amount to absolutely nothing in life. If he did have a large penis and large testicles, obviously his fears would be negated and it would prove that there was no validity to the possibility of castration, and no likelihood of imbecility like Donald. Perhaps, after all, therapy would fulfill his infantile fantasy of rendering him capable of having intercourse with his mother.

***

It should be self-evident that it requires a thoroughly permissive attitude on the part of the therapist to utilize somatic procedures of so dynamic a nature. No pretense on his part will suffice. The suspicious patient—and all maladjusted patients are suspicious—will immediately divine his hidden attitudes of fear, disgust and repulsion. The permissiveness must be wholly sincere. His own unarmored freedom must be the source of his conduct in the consulting room and the origin of his permissiveness to the patient. Whatever taboos lurk unsuspected within the therapist are bound to be exposed by his responsiveness to or withdrawal from the emotional phenomena elicited by the patient's couch work. Some therapists may require considerable re-education and undergo restructuring themselves by means of this therapy to enable them to tolerate willingly and to accept the powerful affective abreactions of their patients.

The results of psychotherapy employing these somatic adjuncts, however, well warrant whatever prolonged discipline the therapist finds imposed upon him. Whereas many sessions would have been previously required to elicit a full personality response from the inhibited patient, the treatment becomes immeasurably more dynamic and considerably shortened by employing these methods. They are to be unequivocally recommended for utilization in all cases where the patient is affect-lame, wholly or in part, and employs fearfully all the forces of his own neurosis to withstand the analytical onslaught. The patient has achieved a precarious equilibrium in relation to his neurosis. As a rule he initially desires only the removal of annoying or crippling symptoms, without interfering with the neurotic character that he has been forced to develop in the preceding years of his life. It is this fear of changing his character that initiates the resistance to psychotherapy and blocks the possibility of emotional growth and development. It is against this resistance to successful change that the heaviest artillery of the therapist has therefore to be directed.

These methods really comprise a reconditioning technique. Within the four walls of the consulting room, the patient is taught to render adequate emotional responses to stimuli. Insight and understanding of his own historical development are also required of him. Both the emotional reconditioning and intellectual understanding render the psychotherapy complete, fitting the patient for healthy biological and intellectual fulfillment in the real world from which he has attempted to protect himself by his emotional contactlessness. This is a genuine and rational psychotherapy grounded securely in the biological core of the organism. Such a dynamic process is capable of engineering within the patient a wholly new creative point of view which is insight in the real sense of the term. I like Rogers' definition of insight. To him, "it involves the re-organization of the perceptual field. It consists in seeing new relationships. It is the integration of accumulated experience. It signifies a reorientation of the self... Insight is essentially a new way of perceiving." (4) And, I would like to add, a new way both of feeling and behaving.

**Some criticisms.** A series of minor objections have been raised as to the theoretical validity—though not to the clinical efficacy—of these methods. It may be worth noting at this juncture that it is quite possible that the diaphragm theory of Groddeck may be totally erroneous, psychologically speaking. It may well be that this does constitute an abuse of symbolism. Character structure may have absolutely nothing to do with anatomical structures, as Reich has insisted. Too, this neurophysiological interpretation may be wholly false or inadequate. All I am concerned with, however, is that the technique *works.* An adequate theory can be constructed around the technique. A more scientific evaluation of the phenomena may evolve at a later date. Meantime, we can and should experiment widely with the method to clarify its specific value in the psychotherapeutic treatment of resistive cases.

A second criticism was that it was inconceivable that this method could produce such extensive clinical results as alleged. Apparently, the critic was under the impression that a single session of hyperventilation was enough to permit a total breakthrough of repressed emotional forces. It is not as simple as that. However, with every single emergence of even slight feelings through the dissolution of muscular tension, the personality structure is dynamically changed. Its previous rigidity, developed as the physical mechanism for repression, is no longer useful and is, in fact, being broken down. Fifty sessions of vegeto-therapy at the rate of one hour per week is far more effectual than several times this amount of conventional psychotherapy. The whole biological core of the patient becomes activated, not merely the intellectual capacity. He becomes capable of living and functioning on a dynamic feeling level.

A more pertinent criticism was phrased thus: "We can understand and analyze by the vehicle of language." Language and ideation are the time-binding characteristics of the human animal. It is through verbalization that we can achieve the exchange of ideas. It is through the same process that we have an opportunity to evaluate some psychical processes. But on the basis not merely of personal experience but of common assent, I must register a profound disbelief in the total efficacy of intellectual insight as a psychotherapeutic goal. All too often skillful therapists have called attention to the sad fact that the patient may develop considerable insight—but his psychoneurotic symptoms persist unchanged and unaltered. Too frequently, also, this viewpoint opens the analytical profession to the quips of psychological amateurs who seem to have a fine penchant for hitting where it hurts most. This is primarily the product of insisting that the goal is merely verbalization, instead of emotional release from the past to which the patient has been thoroughly conditioned and biologically bound. As a result of these somatic methods, significant memories well up spontaneously, and if necessary, can be verbalized on the adult level. These enable the therapist to evaluate them in the light of the patient's history and present symptoms. It is categorically affirmed here that personality insight can be achieved far more satisfactorily after affective discharge.

Another argument was that "many character neurotics habitually act out, but are no nearer improvement by so doing. Rather does the neurosis or pathologic character-trait become more fixed by the display or habit." It is imperative to indicate that these somatic methods are of value mainly in those neurotic reaction patterns where the emotional blocks are so preponderantly developed that the patient has become affect-lame. Moreover, it must be remembered that the dissolution of muscular tensions constitutes the main line of attack on the neurosis. The abreaction of affects is dependent on hyperventilation and the loosening of the muscular armor. Only as the latter becomes dissolved, to that extent also will the gestures release repressed affects.

The notion that the neurotic character trait becomes fixed by display of affects may ordinarily be factual. But under these clinical conditions, nothing could be further from the truth. The apparently fixed character traits change very subtly, but definitely, as the work on the muscular armor proceeds. Before much time has elapsed, usually the armored façade, which is the basis of the pathological character and symptom-formation, is being exposed by the therapeutic process. The character-neurosis becomes undermined, leaving the patient vulnerable to his own hitherto repressed feelings. It is on this basis that personality re-structuring occurs.

"Why all this emphasis on tears?" is still another criticism. The questioner took the stand that as we mature we naturally leave behind us many of the behavior patterns that characterize the infant and child. No longer do we wear diapers; civilized toilet habits have long since replaced them. We no longer reach crudely for food with our fingers; we have been taught table manners and etiquette without any loss of gratification. The childhood patterns of parading naked have been superseded by the wearing of clothes with nudity exposed only on rare and special occasions. Adulthood brings with it a host of other satisfactions that for the child would be both inconceivable and incomprehensible. Is not this crying, then, over-heavily belabored?

There is some justification for such criticism. Many patients argue in this manner when confronted by the therapist's urge that crying need be respected as a legitimate abreactive device. It is significant that those who most use this argument are, in effect, those who are the least capable of crying. The argument represents a simple rationalization to excuse their fear, their unwillingness and their incapacity to behave in this most natural way. They are truly affect-lame.

Furthermore, the initial criticism, which seems on the surface to be so plausible, ignores that whether the infant defecates in diapers or on the stool in a modern bathroom, the fact remains that in both instances a natural function is being fulfilled. Whether fingers or utensils are used to deploy food to the mouth, nonetheless food is being taken to satisfy the normal need for food. So, in all instances a natural urge or physiological drive is gratified regardless of the preliminaries or appurtenances employed to gratify that need.

What, then, shall one do in the face of sorrow, grief, irreparable loss or some other inconsolable frustration? Write poetry? Be silent and heroic? Send a letter to the newspaper? Telegraph one's senator in Washington? Discuss the situation calmly with a friend or with some other member of the family? Or, simply and so naturally, discharge the sadness and hurt feeling in the direct outflow of tears?

Feelings can be hidden away. Repression and displacement can be resorted to, as they have been all too often for so many of us. They can be buried under the hypocritical mask of sophistication and seeming adulthood. But the total personality price in such events is excessive. The physiological sequelae are too extensive and damaging in terms of functional limitation, altogether apart from the ultimate loss of emotional capacity and affective maturity. There is no alternative to tears—no alternative that does not cripple the personality and hamper its further growth. Tears and crying are natural functions. It is impossible to express deep and profound sorrow by any other device. A philosophy or religious outlook or scientific preoccupation often serve merely as a façade behind which the sorrow can hide. Under the circumstances, then, the resort to tears—or any other natural function that has been abused and blocked—is an intelligible attitude. Overemphasis may be necessary to counterbalance the previous under-emphasis.

Still another critical comment consisted in the belief that this kind of therapy was a non-specific abreactive system and that it was more symptomatic than reductive. Without a doubt it could induce a discharge of affect, but it did not and could not remedy the secondary changes that had resulted in the development of the neurosis. In other words, it concerned itself solely with symptoms. It discharged affects in much the same way as would an occasional alcoholic spree, or as if one were a crying spectator at a Hollywood "tear-jerker." This being the case, the method would be subject to severe condemnation when compared to the general trend of all phases of modern medicine where therapy is largely directed towards disclosing those basic factors which initially produced the disease process, and then attempting to eradicate those causative factors and improve function.

More specifically this criticism makes the comparison with psychoanalysis, the parent of all modern psychotherapies. Here the entire burden of therapy is historical and genetic. The patient's life-history becomes the object of prolonged and profound investigation and scrutiny. When the causative factors of present-day neurotic attitudes and symptoms are thoroughly aired and "worked through" by analyzing transference distortions so that the unconscious or infantile motivations no longer remain hidden from conscious examination, the patient is cured—at least in theory. Some re-conditioning or re-education may be required, but the basic problem has been dealt with. The symptoms disappear even though no direct attention has been given to the symptom-complex itself. The latter is considered merely the revealing evidence of hidden emotional disturbance, rooted in pathogenic historical development.

What is not usually realized in connection with this type of criticism is the fundamental theorem which Reich long ago laid down. It is all too often overlooked, mistakenly so I think. Repression is not merely a psychic process divorced from all physiological activity. So long as this viewpoint is rejected, so long will the old psyche/soma dichotomy persist. With this psychobiological viewpoint of the integrated whole organism, it is apparent that *repression and all the other defense mechanisms of the ego must be rooted solidly in somatic processes,* just as all psychic activity is grounded in nervous system activity. Without muscular tension of one kind or another, there can be no repression. This is the basic viewpoint and is experimentally valid.

The difference between a non-specific abreactive therapy and vegeto-therapy lies in both the nature and the purpose of the concerted attack on the muscular armor. The vegeto-therapeutic intent is to help the organism release its own biological and emotional energies that have become bound up in a chronically spastic musculature. An emotional "jag" is very far removed from its intent and function. When the muscles are literally forced to relax, the patient expresses affects. This is what sometimes disturbs the unsuspecting patient. He may leave the consulting room fairly relaxed, and forget the therapist's warning that there is likely to be an eruption of affects from earlier periods of life.

Affects may be expressed by all sorts of devious routes, but if their stronghold in the spastic muscular armor is not attacked and dissolved, nothing of any vital consequence or permanence has been achieved. Vegeto-therapy seeks to reconstruct the personality so that a loose, free and self-regulatory attitude toward living is maintained throughout all life's vicissitudes without the need of the involuntary chronic armor. In the case of neurotic armoring, the muscular rigidity is chronic and automatic, said Reich. But the genital character has his armor at his disposal: he can put it on or take it off at will.

To sum up this discussion, it may be said that some other forms of therapy strive for symptom relief, amelioration of inner strife and adjustment to existing conditions. These goals are largely foreign to this method. Here the goal is the reorganization of the personality and nothing less. Certainly symptoms are removed—and that quite readily in many instances. I have seen bronchial asthma, migraines, myalgias, several types of neuro-dermatitis, cardiac neurosis with skipped systole, spastic colitis, obsessions, compulsions, phobias, alcoholism, anxieties, etc., disappear fairly promptly after the institution of therapy. Should the patient prematurely terminate therapy for any one of a dozen different reasons, so many endopsychic changes have been produced that there is a constant and continuous growth process long after the actual date of termination. Mere relief of symptoms and vegeto-therapy are really antipodal.

What actually is sought after is a thorough-going transformation of the personality. Absence of neurotic symptoms is a negative desideratum of successful therapy. Surrender and the patient's capability of surrendering to his own vegetative excitations in the orgastic convulsion is a positive constructive criterion about which there can be no ambiguity or dubious interpretation. For with the development of this capacity, all of nature is mobilized on the side of the organism. And there is an energetic plunging with eagerness and spontaneity into the stream of life and living that was never and could never have been envisaged before.

Despite the above insistence that relief of symptoms is not essentially the goal of this therapy, the fact remains, however, that there may be occasions when compromise may be forced on the therapist. He may have to be content with lesser goals than the achievement of the orgasm reflex and personality restructuring. By the time many a patient has come to therapy, too much biological mischief and damage may have been perpetrated on the organism. Under these circumstances, amelioration may be all that is left to the therapist.

Age is one factor. The longer the patient has endured his symptoms and his armor, the more inflexible he may have become. This rigidity may make restructuring impossible. Intensity of armoring is certainly another factor. It may have become so intensely stiff and so thoroughly integrated into the life-patterns of the patient as to defy more than mere modification. Actual organic disease may be another factor which may limit therapeutic goals. A coronary obstruction, malignant hypertension, tuberculosis, previous surgical interventions, crippling arthritis that has been in force for a decade or more, these are not to be lightly regarded. Some therapists may legitimately refuse to handle such psychosomatic diseases altogether. Others may be wary of final prognosis. And so far from working toward orgastic potency and the orgasm reflex, they may be content to aim at more limited goals. Symptomatic relief and some insight into character structure with the ability to use some of the operational tools for continued relief from physical harassment may be all that is possible for some patients. But these are goals, however, which many patients will come to welcome and cherish and which, therefore, should not be denied them.

Another possible criticism is that, strictly speaking, hyperventilation is a syndrome and not a therapy. In most instances, the critic has never previously speculated about the possible use of hyperventilation as an operational tool in psychotherapy, but only knows of it as a nosological item in pathology. Attention may very likely be called to those clinical instances where, as a result of anxiety attacks, a chain of rapid respiration is set off. This quick and heavy breathing succeeds rapidly in initiating dizziness, vasoconstriction, trembling, spasms, tetanies, etc.—the clinical symptoms to which attention has constantly been directed here. These, in turn, inspire fearful emotional responses which, further, restimulate the heightened pace of respiration, Panic and a multiplicity of psychological and physical symptoms ensue which, as a rule, can only be terminated by sedation or hospitalization.

Critics will insist that there is nothing therapeutic about the most trivial element in this self-perpetuating chain of events, and, of course, this has to be agreed with. What these critics overlook, however, is the all-important issue so often formulated here—that hyperventilation is used merely as a means to an end. It is employed as an operational tool for several reasons which include: first, the temporary anaesthetization of the cerebral cortex by blowing off carbon dioxide; second, reduction of cortical criticism, inhibition and some learned conditioned responses; third, exaggeration of already existent muscular tension; and finally, these latter can be coaxed into physiological relaxation while simultaneously specific emotional abreactions can be induced.

This therapeutic chain of events has, as indicated, very little relationship to a pathological syndrome. It bears only a distant relationship to the anxiety-induced chain of symptoms elicited by hyperventilation in the unguided and untreated patient. The therapist acts as a clinical policeman and guide to watch over the psychosomatic responses of the patient. He permits and encourages only those events to occur which, on the basis of his own clinical and personal experience, will facilitate the patient's emotional growth and personality restructuring.

The very novelty of hyperventilation as a psychotherapeutic tool evokes resistance from the physician who hears of it for the first time. It seems never to have occurred to him that such a process could have any usefulness. This is intelligible; most of us were at one time in this category. I do not know the events that guided Reich's thinking into juxtaposing breathing with therapy. It was nothing but a stroke of genius that has since amply justified itself. Perhaps it is envy and jealousy that makes some of us hunt furiously for possible criticisms to the employment of hyperventilation as a special approach to psychotherapy. If so, it would be far better to face that fact and come to terms with such undesirable emotions in ourselves. Otherwise we stand a chance of robbing ourselves of all the values that are involved in this operational tool, and then of projecting our own antagonisms onto those therapists who choose to experiment with it in their offices.

In conclusion, I feel compelled to return to a point established in the opening pages of this thesis. One orgonomist who read an earlier version of this manuscript suggested that, as a manual, it was woefully incomplete. It did not even attempt to discuss Reich's orgone theory, nor the experimental and empirical data relating to the cosmic orgone energy, its effects on the personality, disease, social problems, terrestrial climatic conditions, nor with Reich's ultimate adventures in the production of rain and the problem of deserts and arid land wastes.

Admittedly these have been omitted. But this has been done with deliberation and forethought. These are topics that will have to be dealt with by others. I am not willing to handle these concepts at length; they lie outside my immediate province. My chosen sphere has been specifically with the subject of vegeto-therapy.

As indicated earlier, the life work of Wilhelm Reich can be divided for the sake of convenience into at least five separate epochs. The first stage of his life work found him operating as a psychoanalyst, and apparently quite efficiently. This has been written about at great length by others so there is no further need on my part to discuss it. In the second stage he elaborated his technique of character-analysis. Many psychoanalysts now admit that these contributions have become incorporated, wholly or in part, into the mainstream of psychoanalytic thinking. Vegeto-therapy was the third phase. Apart from Reich's writing on this subject, there has been little attempt to organize and consolidate this material. Nor has any interpretation been attempted of this somatic approach in conventional neurophysiological terms. Thus it seems to me that before anyone essays a presentation of the ramifications of the orgone theory which developed many years after Reich developed vegeto-therapy, a good deal of preparatory work is necessary. No understanding of Reich's need for the development of the orgone hypothesis is possible unless one first has experimented with the techniques presented by vegeto-therapy and understood the specific problems that arise in its connection.

This thesis proposes just this—and nothing more. I believe the professional field is in need of a detailed presentation of Reich's approach to the muscular armor treatment of the psychoneuroses and some psychosomatic diseases. My personal experience with it leads me to believe that it possesses a high degree of efficiency. I believe that psychiatrists and psychologists may come to find through it some significant answers to several stubborn clinical problems that have beset them for many years. Reich deserves great credit for his ingenuity and creative thinking. Instead he has been unjustly maligned and defamed for many years with no praise given him for having solved some of these difficult psychotherapeutic problems.

Over the years there has been a variety of spin-offs from the main stream of Reichian therapy.[1] Possibly the most publicized is Rolfing, or structural integration. This system utilizes massage and manipulation of the muscular-fascia from head to toe. It is said to be exquisitely painful and bruises are often found on the areas worked on. I am not sure whether the patient is encouraged to express his pain by shouting or screaming. There is no emphasis on breathing or hyperventilation so the technique is quite different from Reich's. The goals are different, too. Whereas Reich stressed the orgastic reflex as the goal of his therapy, those of Rolfing are to be found in posture.

In offering a neurophysiological interpretation of Reich's vegetotherapy, there is no thought that here is a final theoretical description of the clinical phenomena elicited during the course of this therapeutic process. My major hope is that this thesis may provoke some speculation and organized research which may yield more satisfying results both clinically and theoretically. If I have provided some stimulus in this direction, I shall feel that the labor involved has not altogether been wasted. It is offered just as, in the theater, a single word may act as a prompt to an actor who has momentarily forgotten his lines. This manual, I hope, may serve as the suggested prompt. I

---

[1] The most significant "spin-offs" of Reichian therapy include Alexander Lowen's *Institute of Bioenergetic Analysis* (which was developed after Lowen split from Reich over the issue of orgone around the time this book was being written), and Christopher S. Hyatt's *Radical Undoing* techniques (developed with Regardie), both of which utilize Reich's vegeto-therapy methodology extensively. Ida Rolf's *Structural Integration* and Arthur Janov's *Primal Scream Therapy* are sometimes considered spin-offs, though the methodologies are quite different. [Ed.]

trust it will stimulate the profession to renewed effort and investigation into some complex problems, the solution of which may be of the utmost importance and value to our present harassed generation.

## BIBLIOGRAPHY

1. Adler, Gerhard. *Studies in Analytical Psychology.* N.Y., Norton Co., 1948, p. 49.
2. Mead, Margaret. "What is Human Nature?" *LOOK,* Apr. 19, 1945.
3. Munn, Norman. *Psychology.* Boston, Houghton Mifflin, 1946. p. 203.
4. Rogers, Carl R. *Counseling and Psychotherapy.* Boston, Houghton Mifflin, 1942, p. 206.

# Afterword

### by Fernando P.

"Become what you are. There are no guarantees."
— Christopher S. Hyatt

We are born as we are meant to be, connected to the flow of life through our organic nature. As we grow older and are exposed to "culture and conditioning," we lose our sense of connectedness with the world. Frequently, this process starts as adults neglect their children by using them for their needs instead of providing the safe background where they can grow into unique human beings. As children, we are brainwashed into believing we are somehow flawed, that we need to control ourselves, that we need to act a certain way to survive or get pleasure or avoid pain. We develop a false self, a mask, a persona, that has little to do with our original nature, distracting the true self from inner pain and loneliness. We live with these defensive masks, strengthening them, until we no longer remember who we once were. We have then lost complete connection with our true nature.

Inner emptiness is a result of abandoning ourselves, of feeling ashamed of the way we are. We are afraid of acknowledging our thoughts, desires, emotions, impulses; all of this self-rejection destroys our self-esteem. We repress our instinctual drives and emotions and create muscular armor which is the body's reaction to repression. *This muscular armor is easier to access than the repressed content under traditional therapeutic methods.* Under traditional therapy, we may eventually be able to verbally explain the origin and reason for much of our suffering, but no matter how much we talk about it, it's difficult to actually let it go. It can be especially challenging because of the anxiety and fear of facing certain truths about ourselves.

As a brief anecdote, in my case, I had a nephew who just triggered me the wrong way. He had an enabling-type mother who always seemed to hide his mischief. He was highly narcissistic, needed to win at any game, was constantly seeking attention, and always laughing at another's expense. One Sunday noon, as we were having an extended family lunch, my mother saw how visibly irritated I was with this nephew and pointed out that as a young boy, I was exactly the same way. This was confirmed by an aunt who was also present. All of a sudden, I realized that all of the things I hated about him were things I hated about myself but had refused to see—despite years of traditional therapy. In this refusal to accept the truth, I had lived in inner conflict, and used lots of mental energy to keep me from the fear and anxiety of facing the facts. True healing requires feeling deeply, and much of what needs to be felt is not easily accessed through the conscious mind.

Dr. Wilhelm Reich's work attempts to undo heavy layers of conditioning and unfelt emotion that has been crystallized into our bodies as armor. His techniques help us to bypass *conscious* filters and access our true drives as organic beings—drives that have been repressed as a result of social pressure and moral judgments. In his view, body tension mimics psychological tension. The final aim of this type of therapy is to free our human organic nature with its instincts and drives from the heavy irrational controls of the ego and superego as a result of cultural conditioning and regulation. These controls keep us in a state of both mental anxiety and muscular tension. His techniques allow man to reclaim his organic nature as a true human being and reconnect with the pulsating aliveness that is Life.

The best way I have found to achieve this is the practice of the *Radical Undoing* work of Drs. Regardie and Hyatt.

Fernando P. is a former student of Dr. Hyatt who can be seen in several of the *Radical Undoing* and *Energized Hypnosis* videos.

# MORE ON REICHIAN THERAPY

## RADICAL UNDOING
*The Complete Course for Undoing Yourself*
**Christopher Hyatt, Ph.D.**

For the first time on video, these effective and powerful neo-Reichian methods help you to remove the blocks that have held you back and release your untapped energy. With practice you will learn to harness this powerful sexual energy and experience *The Ultimate Orgasm*.

## ENERGIZED HYPNOSIS
**Christopher Hyatt, Ph.D. & Calvin Iwema, M.A.**

*Energized Hypnosis* is a *breakthrough* program of audios, videos, booklets and a "non-book" for gaining personal power and peace of mind. The techniques of *Energized Hypnosis* were developed many years ago by Dr. Christopher Hyatt and Dr. Israel Regardie, but have remained "in the closet"...until now.

# THE *Original* FALCON PRESS

## Invites You to Visit Our Website:
## http://originalfalcon.com

At our website you can:

- Browse the online catalog of all of our great titles
- Find out what's available and what's out of stock
- Get special discounts
- Order our titles through our secure online server
- Find products not available anywhere else including:
    - One of a kind and limited availability products
    - Special packages
    - Special pricing
- Get free gifts
- Join our email list for advance notice of New Releases and Special Offers
- Find out about book signings and author events
- Send email to our authors
- Read excerpts of many of our titles
- Find links to our authors' websites
- Discover links to other weird and wonderful sites
- And much, much more

## Get online today at http://originalfalcon.com

www.ingramcontent.com/pod-product-compliance
Lightning Source LLC
LaVergne TN
LVHW011928070526
838202LV00054B/4543